S. Hrg. 111–868

THE CURRENT READINESS OF THE U.S. FORCES

HEARING

BEFORE THE

SUBCOMMITTEE ON READINESS AND MANAGEMENT SUPPORT

OF THE

COMMITTEE ON ARMED SERVICES UNITED STATES SENATE

ONE HUNDRED ELEVENTH CONGRESS

SECOND SESSION

APRIL 14, 2010

Printed for the use of the Committee on Armed Services

Available via the World Wide Web: http://www.fdsys.gov/

U.S. GOVERNMENT PRINTING OFFICE

64–544 PDF　　　　WASHINGTON : 2011

For sale by the Superintendent of Documents, U.S. Government Printing Office
Internet: bookstore.gpo.gov　Phone: toll free (866) 512–1800; DC area (202) 512–1800
Fax: (202) 512–2104　Mail: Stop IDCC, Washington, DC 20402–0001

CONTENTS

CHRONOLOGICAL LIST OF WITNESSES

THE CURRENT READINESS OF THE U.S. FORCES

APRIL 14, 2010

Page

Chiarelli, GEN Peter W., USA, Vice Chief of Staff 4

Amos, Gen. James F., USMC, Assistant Commandant, U.S. Marine Corps 9

Greenert, ADM Jonathan W., USN, Vice Chief of Naval Operations, U.S. Navy 18

Chandler, Gen. Carrol H. USAF, Vice Chief of Staff, U.S. Air Force 30

(III)

THE CURRENT READINESS OF THE U.S. FORCES

WEDNESDAY, APRIL 14, 2010

U.S. SENATE,
SUBCOMMITTEE ON READINESS AND
MANAGEMENT SUPPORT,
COMMITTEE ON ARMED SERVICES,
Washington, DC.

The subcommittee met, pursuant to notice, at 2:37 p.m. in room SD–562, Dirksen Senate Office Building, Senator Evan Bayh (chairman of the subcommittee) presiding.

Committee members present: Senators Bayh, Udall, Burris, Inhofe, Chambliss, Thune, and Burr.

Committee staff member present: Leah C. Brewer, nominations and hearings clerk.

Majority staff members present: Peter K. Levine, general counsel; Jason W. Maroney, counsel; John H. Quirk V, professional staff member; and William K. Sutey, professional staff member.

Minority staff members present: Adam J. Barker, professional staff member; David M. Morriss, minority counsel; and Lucian L. Niemeyer, professional staff member.

Staff assistants present: Christine G. Lang and Breon N. Wells.

Committee members' assistants present: Patrick Hayes, assistant to Senator Bayh; Jennifer Barrett, assistant to Senator Udall; Roosevelt Barfield, assistant to Senator Burris; and Jason Van Beek, assistant to Senator Thune.

OPENING STATEMENT OF SENATOR EVAN BAYH, CHAIRMAN

Senator BAYH. Good afternoon, everyone. The hearing will please come to order.

The purpose of today's hearing is to receive testimony on the current readiness of our forces with respect to deployed, deploying, and nondeployed units, and the Services' ability to meet combatant commanders' requirements and respond to unforeseen contingencies. We're all particularly interested in your assessment of strategic risk resulting from the commitment of forces in Iraq and Afghanistan, as well as other areas around the globe. We are also interested in the status of unit reset activities, how you are all managing those vital readiness accounts, your areas of concern, and the impact and expected duration of reset actions on near- and mid-term readiness.

One of my concerns is that we have relied too much on supplemental funding to resource our reset activities. In order to restore the readiness of our Armed Forces, it will be absolutely critical to

(1)

fully fund reset several years beyond our withdrawal dates from Iraq and Afghanistan. I remain concerned that the requirements for combat operations in Iraq and Afghanistan continue to consume readiness as fast as we can create it. I understand that high operational demand and tempo keeps the Services off balance. But, we must strive to find new ways to restore readiness. While I understand the enemy we face gets a vote, we must improve the way we do business, as our current strategy is not sustainable and reduces our full spectrum of capabilities today and in the long run.

My biggest fear is that prolonged stress on our Armed Forces will break our Strategic Reserve. We must increase the dwell time between deployments, not only for the men and women in uniform, of our All-Volunteer Force, but for their families, who are critically important, as well.

In order to reduce risk to our National Military Strategy, we must continue to fully invest in our maintenance accounts to restore readiness. We cannot afford to merely man, train, and equip units "just in time" for deployment. We continue to have a significant difference in readiness between deployed and nondeployed forces. Nondeploying forces, along with our National Guard and Reserve units, continue to bear the burden of being billpayers for deploying units. We are very interested in hearing the Services' goals, priorities, and investment plans for rebuilding the force, and when they expect readiness will begin to improve.

When we talk about supporting the troops, operation and maintenance (O&M) accounts are where we must back up our talk with funding. These are the funds that train, house, and protect our Armed Forces with the food, water, ammunition, flying hours, steaming days, and tank miles that need to accomplish their mission. At a time when readiness is under stress, we must do all that we can to protect these accounts from unreasonable cuts.

Gentlemen, I know you have prepared statements, which will be included in the record. In the interest of time, if you would please summarize, and then we'll have plenty of time for questions and discussions. If you could roughly keep it to about 7 minutes, give or take, with some flexibility there for things you think are particularly important, I think that would be a good place to begin, and then we'll get into the questions and answers, and flesh out the statements, as need be.

I want to sincerely thank all of you for your dedicated service and your sacrifice to our Nation. I also want to thank you all, for making the time to attend our hearing this afternoon. I look forward to your testimony.

I will now turn to my friend and colleague, Senator Burr, for his opening remarks. I want to thank him for his devotion to this committee and to the good citizens of the State of North Carolina.

Senator BURR. Thank you.

Senator BAYH. Senator Burr.

STATEMENT OF SENATOR RICHARD BURR

Senator BURR. Thank you, Mr. Chairman.

Admiral and Generals, welcome. We're delighted to have you here today.

I commend the chairman for calling this hearing as we continue to focus this committee's attention on the critical issue of the readiness of our combat units.

I also want to thank our witnesses for their dedication and for their service. I note that, despite 8 years of sustained combat operations, morale remains high, recruiting remains strong, retention is excellent, and our units, more importantly, continue to accomplish their mission. These are testaments to the leadership of our panelists, and their service.

Mr. Chairman, this is the third year of hearings on current unit readiness. During this time, we've achieved success in Iraq, meeting our goal of an orderly drawdown and transfer of security responsibilities to a democratically elected government of Iraq. The drawdown in Iraq has allowed us to surge forces and resources in Afghanistan in order to establish stability in a country that, for years, served as a training ground for terrorists. By this August, we plan to reduce U.S. force levels in Iraq to 50,000. In Afghanistan, we're surging 30,000 troops over the same period of time. The Marine Corps has completed its withdrawal from Iraq and is now deploying roughly 8,000 of the 30,000 additional troops to support increased combat operations in Afghanistan, bringing the Corps' troop level in there to about 19,400. This combined logistical movement is the largest effort since World War II.

I'd like to hear from each of our witnesses today how this rapid redeployment of forces impacts personnel and equipment readiness, particularly our readiness of nondeployed units at home.

What concerns me is our ability to respond to the next challenge; in other words, our strategic depth. Our Nation expects that our fighting force in all Services has been the best equipped and trained to provide to our most precious resources, the young men and women who choose freely to serve in our military. For them to be consistently ready, we need to look further than those fateful days of September 11, when attacks here, on our Nation, called for an immediate and decisive response to the horrible attacks on New York and Washington.

No better demonstration of what this country expects, in terms of Strategic Reserve, can be found than the understanding of what we've been asked to do in the 82nd Airborne, out of Fort Bragg. Major elements of the division have recently returned from a year in Afghanistan, yet on January 14, 2010, the 82nd Airborne was called upon by the President, with no prior notice, to deploy to Haiti to provide humanitarian assistance, security, and disaster relief. Within days, over 3,000 personnel of the 2nd Brigade Combat Team (BCT), a decorated unit with two rotations in Afghanistan, began providing manpower and security to about 15 food distribution sites around Port-au-Prince, Haiti, as well as running the international airport. Today major elements of the 2nd BCT still remain in Haiti.

This is not only an Army response. The Marine Corps deployed the 22nd Marine Expeditionary Unit (MEU), on January 13 from Camp Lejeune, to support relief operations with a network of sea-based logistics and land-based support, with as many as 1,100 marines and sailors ashore, to conduct immediate aid efforts.

The Navy also contributed invaluable medical assistance offshore by an unnoticed deployment of the hospital ship, the USS *Comfort*, as well as using the medical treatment facilities on board the aircraft carrier USS *Carl Vinson*.

The Air Force supplied critical strategic airlift and air traffic controllers to maintain an essential flow of resources temporarily operating Haiti's main airport at Port-au-Prince.

While our Armed Forces responded magnificently to the disaster in Haiti, I'm concerned that we have our premier combat units still engaged there and not back in the States with their families. This means less time to prepare for their next duty.

In order for our combat forces to be ready to respond to future challenges, our support of these efforts to restore their readiness should be constant and vigilant. This will be tougher to accomplish in a budget climate of soaring deficits and economic hardships. It may be easier to claim victory in Afghanistan and then start drawing down budgets for the Department of Defense (DOD). This would be the same mistake we've made in the past. The best equipment and proper training needs to be in place before our Nation asks for further sacrifice. As such, we should not continue to accept risk across the full spectrum of operations.

I look forward to hearing our witnesses lay out their plans to reset forces, both in the Active and Reserve.

Mr. Chairman, I thank you.

Senator BAYH. Thank you, Senator Burr, for your statement and for your service on the committee. I only wish that every Member of the U.S. Senate could have the kind of cooperative relationship that the two of us have been fortunate enough to enjoy. So, it's been good working with you.

Gentlemen, just one personal note, since this is the last time I'll be chairing this subcommittee hearing. It is my hope that our working together has been rigorous but not painful, because we're all on the same team. I'm very grateful to each and every one of you for your service to our country. I believe that very strongly, as do the 6.5 million people of my State.

General Chiarelli, why don't we begin with you.

STATEMENT OF GEN PETER W. CHIARELLI, USA, VICE CHIEF OF STAFF

General CHIARELLI. Chairman Bayh, Ranking Member Burr, I thank you for the opportunity to appear here today to discuss the readiness the U.S. Army. I've submitted a statement for the record. I look forward to answering your questions at the conclusion of my opening remarks.

As you are all aware, these are challenging times for our Nation's military. Still, our deployed forces represent the best-manned, -equipped, -trained, and -led in the history of our Army. I'm incredibly proud of all they've accomplished in Iraq and Afghanistan and around the world.

America's Army remains a resilient, professional force dedicated to defending the Homeland and defeating our enemies. However, 8-plus years of war continues to strain our soldiers, our civilians, and their families, as well as our ability to build trained and ready forces and respond to unforeseen contingencies. Ultimately, this impacts the overall readiness of our force. Readiness is a reflection of the total number of deployed or deployable soldiers, time to train, and availability to materiel resources. We made progress over the last year in mitigating some of the negative effects of the consistently high demand for forces. If demand continues to come down as forecasted, and budgetary expectations remains consistent, we should be able to restore our operational depth by fiscal year 2012.

That said, this prediction is based upon a number of factors, not the least of which is the projected drawdown of forces in Iraq. We all recognize we live in an uncertain world and there is always the possibility that circumstances may change unexpectedly and dramatically. In any event, we will work very closely with Congress and with DOD to make necessary adjustments. In the meantime, we must continue to work together to ensure all soldiers, from both our Active and Reserve components, and their families, are properly cared for and have the training, equipment, and resources they need to accomplish their mission, now and into the future.

Mr. Chairman, Mr. Ranking Member, I thank you again for your continued generous support and demonstrated commitment to the outstanding men and women of the U.S. Army. I look forward to your questions.

[The prepared statement of General Chiarelli follows:]

PREPARED STATEMENT BY GEN PETER W. CHIARELLI, USA

INTRODUCTION

Chairman Bayh, Ranking Member Burr, distinguished members of the Senate Armed Services Committee's Subcommittee on Readiness and Management Support, I thank you for the opportunity to appear here today to provide a status on the Readiness of U.S. Army forces with respect to deployed, deploying and nondeployed units and the Army's ability to provide forces to meet combatant commanders' requirements and respond to unforeseen contingencies.

On behalf of our Secretary, the Honorable John M. McHugh and our Chief of Staff, General George W. Casey Jr., I would like to take this opportunity to thank you for your continued, strong support and demonstrated commitment to our soldiers, Army civilians, and family members.

As all of you know, it has been a busy time for our Nation's military. We have been at war for the past 8-plus years. With the support of Congress, our forces deployed are the very best manned, equipped, trained and led in the 234-year history of the U.S. Army. That said, this success has come at the expense of our nondeployed and Generating Forces. The consequence is increased strategic risk to the Nation.

The prolonged demand and high operational tempo of this two-front war have undeniably put a strain on the readiness of our Force. Our current readiness is a reflection of the total number of available soldiers, as well as materiel resources—coupled with time to train. This sum measure of readiness is further impacted by the overall global demand for Army forces.

So long as demand exceeds supply, the availability and deployability of soldiers, units, and equipment will be challenged, as will the Army's ability to build trained and ready forces. In particular, heightened, prolonged demand results in periods of degraded readiness for nondeployed forces in order to shift soldiers and equipment to units preparing to deploy.

The Army currently has limited capacity to respond to unforeseen contingencies. However, if demand for Army forces comes down as forecasted and budgetary expectations remain consistent, then we should be able to restore our full operational depth by fiscal year 2012.

Recognizing this process will be dependent upon a number of factors to include the projected drawdown of forces in Iraq; the continued implementation of the rotational Army Force Generation (ARFORGEN) model; and, the continued transition of our Reserve component (RC) force from a Strategic Reserve to an operational force, thus allowing the Army recurrent, assured, predictable access to the RC to meet operational requirements IAW ARFORGEN. By fiscal year 2013, these actions, in part, and the resulting increase in operational depth should enable our Army to mitigate current strategic risk and reliably respond to the full range of potential, unforeseen contingencies.

In the meantime, I assure the members of this subcommittee, the Army is doing everything within its control to improve our readiness and restore balance to the Force. Congress remains a vital partner in this shared endeavor.

OUR PLAN TO RESTORE BALANCE TO THE FORCE

The U.S. Army remains focused on the four imperatives of our plan to restore balance to the Force: our ability to sustain the Army's soldiers, civilians, and families; prepare forces for success in the current conflict; reset returning units to rebuild the readiness consumed in operations and to prepare for future deployments and contingencies; and transform to meet the demands of the 21st century.

SUSTAIN OUR ALL-VOLUNTEER FORCE

Sustaining our All-Volunteer Force is our first imperative. The soldier, as Secretary Gates has said, is our greatest strategic asset. Unfortunately, after 8-plus years of war, we continue to see the high OPTEMPO and prolonged stress and strain on our Force manifested in the increased demand for behavioral health counseling and drug and alcohol counseling; increased divorce rates; and increased numbers of soldiers temporarily nondeployable from nagging injuries from previous deployments.

The Army remains focused on providing vital family programs and services to include welfare and recreation; youth services and child care; Survivor Outreach Services; mental and behavioral health services; and expanded counseling and rehabilitative opportunities for soldiers and family members.

In collaboration with the National Institute of Mental Health, the Army began a 5-year, $50 million seminal study into suicide prevention that will help inform the Army Campaign Plan for Health Promotion, Risk Reduction, and Suicide Prevention (ACPHP). The Army also began instituting our Comprehensive Soldier Fitness (CSF) program, an all-inclusive approach that puts mental health on par with physical fitness. By promoting resiliency and life-coping skills, we hope to help our soldiers, civilians, and family members to better deal with stress and other challenges. By enhancing the quality of life across our Army community, we believe we will see improvement in many other areas of concern, including suicides.

PREPARE FORCES FOR SUCCESS

The centerpiece of our plan to continue to restore balance to our Force is the maturation of the ARFORGEN model. This model represents the core process for generating trained, ready, and cohesive units on a sustained and rotational basis—to meet current and future strategic demands.

The ARFORGEN process includes three force pools—Reset, Train-Ready, and Available. This process increases predictability for soldiers, families, employers, and communities. ARFORGEN enables our Reserve component to remain an integral element of the operational force while providing the Nation with strategic depth (i.e., those nondeployed units which are 2 to 3 years from commitment) and operational flexibility to meet unexpected contingencies.

MANNING

The Army is currently implementing the Active Army temporary end-strength increase of up to 22,000 soldiers approved by the Secretary of Defense in July 2009. More than 8 years of sustained combat operations, coupled with taking the Army off of stop-loss, have increased nondeployable rates in our units. These increasing non-deployable rates (from 9.92 percent in fiscal year 2007 to 12 percent in fiscal year 2009) require us to continue to overfill our deploying units. The soldiers needed to overfill those deploying units come largely from both nondeployed and Generating Force units. The resulting reductions in personnel hamper the affected units' ability to train which ultimately impacts the units' overall readiness.

The decision was made to temporarily increase the Army endstrength by 15,000 soldiers by end of fiscal year 2010. This increase assisted in offsetting the decline in available personnel in our Army units. We added 5,000 soldiers in fiscal year 2009, and will add an additional 10,000 in fiscal year 2010. The resulting temporary Army end-strength will be 562,400 soldiers.

The Army is still assessing the need for the additional 7,000 soldier growth for fiscal year 2011. This would bring us to the total 22,000 end-strength increase. The decision on whether or not to add the additional 7,000 personnel is pending confirmation of our immediate demand, the pace of the drawdown from Iraq, and the requirement for forces in Afghanistan. If the decision is made to add the additional 7,000 soldiers, growth could be complete by end of second quarter, fiscal year 2011. We would hold at that end-strength for the requisite 12 months before beginning the 18-month drawdown. Regardless of the decision on the 7,000 soldier growth, we plan to return to the pre-increase end-strength level of 547,400 by the end of fiscal year 2013.

RESET EQUIPMENT

Equipment Reset is an essential element of readiness and restoring balance to the Army for known and future requirements. Reset is a necessary process that must continue not only as long as we have forces deployed, but an additional 2 to 3 years after major deployments end to ensure future equipment readiness.

Reset is especially challenging given the extraordinary wear on vehicles, aircraft, and equipment in the harsh environments our forces operate in today. Coarse sand, fine dust, extreme temperatures, and high OPTEMPO erode sophisticated mechanical and electronic systems at altitudes and loads which near the edge of the aircraft design capabilities. Our rotary wing fleet, for example, operates up to six times non-combat usage levels.

Reset timelines are directly related to the pace of the Iraq drawdown, operational decisions such as the Operation Enduring Freedom plus-up, available capacity within our industrial base (physical plant capacities, labor and long lead-time parts) and the availability and timing of funding. Over the past year, our depot-level Maintenance Reset workload exceeded ~100,000 items of equipment; and, we expect to sustain this pace for as long as we have substantial forces deployed. In fiscal year 2010, the Army plans to complete the equipment Reset 27 Brigades (25 maneuver and 2 enabling brigades), as well as numerous below Brigade-level units.

Given current projections, we would expect our requirements to decrease in the out-years as we complete the retrograde and Reset of equipment from Iraq. That said, Reset activities alone cannot improve Army Readiness in the near- or midterm. Repairs, recapitalization, or replacement of battle losses experienced in combat does not fix on-hand equipment shortfalls that existed prior to a unit's deployment. However, equipment Reset does ensure our on-hand equipment is maintained at a high state of readiness to prepare units for future combat operations.

READINESS REPORTING

The Army has made progress towards implementing and advancing readiness reporting policy and technology in 2009. Our current readiness reporting system has considerably improved the accurate, reliable measurement of units at the tactical and operational level.

However, significant challenges do still remain. The fast pace of this war, coupled with the rapidly evolving demand for new and improved capabilities means our requirements are constantly shifting and equipment is continually on the move. Our longstanding unit readiness reporting process was not designed to nor is it capable of keeping up with or capturing the full 'velocity' or magnitude of activity in our current operating environments. Our longstanding readiness reporting process has been adapted to support the ARFORGEN model and the Army's new modular force structure.

We are making progress towards improving and expanding this process. For example, the Army expanded the former Percent Effective reporting to include manning and equipping levels for assigned missions. This new rating called the A-Level incorporates assigned mission manning and equipping ratings to better support commanders in their assessments of assigned mission capabilities. These are reported no later than 270 days prior to deployment or even earlier if the command or component directs it.

These and other changes to the Army's overall readiness reporting process represent significant improvements, but challenges still remain. We must continue to make necessary adjustments and educate the Force accordingly.

Army Prepositioned Stocks

Army Prepositioned Stocks (APS) continue—most recently in Operation Enduring Freedom and Operation Iraqi Freedom—to fulfill their primary purpose of enhancing the Army's strategic agility. We have pulled equipment from and rebuilt APS several times over the past 8-plus years. Most recently, we used equipment from APS–3 and APS–5 to support both the surge in Iraq and the ongoing plus-up in Afghanistan.

In order to restore operational flexibility and reduce strategic risk, it is necessary that we continue to try to reconstitute APS, and indeed, all our war reserve stocks. We have a strategy in place and will continue to make appropriate budget requests to restore our APS to full capability by 2015.

TRANSFORMING OUR FORCE

The Army is evolving our capabilities to meet current and future strategic demands. We recognize that we must ensure our Nation has the capability and range of military options to meet the challenges we face in the 21st century. As Army Chief of Staff, General George W. Casey, Jr. has stated, "We need an Army that is a versatile mix of tailorable and networked organizations, operating on a rotational cycle, to provide a sustained flow of trained and ready forces for full spectrum operations and to hedge against unexpected contingencies—at a tempo that is predictable and sustainable for our All-Volunteer Force."

The centerpiece of our efforts is the shift to a modular construct focused at the brigade level, thus creating a more deployable, adaptable, and versatile force. This ongoing transformation has greatly enhanced the Army's ability to respond to any situation, quickly and effectively. However, the degree of impact continues to vary, for example, between Brigade Combat Teams (BCTs), "enablers," the Reserve components, and individual soldiers.

STRATEGIC RISK

Our Army remains a resilient, professional force dedicated to defending the homeland and defeating our Nation's enemies. However, 8-plus years of war continue to strain our soldiers, civilians, families, equipment and infrastructure. We made considerable progress over the last year in mitigating the negative effects of consistently high demand for forces; nonetheless, high deployment-to-dwell ratios for Army units and individuals continue to stress the All-Volunteer Force, and challenge the Army's ability to respond to unexpected contingencies. Strategic risk has been identified in the following areas:

SUSTAINED DEMAND

Since September 11, 2001, all deploying Army units are trained, led, and equipped to achieve the highest readiness standards prior to deployment. However, due to sustained demand, Army units are achieving this deployment readiness closer and closer to their arrival dates in theater. This creates operational risk by reducing the near-term flexibility for adapting to mission-driven adjustments to arrival dates or other requirements.

LIMITED DWELL TIME

Prolonged, heightened demand for Army forces continues to limit availability of unit and individual dwell time. As a result, soldiers often have minimal time to train, rest, and recuperate prior to their next deployment. This also restricts the geographic combatant commander's operational flexibility for altering unit arrival dates or shifting areas of responsibility.

Projected increases to unit and individual dwell times depend on a number of factors to include: absence of any significant new missions; Iraq drawdown will proceed on time and year-end end-strength in Iraq will be less than 50,000 personnel; we will maintain continued access to RC forces; and, Afghanistan surge will proceed on time and not increase beyond the planned level.

LIMITED RESOURCES

Army and Defense resources are set within national affordability parameters, yet demand is unconstrained. Over time, the Army (in complete transparency with the Office of the Secretary of Defense, the Joint Staff, and combatant commanders) has directed resources away from non-deployed Operational Forces and our Generating Force to support our forces deployed. The result is increased strategic risk in the Army's ability to respond to unforeseen contingencies.

UNFUNDED READINESS PRIORITIES

While the Army does not have any unfunded requirements, as with any budget request, there are areas where additional resources could enhance existing programs. The continuous assessment of lessons learned provides us with new information on possible items that, if accelerated, would provide added value to commanders in the field.

UNKNOWN RISK

We recognize that much of the risk we assume depends on minimal projected reductions in demand and corresponding savings; and the absence of unplanned events or a resurgence of tensions in 'hot spots' around the world. If such unforeseen events occur, we will have to make the necessary adjustments, to include reallocation of resources.

However, based on the current situation and known risks, we are confident the fiscal year 2011 budget request, if appropriated in full, would improve the overall readiness of our Force by ensuring the Army is able to properly care for, train, equip and support our soldiers, civilians, and family members around the world.

CONCLUSION

These continue to be challenging times for our Nation and for our military. With the support of Congress, we have deployed the best manned, equipped, trained, and led forces in the history of the U.S. Army over the past 8-plus years. However, the fact remains that we have asked a great deal from our soldiers, civilians, and their families.

Looking ahead, the Army must continue to sustain our All-Volunteer Army, modernize, adapt our institutions, and transform our Force. We must ensure we have a trained and ready Force that is well-prepared, expeditionary, versatile, lethal, sustainable, and able to adapt to any situation.

I assure the members of this subcommittee—the Army's senior leaders are focused and working hard to address these challenges and to determine the needs of the Force for the future.

Chairman, members of the subcommittee, I thank you again for your continued and generous support of the outstanding men and women of the U.S. Army and their families. I look forward to your questions.

Senator BAYH. Thank you, General Chiarelli.

General Amos, why don't we proceed next with you.

STATEMENT OF GEN. JAMES F. AMOS, USMC, ASSISTANT COMMANDANT, U.S. MARINE CORPS

General AMOS. Thank you, sir.

Chairman Bayh, Senator Burr, distinguished members of the committee, thank you for the opportunity to report on the readiness of your U.S. Marine Corps. On behalf of the more than 242,000 Active and Reserve marines and their families, I'd like to extend my appreciation for the sustained support Congress has faithfully provided its Corps.

As we begin this hearing, I would like to highlight a few points from my written statement.

Within the U.S. Central Command (CENTCOM) theater of operations, we have successfully completed a responsible drawdown of marines in Iraq. After 7 straight years of sustained combat operations and nation-building, our work in Iraq's Anbar Province is done. With the exception of our eight training teams and the support to higher headquarters staff, 100 percent of our marines and 100 percent of their equipment have left Iraq.

As we sit in this hearing room today, more than 31,000 marines remain deployed across the globe, supporting oversees contingency operations (OCO) and security cooperation activities and exercises. Specifically, your Corps has reoriented its principal efforts towards Afghanistan. To date, we have 20,525 marines and sailors on the ground in Afghanistan. We will close the remainder of this surge force by the end of this month.

All of our forward-deployed units were manned, trained, and equipped to accomplish their assigned missions. These units continue to report the highest levels of readiness for those missions.

For the past 8 years, we have been fully engaged in winning combat operations as part of this generational struggle against global extremism. As I testified last year before this subcommittee, this sustained effort in performance does not come without cost to the institution, to our equipment, and to our strategic programs, and most importantly, to our marines and their families.

Equipment readiness of our nondeployed units is of great concern to our senior leadership. We have taxed our home-station units, as the billpayer, to ensure that marines in Afghanistan in our MEUs have everything that they need. As a result, the majority of our nondeployed forces are reporting degraded materiel readiness levels. This degraded state of readiness within our nondeployed forces presents risk to our ability to respond rapidly to other unexpected contingencies around the globe.

The tempo of operations in the harsh environments that we have been in since 2003 have accelerated the wear and tear on our equipment. Necessarily, the diversion of equipment in theater from Iraq to Afghanistan has delayed reset actions at our logistics depots within the United States. Our current estimate of the cost of reset for the Marine Corps is $8 billion. Additionally, validating the lessons learned from 8 years of combat has necessitated that we update and approve the way we equip our units. The cost for these changes to our equipment sets is estimated to be an additional $5 billion. Money to reset and rebuild the Marine Corps will be required for several years after the end of the war. I ask for your continued support for that continued funding as we rebuild our Nation's Corps. With your steadfast support, we will succeed in current operations, take care of our marines and their families, reset and modernize our equipment, and train the marine air/ground task forces for the challenges of the future. We continue to stand ready as the Nation's expeditionary force in readiness.

I thank you, each of you, for your faithfulness to our Nation, and I request that my written testimony be accepted for the record. I look forward to your questions.

[The prepared statement of General Amos follows:]

PREPARED STATEMENT BY GEN. JAMES F. AMOS, USMC

INTRODUCTION

Chairman Bayh, Ranking Member Burr, and distinguished members of the committee, on behalf of your Marine Corps, I want to thank you for your generous support and for the opportunity to speak with you today about the readiness of the U.S. Marines. My statement will address our efforts to create a balanced force capable of prevailing in current conflicts while preparing for other contingencies, the readiness challenges facing marines today, and the critical steps needed to reset and reconstitute our Corps for today's complex challenges and tomorrow's uncertain security environment.

Despite high operational tempo, your marines are resilient, motivated, and performing superbly in missions around the globe. This sustained effort and performance does not come without costs—to the institution, to our equipment, to our strategic programs, and most importantly, to our marines and their families. Continued congressional investment in our marines and families, resetting and modernizing our equipment, and training Marine Air Ground Task Forces (MAGTFs) for the future security environment are critical to the Marine Corps' success as the "Nation's Force in Readiness."

READINESS ASSESSMENT

The pace of operations for your marines remains high, with over 31,000 marines forward-deployed across the globe. In the U.S. Central Command area of operations, there are over 23,000 marines deployed in support of Operations Iraqi Freedom (OIF) and Enduring Freedom (OEF). Our mission in Iraq is now complete. After 7 years of intense combat and nation building operations, the Marine Corps returned the Anbar Province to the leadership of Iraq. With exception of some Training Team members, our last piece of equipment and our last marine departed Iraq this past week. In the course of the last 8 years, your Marine Corps has been battle-tested, combat-hardened, and has accumulated tremendous experience in irregular warfare and counter-insurgency operations. Forward deployed units are manned, trained, and equipped to accomplish their assigned missions, and these units are reporting the highest levels of readiness for those missions. However, resources are limited, and non-deployed units incur the costs of ensuring deployed and next-to-deploy units have sufficient personnel, equipment, and training. As a result, our non-deployed forces continue to report degraded readiness levels. This degraded state of readiness within our non-deployed forces presents risk in our ability to rapidly respond to other unexpected contingencies.

Because our equipment, personnel, and training priorities are focused on counter-insurgency operations, we have experienced degradation in some of our traditional, full spectrum, core competencies such as integrated combined arms operations and large-scale seaborne operations. These skills are critical to maintaining the Marine Corps' primacy in theater access operations that enable follow-on joint forces. The OIF/OEF demand for units has also limited our ability to fully meet combatant commander requests for theater engagement activities. The current security environment has clearly justified the tradeoffs we have made to support Overseas Contingency Operations, but the uncertainty of the future makes it prudent to regain our capabilities to operate across the full range of military operations.

In addressing the challenges facing the Marine Corps, I have structured my statement along the lines of our key readiness concerns—equipment, personnel, military construction, training, amphibious shipbuilding, and caring for our warriors and their families. I will discuss the positive steps and proactive initiatives we are undertaking, with your support, to reset, modernize, and reconstitute the Marine Corps for an uncertain future. Finally, I will conclude with some of our ongoing initiatives and programs that address the care and welfare of our marines and their families.

EQUIPMENT READINESS

Ensuring that our marines are equipped with the most modern and reliable combat gear is a necessity. However, the requirement to fully resource deployed forces, often in excess of our tables of equipment, has reduced the availability of materiel essential to outfit and train our nondeployed units. Approximately 21.5 percent of all Marine Corps ground equipment and 42 percent of our aviation assets are deployed overseas. Most of this equipment is not rotating out of theater at the conclusion of each force rotation; it remains in combat, to be used by the relieving unit. As of 1 Mar 2010, Marine Corps Logistics Command folded its flag, redeployed, and the final 21 trucks headed for Kuwait; we have completed the responsible drawdown from Iraq, our mission there is complete. While we reorient our effort to OEF operations, we have been transitioning a significant amount of equipment to Afghanistan. We continue to face significant home station equipment readiness challenges.

GROUND EQUIPMENT READINESS

After 8 years of sustained combat operations, our deployed equipment has been subject to significant wear and tear, harsh environmental conditions, and increased operating hours and mileage. Additionally, the weight associated with armor plating further increases the wear on our deployed vehicle fleet and accelerates the need for repair and replacement of these assets. Despite these challenges and higher utilization on already aging equipment, our young marines are keeping this equipment mission-ready every single day. The high equipment maintenance readiness rates throughout the Marine Corps are a testament to their dedication and hard work.

The policy to retain equipment in theater as forces rotate in and out was accompanied by increased in-theater maintenance presence. This infusion of maintenance support has paid great dividends, with deployed ground equipment maintenance readiness above 90 percent. However, the Marine Corps is experiencing challenges with the supply availability of a number of critical equipment items at home stations. Supply readiness rates (On-hand vs Required) have decreased for home station units, while we work to meet the demand of deployed forces and those next-to-deploy. Shortages of critical equipment limit home station units' ability to prepare and train to their full core competencies and present additional risk in availability of equipment necessary to respond swiftly to unexpected contingencies.

The sourcing of equipment for the Marine Expeditionary Brigade (MEB) in Afghanistan over the past year, and the transition to a much larger Marine Expeditionary Force Forward (MEF(Fwd)), illustrates our equipment availability challenge. Equipment assets were pulled from across the entire Marine Corps to accomplish this task. To ensure the MEF(Fwd) is provided the newest and most capable equipment, over 34 percent of their equipment came via new procurement provided by Marine Corps Systems Command. Approximately 42 percent of the equipment came from within the Central Command area of operations, including items made available from units retrograding from Iraq; and about 4 percent of the required assets were sourced from our Logistics Command Maritime Prepositioning Ships Program and the Marine Corps Prepositioning Program in Norway. Although a concerted effort was made to minimize the impact on home station unit readiness, 20 percent of the equipment for I MEF(Fwd) needed to be drawn from our non-deployed operating forces. The net effect has been degradation in readiness at home station. For instance, the overall supply rating of Marine Corps units in Afghanistan is near 100 percent, while the supply rating of units at home station is less than 60 percent.

Ground equipment age continues to be a top readiness challenge as well. As equipment ages, more time, money, and effort are expended repairing it. Ultimately, the answer to achieving sustained improvements in ground equipment readiness is to improve logistics processes and to modernize with highly reliable and maintainable equipment. The Corps is achieving efficiencies by improving supply-chain processes, adopting best practices, and leveraging proven technological advances to facilitate responsive and reliable support to the Operating Forces.

AVIATION EQUIPMENT

Our aviation capability is a critical part of the MAGTF. Just like our ground force units, deployed Marine aviation units receive priority for aircraft, repair parts, and mission essential subsystems such as forward-looking infrared (FLIR) pods. Non-deployed forces, therefore, face significant challenges for available airframes and supply parts. Exacerbating the readiness challenges in our aviation fleet, most Marine aircraft are older, or are "legacy" platforms no longer in production, thus placing an even greater strain on our logistics chain and maintenance systems.

Our Marine Corps aviation platforms are supporting ground forces in some of the world's harshest environments: Afghanistan, the Horn of Africa, and aboard ships around the world. While operating in these demanding areas, our aircraft are often doubling—sometimes, nearly tripling—the utilization rates for which they were designed.

Maintaining the readiness of aviation assets while training aircrew is a large effort, and one which Marine Corps aviation is meeting through a careful and ongoing program of mitigation, bridging legacy platforms to new aircraft. We are replacing our assault support and tactical aviation airframes through programs of record, which will provide the MAGTF with dependable and tactically dominant capabilities for decades to come. The key to our steady improvement of Marine Corps aircraft flexibility is maintaining the "ramp rates" at which we purchase these improved airframes.

Fleet Readiness Centers have been able to mitigate the strain on our aircraft materiel readiness through modifications, proactive inspections, and additional maintenance actions. These efforts successfully bolstered aircraft reliability, sustainability, and survivability. We expect requirements for depot-level maintenance on airframes, engines, weapons, and support equipment will continue well beyond the conclusion of hostilities.

PREPOSITIONING EQUIPMENT AND STORES

Marine Corps Prepositioning Programs are comprised of the Maritime Prepositioning Force (MPF), with three Maritime Prepositioning Ships Squadrons, and the Marine Corps Prepositioning Program-Norway (MCPP–N). Since 2002, we have drawn equipment from our strategic programs and stocks to support combat operations, Operation Unified Response, growth of the Marine Corps, and other operational priorities. While the readiness of the strategic prepositioning programs continues to improve, equipment shortages in our strategic equipment prepositioned stores have forced the Marine Corps to accept necessary risk in our ability to rapidly respond to worldwide contingency operations. With Congress' support, our end item shortfalls in the MPF and MCCP–N programs will be reset, in accordance with operational priorities, as equipment becomes available.

IN-STORES EQUIPMENT

In-stores equipment refers to our pool of assets that serves as a source of equipment to replace damaged or destroyed equipment in the operating forces, and potentially fill shortfalls in the Active and Reserve components. This equipment was used heavily to meet equipment requirements in Iraq, and it continues to support our forces in Afghanistan. The availability, or supply rating, for in-stores assets has been degraded over the past years and limits our ability to rapidly respond to unexpected contingencies and to replace damaged equipment in the operating forces.

EQUIPMENT INITIATIVES

To counter the readiness impact of damaged, destroyed or worn out equipment, the Marine Corps initiated a program to reset and modernize our force. The goal of our reset and modernization programs is to sustain the current fight by repairing or replacing worn out or damaged/destroyed equipment while enhancing our support to the warfighter by reconstituting our force with newer, more capable equipment. Over time, these initiatives will help to increase nondeployed unit readiness by enhancing home station equipment pools and predeployment unit training requirements.

EQUIPMENT RESET

Reset consists of actions taken to restore units to a desired level of combat capability commensurate with a unit's assigned mission. It encompasses maintenance and supply activities that restore and enhance combat capability to equipment that has been damaged, rendered obsolete, or worn out beyond economical repair due to combat operations by repairing, rebuilding, or procuring replacement equipment. In light of the continued high tempo of operations in the CENTCOM AOR, and the delay in reset actions due to the diversion of equipment to Afghanistan, we estimate the cost of reset for the Marine Corps to be $8 billion ($3 billion requested in the fiscal year 2011 OCO and an additional $5 billion reset liability upon termination of the conflict.

To prepare for the reset of equipment redeployed from Iraq, we created an OIF Reset Plan. The plan synchronizes Marine Corps reset efforts to ensure we effectively and efficiently reset equipment to support follow-on operations. Equipment being redeployed is inspected, sorted and redistributed in theater, or redeployed to the continental United States to maintenance facilities. This equipment will then be repaired and distributed to fill shortfalls for established priorities. Equipment determined to be beyond economical repair will be disposed of and replacements procured.

MODERNIZATION

As the Nation's expeditionary force in readiness, the Marine Corps is required to prepare for the unexpected. We are making progress in repairing and resetting existing equipment, but this effort must be augmented with continued investment to modernize our capabilities. Equipment modernization plans are a high priority within our Corps. Our Commandant's Marine Corps Vision and Strategy 2025 will help guide our modernization efforts as we continue to be the agile and expeditionary force for the Nation.

GROUND MODERNIZATION

Prompted by a changing security environment and hard lessons learned from 8 years of combat, the Marine Corps completed a review of its Operating Force's ground equipment requirements. Recognizing that our unit tables of equipment (T/Es) did not accurately reflect the challenges and realities of the 21st century dispersed battlefield, the Corps revised T/Es for our operating units. This revision was synchronized with our modernization plans and programs, and provides enhanced mobility, lethality, sustainment, and command and control across the MAGTF. The new equipment requirements reflect the capabilities necessary, not only for the Corps' current mission, but for its future employment across the range of military operations, against a variety of threats, and in diverse terrain and conditions. We estimate the cost associated with our revised tables of equipment to be $5 billion.

AVIATION MODERNIZATION

We are modernizing the aircraft we fly, even as we continue our long-range plan to replace our entire operational aircraft fleet with new or rebuilt airframes; changing the way we think about aviation support to our ground forces; and improving our capabilities to conduct operations in any clime and place. We are committed to an "in-stride transition" from 12 legacy type/model/series aircraft to 6 new aircraft, including the F–35B Joint Strike Fighter, the MV–22 Osprey, the KC–130J, the CH–53K, and upgrades to our H–1 series helicopters. To help meet the growing intelligence, surveillance, and reconnaissance requirements of our operating forces, the Marine Corps is fielding three groups of unmanned aircraft systems. It is critical that these programs stay on track, and on timeline, with full funding support, due to the declining service life of our legacy tactical aviation platforms. These improvements will increase the Corps' aviation capability and MAGTF flexibility, and ensure our continued warfighting advantage.

PERSONNEL READINESS

The Marine Corps is meeting all Operation Enduring Freedom (OEF), and Operation Unified Response requirements. The demand and associated operational tempo for marines will remain high as we provide requested forces to Afghanistan. Meeting this global demand resulted in short deployment-to-dwell ratios for many units, with some deployed for as many months as they spend at home. Some of our low-density/high-demand units such as Intelligence, Communications, Explosive Ordnance Disposal, and certain aviation units, remain at about a 1:1 dwell ratio, with only moderate relief in sight for the near future. Insufficient dwell time negatively impacts our total force readiness because it leaves inadequate time to conduct full spectrum training and reconnect with families.

Another readiness detractor has been the need to task combat arms units, such as artillery, air defense, and mechanized maneuver to perform "in-lieu-of" (ILO) missions such as security, civil affairs, and military policing. Shortages of those skill sets created the need for ILO missions to meet the requirements for counter-insurgency operations in Iraq and Afghanistan. Although these mission assignments are necessary, they have degraded our readiness because these combat units are unable to train to and maintain proficiency in their primary skill sets.

Additionally, the Marine Corps is tasked to fill a variety of assignments for forward-deployed staffs, training teams, and joint/coalition assignments that exceed our normal manning structures. The manning requirements for these uncompensated Individual Augments (IAs), Training Teams (TTs) and Joint Manning Documents (JMDs) seek seasoned officers and staff noncommissioned officers because of their leadership, experience, and training. We understand that these augmentees and staff personnel are critical to continued success in Iraq and Afghanistan, but their extended absence has degraded home station readiness, full spectrum training, and unit cohesion. This has become most evident in our field grade ranks. In addition to the IA, TT, and JMD billets, emerging requirements associated with activation of USCYBERCOM, the AF–PAK Hands program, AFRICOM, and increased SOCOM support have compounded the demand for Marine majors, lieutenant colonels, and colonels who would otherwise be assigned to key leadership positions in the operating force.

PERSONNEL INITIATIVES

In order to better meet the needs of a nation at war, the Corps has grown to its authorized active duty end strength of 202,000 marines. This increase in manpower will ultimately result in a Marine Corps with three balanced Marine Expeditionary Forces (MEFs), and will help mitigate many of our operational tempo challenges described in the previous section. A balanced Marine Corps will provide combatant commanders with fully manned, trained, and equipped MAGTFs that are multi-capable, responsive, and expeditionary. Additionally, our current end strength growth will increase our capacity to deploy forces in response to contingencies and to participate in exercises and operations with our international partners in support of the Nation's broader security objectives. It will also allow more time at home for our marines to be with their families, to recover from long deployments, regain proficiency in core skills, and prepare for their next mission.

Thanks to the continued support of Congress, we have increased our infantry, reconnaissance, intelligence, combat engineer, unmanned aircraft, military police, civil affairs, and explosives ordnance disposal communities. Most of these units have already deployed to Iraq and Afghanistan, mitigating the need for additional ILO missions. We have realized improvements in dwell time for a number of stressed communities. Although the plan is progressing well, the growth in end strength will not result in an immediate improvement in reported readiness, because it takes time to train and mature our newly recruited marines and units.

MILITARY CONSTRUCTION

In conjunction with the Marine Corps' growth, military construction is critical to supporting and sustaining the new force structure and maintaining the individual readiness and quality of life for our marines. Thanks to your support, we recently expanded our construction efforts and established a program that will provide adequate bachelor housing for our entire force by 2014. Since the announcement of the Commandant's Barracks Initiative in fiscal year 2008, Congress has funded approximately 19,700 barracks spaces for our marines. We ask for your continued support of this program to meet our 2014 goal. Concurrent with our new construction efforts is our commitment for the repair and maintenance of existing barracks to improve morale and quality of life.

TRAINING MARINES TO FIGHT

In preparing marines to fight in "any clime and place," the perennial challenge to our Corps is to attain the proper balance between core warfighting capabilities and those unique to current operations. Decreased unit dwell times and shortages of equipment in our non-deployed forces translate to a limited ability to conduct training on tasks critical to our core competencies, such as integrated combined arms, large force maneuver, and amphibious operations. Short dwell times between deployments and the need for many units to perform "in lieu of missions" have resulted in a singular focus on counter-insurgency training. Our marines continue to be well trained for current operations through a challenging pre-deployment training program that prepares them for all aspects of irregular warfare.

PREDEPLOYMENT TRAINING PROGRAM

We have continued to improve our demanding, realistic and adaptive pre-deployment training program in order to properly prepare our operating forces for the rigors and challenges they face in OEF. The Predeployment Training Program (PTP) contains standards-based, skill progression training which is evaluated by commanders and assessed by our Training and Education Command at the final Mission Rehearsal Exercise. The PTP includes counter-insurgency combat skills, training in joint/coalition operations, working with our interagency partners, and increasing operational language sets and cultural skills. Unit after-action reports and unit surveys conducted by the Marine Corps Center for Lessons Learned (MCCLL) are shared Corps-wide and have influenced training changes to keep PTP relevant. For example, the Afghanistan Pre-Deployment Training Program, while similar in many facets to the PTP for Iraq, includes mountain warfare training, an increased emphasis on MAGTF combined arms training, and a focus on partnering and mentoring of host nation security forces.

While our PTP focuses on preparing Marine units for their next deployment, we are further enhancing our education and training programs to respond to ongoing changes in the security environment. Through the efforts of the MAGTF Training Command and organizations such as Marine Aviation Weapons and Tactics Squadron One, Marine Corps Tactics and Operations Group, the Center for Advanced Operational Culture Learning, the Security Cooperation Education and Training Center, Marine Corps Advisor Training Group, and the Marine Corps University, we are providing holistic training and education for our marines across the range of military operations. Based on a continuous lessons learned feedback process, supported by the Marine Corps Center for Lessons Learned, we are building Enhanced MAGTF Operations capability which will make all of our MAGTFs more lethal, agile, and survivable.

PREPARING FOR FUTURE CONFLICT

As challenging as it is to prepare marines for the current fight, our forces must adapt to the ever-changing character and conduct of warfare to remain relevant. To meet the complex challenges in the emerging security environment, we are improving training and education for the fog, friction and uncertainty of the 21st century battlefield. We are focusing efforts on our small unit leaders—the "strategic non-commissioned officers" and junior officers—who will operate more frequently in a decentralized manner and assume greater responsibility in operations against hybrid threats.

To better prepare our MAGTF to operate across the spectrum of conflict, we are developing an improved training and exercise program. When implemented, this program will increase our ability to maintain proficiency in core warfighting capabilities, such as combined arms maneuver and amphibious operations, while continuing to meet current commitments. Three important training concept exercises being developed are the Combined Arms Live Fire Exercise (CALFEX), the Marine Air Ground Task Force Large Scale Exercise (MAGTF–LSE), and a joint Navy-Marine Corps initiative titled Bold Alligator. The CALFEX will be a live-fire training exercise aimed at developing combined arms maneuver capabilities from individual marine to regimental-sized units. It will incorporate lessons learned from today's conflicts, while training adaptable and flexible MAGTFs for the future. The MAGTF–LSE will be a scenario-based, service-level training exercise, scalable from MEB to Marine Expeditionary Force levels. It will develop the MAGTF's capability to conduct amphibious power projection and sustained operations ashore in a combined, joint, whole-of-government environment. Lastly, Bold Alligator is specifically designed to re-energize the Navy/Marine Corps' understanding of the intricacies of amphibious operations. The initial audience is Expeditionary Strike Group 2 (ESG2) and the 2nd MEB who will participate in a number of planning seminars and simulated exercises in preparation for the fleet exercise scheduled in fiscal year 2011. We envision that the Bold Alligator series will continue indefinitely and progress to include a wider range of participants.

AMPHIBIOUS SHIPBUILDING

Amphibious warships provide distributed forward presence to support a wide range of missions from theater security cooperation and humanitarian assistance to conventional deterrence to assuring access for the Joint Force. In support of day-to-day Combatant Commander demands and in major combat operations, the number of amphibious ships in the Department of the Navy's inventory is critically important. As discussed in the fiscal year 2011 Shipbuilding Report to Congress, the Navy is reviewing options to increase the assault echelon to reflect a minimum of 33 amphibious ships to support assured access operations conducted by the assault echelons of 2.0 MEBs. The Navy and Marine Corps have determined a minimum of 33 ships represents the limit of acceptable risk in meeting the 38-ship amphibious force requirement.

CARING FOR OUR WARRIORS AND FAMILIES

A critical part of our overall readiness is maintaining our solemn responsibility to take care of our marines and their families. While marines never waiver in the ideals of service to Country and Corps, the needs of our marines and their families are constantly evolving. With more than 45 percent of our marines married, we believe that investment in our families is critical to the long-term health of our institution. Marines have reasonable expectations regarding housing, schools, and family support. It is incumbent upon us, with the generous support of Congress, to support them in these key areas. Marines make an enduring commitment to the Corps when they earn the title, Marine. The Corps, in turn, makes an enduring commitment to every marine and his or her family.

PERSONNEL AND FAMILY READINESS PROGRAMS

Taking care of marines and their families remains one of our highest priorities. With your help, we initiated a myriad of personnel and family readiness program reforms during fiscal years 2008 and 2009 with supplemental appropriations. As a result of extensive program assessments and evaluations, we have built these programs into our baseline, and our baseline budget in fiscal years 2010 and 2011 is $399 million per year. Key accomplishments through our transition phase include:

- Establishment of over 400 full-time Family Readiness Officer positions at the unit level to provide direct support to the unit commander and families.
- Development of an inventory of Lifeskills training courses supported by full-time Marine Corps Family Team Building trainers.
- Transformation of the Exceptional Family Member Program (EFMP) to ensure enrolled family members have access to a continuum of care, while providing the sponsor every opportunity for a successful career. The Marine Corps EFMP has been recognized as a premier, full-service program to be used as a template for other services. Since 2007, sponsor enrollment has increased by 40 percent.
- Direct attention to suicide prevention. The loss of any marine through suicide is a tragedy. With 52 suicides confirmed or suspected in 2009, the

Marine Corps recorded its highest suicide rate since the start of OEF/OIF. We are taking proactive action, focusing on the important role of leaders of all ranks in addressing this issue.

• Enhancing Combat and Operational Stress Control capabilities to further assist leaders with prevention, rapid identification and early treatment of combat and operational stress. Through the Operational Stress Control and Readiness (OSCAR) program, we are embedding mental health professionals in deploying operational units to directly support all Active and Reserve ground combat elements. This will be achieved over the next 3 years through the realignment of existing Navy structure supporting the operating forces, and by increasing the Navy mental health provider inventory. The OSCAR capability is also being extended down to infantry battalions and companies by providing additional training to OSCAR Extenders (existing medical providers, corpsmen, chaplains, and religious program specialists) to make the OSCAR expertise more immediately available to marines. In addition, we are training senior and junior marines to function as OSCAR Mentors. In this capacity, they will actively engage marines who evidence stress reactions, liaison with OSCAR Extenders, and advocate for fellow marines regarding stress problems. OSCAR Mentors will also greatly decrease the stigma associated with stress reactions, and help marines take care of their own.

As we move forward, we are continuing to assess the efficacy of our programs and to empower marines and their families to improve family readiness and maintain a positive quality of life. These initiatives and others demonstrate the commitment of the Marine Corps to our families, and highlight the connection between family readiness and mission readiness. We are grateful to Congress for your unwavering support of these important programs.

IMPROVING CARE FOR OUR WOUNDED WARRIORS

The Marine Corps is proud of the positive and meaningful accomplishments of the Wounded Warrior Regiment in providing comprehensive recovery and transition support to our wounded, ill, and injured marines and sailors and their families. The Regiment provides all Active and Reserve marines with non-medical care without regard to the origin of the Marine's condition. Whether the road to recovery keeps wounded warriors in the Marine Corps or helps them transition to civilian life, the Regiment continues to develop programs that focus on Wounded Warriors' abilities and facilitates their recovery.

The Regiment's Recovery Care Coordinators serve as the primary point of contact for wounded, ill and injured marines and their families. These coordinators help marines meet individual goals for recovery, rehabilitation and reintegration. They also work with families and family caregivers to ensure they have the necessary information, care and support during these difficult times.

The Sergeant Merlin German Wounded Warrior Call Center, a Department of Defense Best Practice recipient, receives calls from active duty members, veterans and families seeking assistance in matters of Wounded Warrior care and transition. The call center also conducts important outreach calls to monitor injury recovery and distribute information on new programs offered by the Regiment, the Department of Defense, the Department of Veterans Affairs and other entities. Augmented by a staff of psychological health professionals, the call center also provides critical assistance to those seeking help for post traumatic stress disorder and traumatic brain injury.

Our Wounded Warrior Employment Cell, manned by marines and representatives of the Departments of Labor and Veterans Affairs, identifies and coordinates with employers and job training programs to help wounded warriors obtain positions in which they are most likely to succeed and enjoy fulfilling careers.

The Marine Corps' commitment to our wounded, ill, and injured is steadfast. We are grateful for the support and leadership of Congress on their behalf. I would like to extend my personal thanks to you and all Members of Congress for your visits to our wounded, ill, and injured marines and sailors and their families in the hospitals and other facilities where they are being treated.

CONCLUSION

This Nation has high expectations of her Corps—and marines know that. Your marines are answering the call around the globe while performing with distinction in the face of great danger and hardships. The Corps provides the Nation unrivaled speed, agility, and flexibility for deterring war and responding to crises; our ability to seize the initiative and dominate our adversaries across the range of military operations requires the right people, the right equipment, and sufficient time to train and prepare.

As marines continue to serve in combat, we must provide them all the resources required to complete the tasks we have given them. Now, more than ever, they need the sustained support of the American people and Congress to maintain readiness, reset the force during an extended war, modernize to face the challenges of the future, and fulfill the commitments made to marines, sailors, and their families.

On behalf of your marines, I offer our sincere appreciation for your faithful support and thank you in advance for your ongoing efforts to support our brave warriors. The Corps understands the value of each dollar provided by the American taxpayer, and will continue to provide maximum return for every dollar spent. Today over 203,253 Active and 39,400 Reserve Force marines remain ready and capable as the "Nation's Force in Readiness" ... and with your continued support, we will stay that way.

Senator BAYH. Without objection, all the written testimony will be accepted into the record.

General Amos, thank you very much.

Oh, and by the way, let me note the presence of Senator Burris.

Thank you for your devotion to the committee, and your attention here today.

Admiral Greenert.

STATEMENT OF ADM JONATHAN W. GREENERT, USN, VICE CHIEF OF NAVAL OPERATIONS, U.S. NAVY

Admiral GREENERT. Thank you, Mr. Chairman.

Chairman Bayh, Senator Burr, distinguished members of the Readiness and Management Support Subcommittee, it's my honor to appear before you to testify on the readiness of our Navy.

Mr. Chairman, I have a brief opening statement, and, as you said, please accept my full statement for the record.

I'd like to make three points, if I may. My first point addresses our increase in our fiscal year 2011 base budget O&M request. During the past 9 years, sustaining the readiness of our force in a high-demand operational environment has been aided by OCO funds or similar supplemental funding. Despite this, both the high operational tempo and the reduced turnaround ratio continue to increase risk to fleet readiness, force structure, and personnel.

As we look to the future, we have to balance global demand with the global management of our forces, and we should transition a supplemental resource dependency toward a baseline budget that provides the level of resources and resource support needed to meet an operational level that we refer to now as the "new normal." To do this, we have increased our base budget O&M request by about 6 percent; that's $3.5 billion, when compared to last year. This request is designed to meet our global obligations, properly sustain ships, aircraft, and expeditionary equipment to reach the end of their expected service lives, fund enduring flying readiness requirements, and fund price increases—notably, fuel. We request the support of Congress to fully fund the O&M request in the base budget and to fund contingency operations and maintenance in the OCO funding. This level of funding request, appropriately, represents our "new normal."

My second point addresses reset. Navy ships and aircraft are capital-intensive forces procured to last for decades. Scheduled maintenance of our force structure, training and certification of our crews between deployments, is a key element in Navy's reset of the

19

force. This interdeployment, maintenance, and training, we refer to as "reset in stride." It helps assure timely rotational deployment of our forces, ensures capability and capacity for future missions, and enables forces to surge for operations such as Operation Unified Response in Haiti. Reset translates into decades of readiness for each ship and aircraft, and it's a good return on investment. We rely on OCO, if you will, to fund the requisite OCOs and, in part, to reset in stride.

My third and final point addresses family readiness programs. We remain committed to the professional and personal development of our sailors, our Navy civilians, and the support to their families. Our budget request will enhance support to our sailors and their families, including those who are wounded, ill, and injured. Our Navy child and youth programs provide high quality educational and recreational programs for our children. We are leveraging military construction, Recovery Act funding, commercial contracts, and military-certified in-home care expansion to increase our childcare spaces and to meet our goal for placing children under care.

I request your strong support for our fiscal year 2011 readiness budget request and our identified priorities.

Thank you very much for your unwavering support to our sailors, civilians, and families, and for all that you do to make our Navy effective and an enduring global force for good.

Thank you. I look forward to your questions, sir.

[The prepared statement of Admiral Greenert follows:]

PREPARED STATEMENT BY ADM JONATHAN GREENERT, USN

Chairman Bayh, Senator Burr, and distinguished members of the Senate Armed Services Readiness and Management Support Subcommittee, it is my honor to appear before you to testify on the readiness of our Navy. Our Navy remains the preeminent maritime power, providing our Nation a global force for good. Our sailors and civilians continue to perform exceptionally well around the world under demanding conditions. Many of them are engaged in combat operations ashore, and assisting the people of Iraq and Afghanistan by providing security and helping to build an enduring infrastructure. Many are working with coalition partners to enable safe passage of shipping, reassuring relationships with allies; building partnership capacity, providing security force assistance and providing deterrence through ballistic missile defense and coalition operations. Still, others are responding to emergent calls for disaster relief and providing humanitarian assistance in Haiti. These diverse operations are tangible examples of our Navy's core capabilities as described in our Maritime Strategy—"A Cooperative Strategy for 21st Century Seapower". The 2010 Quadrennial Defense Review (QDR) validated the underlying principle in our Maritime Strategy: preventing wars is as important as winning wars. Additionally, the QDR found that U.S. security and prosperity are connected to the global commons; that deterrence is a fundamental military capability; and that partnerships are key to our strategy's success, and essential to the global stability. QDR's outcomes are consistent with the tenets of our Maritime Strategy. Naval operations are often one component of a joint force. Accordingly, it is my privilege to address the committee alongside my fellow Service Vice Chiefs and the Assistant Commandant.

Coincident with our endeavor to build our future force, we remain engaged in supporting operations in Afghanistan, Iraq and all other Combatant Commander (COCOM) Areas of Responsibility. For the second year in a row, Navy has more sailors on the ground than at sea in the Central Command (CENTCOM) area of responsibility. At sea in CENTCOM, we have more than 9,000 sailors, including a Carrier Strike Group dedicated to providing air support to U.S. and coalition ground forces in Afghanistan, and combatants supporting ballistic missile defense, anti-piracy, maritime security, counter-terrorism, theater security and security force assistance. Navy Riverine forces are on their sixth deployment to Iraq, conducting interdiction patrols and training their Iraqi counterparts. On the ground, we have more than

12,000 Active and Reserve sailors supporting Navy, Joint, and Coalition Forces, and Combatant Commander requirements. In Afghanistan, Navy Commanders lead seven of the 13 U.S.-led Provincial Reconstruction Teams. We have doubled the capacity of our Seabee construction battalions in Afghanistan, to support U.S. and coalition forces and provide critical infrastructure. Our Naval Special Warfare forces continue to be heavily engaged in combat operations. Our Explosive Ordnance Disposal detachments, many embedded in ground units, continue to conduct counter-improvised explosive device (C–IED) operations and train Iraqi and Afghan C–IED units. As we shift effort from Iraq to Afghanistan, demand for Navy Individual Augmentees (IAs) has increased. During a recent trip to CENTCOM in mid-February, I met many of our dedicated Navy men and women supporting these efforts and I could not be prouder of their contribution. Their professionalism, dedication and skill, are unmatched.

While operations in Iraq and Afghanistan continue to be the primary effort, our Navy remains globally engaged. We have 120 ships deployed—over 40 percent of our fleet—providing U.S. presence in every region of the world and demonstrating the capabilities of our Maritime Strategy. Our ballistic missile submarines are providing strategic nuclear deterrence, while our Aegis cruisers and destroyers are providing conventional deterrence in the form of ballistic missile defense in CENTCOM, the eastern Mediterranean, and western Pacific. Our Carrier Strike Groups and Amphibious Ready Groups continue to prevent conflict and deter aggression in the western Pacific, Persian Gulf, Arabian Sea and Indian Ocean. Their rotational deployments afford the U.S. the ability to influence events abroad, and the opportunity to rapidly respond to crises. Our Navy continues to confront irregular challenges associated with regional instability, insurgency, piracy, and violent extremism at sea, in the littorals, and on shore. We recently published the "Navy Vision for Confronting Irregular Challenges" to refine how our Navy will plan, resource, and deliver a wide range of capabilities through tailored forces (e.g.: riverine, maritime civil affairs and security, and special operations), and through our multi-mission general purpose forces (ships and aircraft). We are partnering with U.S. Coast Guard law enforcement teams in the Caribbean to conduct counter-narcotics and to deny illegal traffickers use of the sea. We recently deployed USS *Freedom* (LCS1), our first Littoral Combat Ship, to U.S. Southern Command. She is currently operating with counter-narcotics units in the Caribbean, and has already executed three successful drug interdictions. Her deployment, 2 years ahead of schedule, will allow us to more quickly evaluate her capabilities and incorporate operational lessons into the tactics, techniques and procedures of this new class of ships. We continue to strengthen relationships and enhance the capabilities of our international partners through maritime security activities such as global partnership stations in Africa, South America, and Southeast Asia. We reassure our allies through high-end training and operations in the Western Pacific and Europe.

Humanitarian assistance and disaster response operations continue in Haiti after a 7.0-magnitude earthquake devastated the nation. Within hours of the earthquake, we mobilized the aircraft carrier USS *Carl Vinson* (CVN70) with over a dozen helicopters, cargo aircraft, and extensive water-making capability; and quickly thereafter, the USS *Bataan* (LHD5) amphibious ready group with heavy lift helicopters and command and control capability, a Reserve Cargo Handling Battalion, a Seabee construction detachment, and a Marine Corps expeditionary unit; our hospital ship USNS *Comfort* (T–AH1) with medical personnel and supplies has completed over 850 major surgeries; a Navy dive and salvage team is working with Army dive teams to rebuild piers in the port facility; P–3 surveillance aircraft have flown over 90 intelligence, surveillance, reconnaissance missions; several surface ships with helicopters, and Military Sealift Command ships with fuel and cargo. Navy helicopters have transported over 900 medical evacuation patients to our off-shore hospitals and flown over 2 million meals-ready-to-eat throughout the disaster zone. Our disaster relief effort continues there today as part of a comprehensive U.S. Government and nongovernmental organization response. Global demand for Navy forces remains high and continues to rise because of the ability of our maritime forces to overcome diplomatic, geographic, and military impediments to access while bringing the persistence, flexibility and agility to conduct a broad spectrum of operations from the sea.

Our readiness programs and their processes, which are designed to maximize the operational availability of our Navy force structure and infrastructure, have been able, thus far, to satisfy the evolving and dynamic requirements of the COCOMs. Demand for naval forces continues to increase and shows no signs of abating in the near future. Your Navy is ready, responsive, agile, flexible—and actively engaged around the world.

Realistically, our ability to meet increasing demand requires that we continue our efforts to balance resources to sustain afloat and ashore readiness, force structure, and the readiness of our sailors and their families. In the aggregate, the health of all of these programs describes our total capability and capacity to deliver capable forces ready for tasking. During the past 9 years, sustaining the readiness of our force in a high demand operational environment has been aided by Overseas Contingency Operations (OCO) funds or similar supplemental funding. Despite this, both the high operational tempo and the reduced turn-around ratio (dwell) caused a high global demand for forces continue to increase risk to fleet readiness, force structure and personnel. As we look to the future, we must holistically address the fleet's operational availability requirements versus our global force management (GFM); and transition a supplemental resource dependency to a baseline budget that provides the level of resource support necessary to meet the Nation's maritime interests in an era of increasingly diverse, concurrent crises—the "new normal".

We remain focused on ensuring we are ready to answer the call now and in the future. Last year, we stated our risk was moderate, trending toward significant, because of the challenges associated with fleet capacity; increasing operational requirements; and growing manpower, maintenance, and infrastructure costs. This risk has increased over the last year. Trends in each of these areas have continued. We are able to meet the most critical COCOM demands today. But we are increasingly concerned about our ability to meet additional demands while sustaining a ready force through its expected service life by conducting essential maintenance and modernization to "reset" our fleet; and procuring the future Navy so we are prepared to meet the challenges of tomorrow.

The cost to operate and maintain our fleet has outpaced inflation by almost 2 percent each year. The need to balance between future fleet readiness and current readiness for operational requirements has resulted in risk. We increased our base budget OMN request by $3.5 billion, a 5.9 percent real increase in fiscal year 2011 compared to last year. This request is tightly focused on meeting global COCOM operations tempo (OPTEMPO) requirements, and on properly sustaining ships and aircraft to reach expected service lives, funding enduring flying readiness requirements in the base budget, and funding price increases, most notably in fuel. We request the support of Congress to fully fund the OMN request as we endeavor to fund enduring operations and maintenance in our base budget, and resource contingency operations and maintenance in OCO. The level of funding requested appropriately represents our "new normal".

Our fiscal year 2011 budget request achieves the optimal balance among our priorities to build tomorrow's Navy, maintain our warfighting readiness and develop and support our sailors, Navy civilians, and their families. It is aligned with Presidential and Department of Defense (DOD) guidance and it represents our Maritime Strategy and the 2010 QDR.

RESETTING THE FORCE: PREVAILING TODAY AND READY FOR TOMORROW

In addition to conducting rotational deployments, we are meeting emerging combatant commander requirements for ballistic missile defense; electronic attack; intelligence, surveillance, and reconnaissance; combat support and combat service support; and maritime security force assistance. Our OPTEMPO in CENTCOM will continue as the combat mission ends in Iraq. Navy enabling forces will remain in CENTCOM to provide various combat support/combat service support to joint and coalition forces in the region. Concurrently, we will continue to maintain a forward-deployed force of about 100 ships globally to prevent conflict, support allies, and respond to crises.

The high OPTEMPO has placed additional stress on our sailors and their families, ships, and aircraft. We are operating (and therefore consuming) our fleet at a higher than expected rate. Over the last decade, the size of our fleet has decreased while our operational requirements have grown. Consequently, there are more ships at sea assigned to COCOMs today and fewer ships available for at-sea training, exercises, or surge operations. Our challenge is to balance the need to meet current operational requirements with the need to sustain sailors' proficiency, and our ship and aircraft expected service lives.

Navy ships and aircraft are capital-intensive forces, procured to last for decades. Scheduled maintenance of our force structure, and training and certification of our crews between deployments is a key element in the "reset" of the force. This "reset in stride" process is perhaps different from other Services. It enables our ships and aircraft to rotate deployments and provide continuous forward presence as well as be ready for sustained surge operations, such as the humanitarian assistance and disaster relief in Haiti recently. For Navy, "reset in stride" translates into decades of readiness for each ship and aircraft, a good return on investment. However, deferring maintenance and modernization risks sustained combat effectiveness of force structure and reduces expected service lives. Almost three-quarters of our current fleet will still be in service in 2020. These "in-service ships" and submarines are a critical part of our 30-year Shipbuilding Plan and future inventory. Investment in the readiness of today's fleet will yield dividends in future capability and capacity.

Navy has a "current value" in ships and aircraft of approximately $640 billion. We are perhaps unique in that our maintenance accounts maintain the force, modernize, and "reset in stride" for the service life of our platforms. Since increased emergent operations are consuming the expected service lives of fleet units, at an advanced rate, Navy relies on OCO to fund OCOs and "reset-in-stride". Annual costs to own and operate the fleet represent about 3 percent of the capital value of our fleet assets. As we continue Operation Iraqi Freedom (OIF)/Operation Enduring Freedom (OEF), and sustain operating at a "new normal", operating and maintenance costs in our baseline accounts must keep pace.

FLEET READINESS: OPERATIONS, MAINTENANCE, EXPEDITIONARY (COMBAT SUPPORT)

Fleet Response Plan

The Fleet Response Plan (FRP) is Navy's force generation construct and has an operational framework of four phases (maintenance, basic, integrated, and sustainment). FRP has proven to optimize the return on training and maintenance, enhance sailor proficiency, and ensure units and forces are trained and certified in defined, progressive levels of employable and deployable capability. It provides COCOMs and the National Command Authority a transparent readiness assessment of Navy forces—ready for tasking. An FRP cycle is defined as: that period from the end of a maintenance phase to the end of the next maintenance phase. For surface combatants, an FRP cycle is nominally 24–27 months. Maintenance completed during the "maintenance phase" supports the appropriate readiness during remaining phases of a cycle. Personnel manning processes within the FRP cycle maintain appropriate defined unit manning readiness levels throughout the entire FRP cycle. We do not allow personnel readiness levels to atrophy and then peak just before a deployment. Training processes in the FRP provide appropriate required levels of unit readiness in the Fleet Response Training Plan (FRTP), and sustain deliberate unit readiness levels throughout the phases of the FRP. In the aggregate, the FRP provides Navy forces with the capability to respond to the full spectrum of Navy roles and missions through traditional rotational deployments as well as emergent COCOM needs (Request for Forces (RFF)).

Today's global security environment has created emerging demands for Navy forces requiring more flexibility to respond to rotational deployments, and emergent RFFs from geographic COCOMs. While reaffirming the importance of Navy forward presence resourced through rotational deployments, changes in the global security landscape have highlighted the need for trained and ready Naval forces capable of responding on short notice "surge" requirements. The rotational aspect of the FRP makes it an inherently sustainable plan if properly resourced. Risk in achieving the desired level of presence or surge is determined by force structure decisions, the OPTEMPO of assets while deployed, personnel manning, a proper maintenance phase and the length and rigor of an FRTP.

The FRP is applied to every unit and group (carrier strike groups and amphibious ready groups). The required operational availability of forces is derived from the GFM Plan and the "surge" requirements needed to support the most stressing operational plan. Our top priority is ensuring that forces are fully maintained, trained and ready to deploy.

Ship Operations

The fiscal year 2011 ship operation budget request (including OCO) provides funding for ships to steam an average of 58 days per quarter (while deployed) and 24 days per quarter (non-deployed). This OPTEMPO enables the Navy to meet FRP and training/certification requirements with acceptable risk. Risk is mitigated through increased use of simulators, concurrent training and certification events while underway, and judicious use of fuel.

While Navy met all fiscal year 2009 GFM commitments, and the operational requirements in support of OIF and OEF, some fiscal constraints resulted in degradation of readiness. Some unit training was prioritized to support FRTP training/certification only, and exercise and U.S. port visits were deferred. Some ships deployed to theater "surge capable" and certified for planned theater operations, but not "Major Combat Operation (MCO)" ready. MCO is the FRTP goal. The fiscal year 2009 mitigation strategy was intended to be the exception—sustaining Navy training readiness at these levels will have a cumulative risk to mission success in future operations. Crew proficiency can degrade in these circumstances.

Navy ships require routine corrective and preventive maintenance, assigned and conducted within the capability and capacity of the ship's crew. Deferring repair parts re-stock results in eventual inventory shortages, and will likely result in eventual deferred preventive maintenance. Deferred corrective maintenance by the crew reduces unit readiness and can result in increased workload and cost for shore-based repair facilities. Deferred preventive and corrective maintenance will cause degraded performance or failure of installed equipment during critical training events or deployments. Annual ship repair part obligations have remained relatively unchanged for several years. During fiscal year 2009, fleet operation mitigations (reduced OPTEMPO) helped reduce the impact of ship repair parts shortfalls until OCO funds were appropriated. However, an uneven temporal allocation of funds results in:

- Delayed funding (planning) for ship maintenance periods
- Delayed repairs (e.g., cross-decking parts to satisfy emergent requirements and requisitions)
- Deferred preventative maintenance
- Delayed storeroom re-stock of repair parts

Another factor in ship operations is the price of fuel. Fluctuations in fuel prices complicate the ability to precisely budget operating costs.

Ship Maintenance

The fiscal year 2011 budget request (including OCO) resources the ship maintenance account to 99 percent of requirement. This includes carrier, submarine and surface ship dry-docking availabilities, anticipated voyage repair and 40 of 49 non dry-docking surface ship availabilities. We assess this to meet currently known requirements with an acceptable level of risk. A key factor in the Navy's 30-Year Shipbuilding Plan is the ability to reach the expected service life of our ships. Reaching full service life requires an integrated engineering approach to ensure the right maintenance is planned, funded and executed over a ship's lifetime. We are committed to the right level at the most efficient cost. An example of our effort to reduce the total cost of ownership, the submarine technical community has increased the operating interval for SSN 688 and SSN 774 class submarines through analysis of engineered technical requirements and assessment of recently completed availabilities. This change will improve operational availability while reducing the cost of submarine life-cycle maintenance.

We made significant improvements in the way the Navy manages the maintenance and modernization of its surface force through efforts such as the Surface Ship Life Cycle Management (SSLCM) Activity and the Surface Ship Life Cycle Assessment Pilot Study. Partnering with the fleet, the SSLCM Activity will assess and manage the maintenance requirements throughout the life cycle of surface ships, enabling more precise and accurate planning and budgeting. The SSLCM is modeled after two successful and similar programs; the Submarine Maintenance Engineering Planning and Procurement Activity and the Carrier Planning Activity.

SSLCM is conducting a detailed technical review of surface ship class maintenance plans to make certain we understand the full maintenance requirement necessary to reach expected service life for these platforms. We have completed the update on two of our larger ship classes, the DDG 51 and the LSD 41/49 classes. SSLCM is now the designated life cycle organization responsible for maintaining the Integrated Class Maintenance Plans, building availability work packages, and providing technical oversight/approval for fleet work deferral requests.

The cyclical nature of ship and submarine depot availabilities from year to year causes variations in budget requests and in annual obligation levels. Budget years with multiple ship-docking availabilities increase required funding. More maintenance scheduled in the private sector tends to increase funding in a given year. Nuclear powered carriers and submarines are on a strict time-based maintenance interval in order to maintain certification for unrestricted operations.

Surface ship availabilities are conducted almost exclusively in the private sector. Nuclear submarine and aircraft carrier availabilities are primarily conducted in the public sector, with selected availabilities completed by nuclear capable private shipyards (Electric Boat (Subs) and Northrop Grumman Shipbuilding (Subs/Carriers)). Whenever practical, maintenance is performed in the ship's homeport to minimize the impact on our sailors and their families. The Navy recognizes that both public and private sector maintenance organizations need a stable and level workload to maximize efficient execution. Navy works to level the workload to the maximum extent possible within operational constraints.

Air Operations (Flying Hour Program)

The Flying Hour Program (FHP) account provides for the operation, maintenance, and training of ten Navy carrier air wings (CVWs), three Marine Corps air wings, Fleet Air Support (FAS) squadrons, training commands, Reserve forces and various enabling activities. The fiscal year 2011 budget request (including OCO) resources the FHP account to achieve Training-rating (T-rating) levels of T2.5 for Navy and T2.0 for the Marine Corps. TACAIR (Tactical Aviation) squadrons conduct strike operations, provide flexibility in dealing with a wide range of conventional and irregular threats, and provide long range and local protection against airborne surface and sub-surface threats. FAS squadrons provide vital fleet logistics and intelligence. Chief of Naval Air Training (CNATRA) trains entry-level pilots and Fleet Replacement Squadrons (FRS) provide transition training to our highly capable, advanced fleet aircraft. Reserve component (RC) aviation provides adversary and logistics air support, makes central contributions to the counter-narcotics efforts, conducts mine warfare, and augments Maritime Patrol, Electronic Warfare, and Special Operations Support to OCO missions.

The aviation spares account supports 100 Type/Model/Series (TMS) aircraft and approximately 3,700 aircraft in the fleet. Aviation spares are funded to 75 percent of the requirement and is a part of the Navy's Unfunded Programs List for fiscal year 2011. The Navy is evaluating alternatives to manage this risk.

Aviation Maintenance

The Aviation Depot Maintenance account ensures operational aviation units have sufficient numbers of Ready for Tasking (RFT) aircraft to accomplish assigned missions. Shortages in the number of airframes, engines, or other components can detract from the number of RFT aircraft. The fiscal year 2011 budget request (including OCO) resources the Aviation Depot Maintenance account to 96 percent of requirement. The 4 percent unfunded will result in a projected cumulative backlog of 21 of 829 airframes and 342 of 1,998 engines, leaving a backlog of acceptable technical and operational risk. The fiscal year 2011 budget request ensures deployed squadrons have 100 percent of their Primary Authorized Aircraft (PAA), and supports achieving our 100 percent zero bare firewall engine goal. The Naval Aviation Enterprise (NAE) AIRSpeed strategy continues to deliver cost-wise-readiness by focusing efforts on reducing the cost of end to end resourcing, increasing productivity, and improving the operational availability of aircraft.

We request that you fully support our baseline and OCO funding requests for operations and maintenance to ensure the effectiveness of our force, safety of our sailors, and longevity of our aircraft.

Strike Fighter Inventory Management

Our current force management measures are targeted at preserving the service life of our existing legacy strike fighter aircraft (F/A–18 A–D). Therefore, we will reduce the number of aircraft available in our TACAIR squadrons during non-deployed FRTP phases, to the minimum required in order to meet training and certification. We will reduce our Unit Deployed TACAIR squadrons (UDP) from twelve aircraft to ten aircraft per squadron to match the corresponding decrease in Marine Corps expeditionary squadrons. We are accelerating the transition of five legacy F/A–18C squadrons to F/A–18 E/F squadrons, using available F/A–18 E/F aircraft, and will transition two additional legacy squadrons using F/A–18 E/F attrition aircraft. These measures make available legacy strike fighter aircraft for High Flight Hour (HFH) inspections and, potentially, the Service Life Extension Program (SLEP). Taken together, these would provide the option to extend the service life of legacy aircraft and help manage the inventory. These measures will expend the service life of some F–18 E/F aircraft earlier than programmed. Accordingly, we are refining our depot level production processes to maximize throughput and return legacy strike fighter aircraft to the fleet expeditiously to ameliorate Super Hornet life expenditure.

There are initiatives in place to extend the service life of our F/A–18 A–D aircraft. HFH inspections, which have been in place for 2 years, provide the ability to extend the service life of our legacy F/A–18 A–D aircraft to 8,600 flight hours. Further engineering analysis is underway to determine the SLEP requirements necessary to reach the service life extension goal of 10,000 flight hours should this course of action be required.

Naval Expeditionary Forces (Combat Support)

Our Navy continues to place significant emphasis on strengthening its expeditionary warfare forces to confront irregular challenges. The fiscal year 2011 budget request continues to support Irregular Warfare (IW) requirements and promotes synergy in IW with the Marine Corps and U.S. Coast Guard. But despite efforts to increase capacity, stress on the high demand and limited supply of expeditionary forces (EOD, Riverine, Seabee) requires continuous monitoring and the employment of mitigation strategies to ensure our forces meet Chief of Naval Operations (CNO) PERSTEMPO guidelines including deployment length, deployment periodicity (dwell goal 1.0:2) and homeport tempo (greater than 50 percent). During fiscal year 2007 the EOD community dwell ratio was averaging 1.0:1. In fiscal year 2008, EOD introduced mitigation options that increased their average dwell ratio above both CNO dwell minimum (1.0:2). Other communities such as P–3, Seabee, Riverine and EA–6B (Prowler) are currently above the minimum dwell ratio, but remain below the CNO's goal (1.0:2).

The budget request provides for the manning, training, operations, and maintenance of expeditionary forces under the purview of the Navy Expeditionary Combat Command (NECC) including: the Naval Construction Force, Explosive Ordnance Disposal/Mobile Diving and Salvage, Riverine Forces, Maritime Expeditionary Security Forces, Navy Expeditionary Logistics Support Group, Expeditionary Combat Readiness Center, Maritime Civil Affairs and Security Training, Navy Expeditionary Intelligence Command, and Combat Camera.

Evolving warfighting missions and increases in COCOM demand for Theater Security Cooperation Programs missions, building partner capacity, and security force assistance, have expanded the training and operational requirements for NECC Forces in every theater. For example, within the past 14 months, Navy Seabees have twice been called upon to enable the troop surge in Afghanistan. First, performing a "lift and shift" from Iraq to Afghanistan to support the arrival of the Marine Expeditionary Force, and subsequently, preparing for the arrival of the 30,000 additional troops directed by the "surge". The Seabees constructed Forward Operating Bases, Combat Outposts, and support facilities. To meet emergent training and global operational requirements associated with OCOs, NECC leverages OCO funding to provide the critical training and outfitting in theater and meet the dynamic missions they execute throughout the theater.

Based on GFM requirements, NECC deploys mission-specific units to fulfill COCOM requests. This involves employing traditional core capabilities in the Navy Expeditionary Combat Force, as well as emerging new mission capabilities that have been requested and developed over the last several years. Combining the disparate capabilities and capacity of these forces under a single type command structure has increased Navy's responsiveness to support existing and evolving irregular warfare missions in both rotational deployments and emergent COCOM needs (RFFs). Navy Riverine forces are now on their sixth deployment to OIF conducting interdiction patrols in southern Iraq and training their Iraqi counterparts.

NECC is providing the training, preparation, and administrative support oversight for the more than 13,000 IA and ad-hoc forces performing enabler missions in support of ground forces. At 40,000 sailors, NECC represents about 12 percent of Navy manpower, yet operates with 1.5 percent of Navy Total Obligation Authority—a bargain considering the extensive capabilities they bring to COCOMs.

TRAINING READINESS: CONNECTING US TO OUR FUTURE FORCE

Ballistic missile proliferation continues to be a growing security concern to our nation. Maritime Ballistic Missile Defense (BMD) is a core U.S. Navy capability. Our Navy's ability to train the force in a flexible and agile fashion remains a necessity in an uncertain strategic environment. We conducted our first BMD Fleet Synthetic Training event this past year, proving the viability and effectiveness of integrated Navy, Joint and partner-nation BMD training. Our budget request continues to build this momentum to develop a comprehensive BMD training program.

The Fleet Synthetic Training program provides realistic operational training including seamless integration of geographically dispersed Navy, Joint, Interagency, and coalition forces. Providing efficient and effective synthesized training optimizes the FRTP.

The proliferation of advanced, stealthy, diesel submarines continues to challenge our Navy's ability to guarantee access in all global regions. Effective Anti-Submarine Warfare (ASW) training at sea with active sonar systems is a necessary part of our FRTP. Synthetic training can supplement, but not completely substitute for at-sea training. Navy remains a world leader in marine mammal research and we will continue our robust investment in this research in fiscal year 2010 and beyond. Through such efforts, and in full consultation and cooperation with appropriate Federal agencies, Navy has developed protective measures to mitigate the potential effects to marine mammals and the ocean environment from the use of mid-frequency active sonar, while meeting ASW training. We will continue to work closely with our interagency partners to further refine our protective measures, as scientific knowledge evolves.

Over the last year, we completed environmental planning documentation for eight existing and proposed at-sea training and combat certification areas. We anticipate completion of planning documentation for another six areas over the next year, as we continue to balance our responsibility to prepare naval forces for deployment and combat operations with our responsibility to be environmental stewards of the marine environment.

Conducting night and day field carrier landing practice (FCLP) prior to at-sea carrier qualifications is a critical training requirement for our fixed-wing, carrier-based pilots to develop and maintain proficiency in the fundamentals of carrier aviation. We continue to seek additional airfield capacity in the form of an outlying landing field (OLF) that will enhance our ability to support FCLP training for fixed-wing, carrier pilots stationed at and transient to Naval Air Station Oceana and Naval Station Norfolk. The additional OLF capacity will allow Navy to meet training requirements and overcome challenges related to capacity limits, urban encroachment, and impacts from adverse weather conditions at existing East Coast facilities. Navy is committed to developing, with local, State, and Federal leaders, a plan to ensure the OLF provides positive benefits to local communities while addressing Navy training shortfalls.

Learning and Development

Quality education and training of our sailors provides unique skills that give us an asymmetric advantage over potential adversaries and sets us apart from every other Navy. To develop a highly-skilled, combat-ready force, we have 15 learning centers around the country providing high quality, tailored training to our sailors and Navy civilians. We remain committed to the professional development of the Navy Total Force, and continue to balance current and traditional education and training requirements with emerging mission areas such as cyber warfare, ballistic missile defense, and counterterrorism. We have completed 40 of 82 enlisted learning and development roadmaps, which describe in detail the required training, education, qualifications, and assignments required throughout a sailor's career. We recognize the importance of providing our officers with meaningful and relevant education, particularly our Naval War College and Joint Professional Military Education, to develop leaders who are strategically-minded, critical thinkers, and adept in naval and joint warfare. Cultural expertise, regional focus and linguistic expertise remain essential to Navy's global mission, and our budget request supports expansion of the Language, Regional Expertise, and Culture majors program for Naval Reserve Officers Training Corps NROTC midshipmen as well as implementation of the AF–PAK Hands Program, which will provide the joint force with enhanced language and cultural capabilities in Afghanistan and Pakistan.

SHORE READINESS

Shore infrastructure supports and enables operational and combat readiness. It is an essential element to the quality of life and quality of work for our sailors, Navy civilians, and their families. Increasing costs in manpower and afloat-readiness, combined with emergent requirements compel us to take risk in Shore Readiness. To manage this risk, our fiscal year 2011 shore readiness budget request places a priority on supporting Navy and Joint mission readiness, ensuring nuclear weapons security and safety, and improving our bachelor and family quarters, including sustained funding for our Homeport Ashore initiative. We are taking risk in other shore readiness areas and at current levels, the recapitalization of our facilities infrastructure is at risk.

To ensure our limited resources are applied to projects with the highest return on investment, we continue to use a capabilities-based Shore Investment Strategy to target shore investments where they will have greatest impact on critical capabilities, specifically investments associated with Navy warfighting requirements, improved quality of life, and Family readiness.

Despite challenges, we have made essential progress and improvements in nuclear weapons security, child care facilities, and bachelors' quarters.

American Recovery and Reinvestment Act

Your support and assistance through the American Recovery and Reinvestment Act (ARRA) of 2009 was very helpful. As you requested, we identified Military Construction projects for Child Development Centers and barracks and prioritized them while considering the ability to obligate funds quickly. We selected infrastructure and energy projects based on mission requirements, quality of life impact, environmental planning status, and our ability to execute quickly. Our aggressive execution schedule is on track, and construction outlays are ramping up swiftly. Due to a very favorable bidding climate, savings of over $100 million have been realized as of the end of December 2009. Following the Office of the Secretary of Defense (OSD) guidance to invest in the 19 States and the District of Columbia with the highest unemployment rates, additional projects for use of these savings have been developed by Commander Navy Installations Command and submitted by OSD for approval. The list of supplemental projects contains a continued emphasis on critical repairs, Quality of Life and Work, energy consumption related projects, enlisted housing, and child development centers.

Energy and Climate

Energy reform is a strategic imperative. We are committed to changing the way we do business to realize an energy-secure future. In alignment with the Secretary of the Navy's goals, our priorities are to advance energy security by, assuring mobility, expanding tactical reach, protecting critical infrastructure, "lightening the load", and greening our footprint. We will achieve these goals through energy efficiency improvements, consumption reduction initiatives, and adoption of alternative energy and fuels. Reducing our reliance on fossil fuels will improve our combat capability by increasing time on station, reducing time spent alongside replenishment ships, and producing more effective and powerful future weapons. Most of our projects remain in the demonstration phase; however, we are making good progress in the form of an electric auxiliary propulsion system delivered last year on the USS *Makin Island* (LHD 8), testing and certification of bio-fuels as drop-in replacements for petroleum, advanced hull and propeller coatings, solid state lighting installations, and policies that encourage sailors to reduce their consumption through simple changes in behavior.

Thanks to your support, the ARRA funded Navy energy conservation and renewable energy investment in 11 tactical and 42 shore-based projects totaling $455 million. Tactical projects included alternative fuel, drive, and power systems for ships, aircraft and tactical vehicles. Ashore projects included alternative energy (wind, solar and geothermal) investments in 10 States and the installation of advance metering infrastructure in three regions. Our fiscal year 2011 budget continues to invest in tactical and ashore energy initiatives, requesting $128 million for these efforts.

In our Maritime Strategy we addressed maritime operations in an era of climate change, especially in the ice diminished Arctic. The CNO established the Navy's Task Force on Climate Change to develop policy, investment, and force-structure recommendations regarding climate change in the Arctic and globally over the long-term. Our focus will be to ensure Navy readiness and capability in a changing global environment.

FAMILY READINESS AND SAILOR CARE

We remain committed to the professional and personal development of our sailors and Navy civilians, and support to their families. We are in the process of expanding opportunities for service at sea to women in the Navy by offering assignments on submarines. Current plans are to accept the first cadre of female officers into the submarine training pipeline this year to facilitate their assignment aboard submarines as early as fiscal year 2012. We intend to enhance support to our sailors and their families, including those who are wounded, ill and injured, through expanded child and youth care, Fleet and Family Support services, Navy Safe Harbor, and the Operational Stress Control program. We are aggressively addressing the rise in suicides over the last 12 months by implementing revised training and outreach programs for Navy leadership, sailors, Navy civilians, and families to increase suicide awareness and prevention. To reduce sexual assaults, we will refocus our leadership, change our cultural approach and insist on accountability. Led by the Sexual Assault Prevention and Response Office, a new direction for intrusive leadership by unit commanders and an emphasis of intolerance for sexual assault and related behavior in our Navy is underway. We remain committed to providing our sailors and their families a comprehensive continuum of care that addresses all aspects of medical, physical, psychological, and family readiness. Our fiscal year 2011 budget request expands this network of services and caregivers to ensure that all sailors and their families, and our wounded, ill, and injured receive the highest quality healthcare available. Navy Safe Harbor, Navy's Operational Stress Control Program, Reserve Psychological Health Outreach Program, Warrior Transition Program, Returning Warrior Workshop and Behavioral Health Needs Assessments are critical elements of this continuum.

Navy Safe Harbor has been expanded and continues to provide non-medical support for all seriously wounded, ill, and injured sailors, coast guardsmen, and their families through a network of Recovery Care Coordinators and non-medical Care Managers at 16 locations across the country. Over the past year, Safe Harbor's enrollment has grown from 387 to 542. Over 84,000 sailors have participated in Operational Stress Control (OSC) training, which is providing a comprehensive approach designed to actively promote the psychological health of sailors and their families throughout their careers while reducing the traditional stigma associated with seeking help. Our individual augmentees receive OSC training prior to deployment while the Warrior Transition Program (WTP) and Returning Warrior Workshops (RWW) are essential to post-deployment reintegration efforts. WTP, established in Kuwait and expanded via Mobile Care Teams to Iraq and Afghanistan, provides a place and time for individual augmentees to decompress and transition from life in a war zone to resumption of life at home. The RWW identifies problems, encourages sailors to share their experiences, refers family members to essential resources, and facilitates the demobilization process.

Stress on the Force

As we continue to operate at a high operational tempo to meet our nation's demands around the world, the tone of the force remains positive. We continue to monitor the health of the force by tracking statistics on personal and family-related indicators such as stress, financial health and command climate, and sailor and family satisfaction with their services in Navy. Recent detailed survey results indicate that sailors and their families remain satisfied with command morale, the quality of leadership, education benefits, health care, and compensation. We remain focused on our connection with the family at the unit level so that we have informed, prepared, and resilient families.

Suicide is a tragic event affecting sailor, family, and unit readiness. We continue efforts at suicide prevention through a multi-faceted approach of communication, training, and command support designed to foster resilience and promote psychological health among sailors. Navy's latest 12-month suicide rate of 13.3 per 100,000 sailors represents a small decrease from the previous year's rate of 13.8 per 100,000 sailors. Although suicides are significantly below the national rate for the same age and gender demographic (19.0 per 100,000 individuals), we are not satisfied. Any loss is unacceptable. We remain committed to creating an environment in which stress and other suicide-related factors are more openly recognized, discussed, and addressed. We continue to develop and enhance programs designed to mitigate suicide risk and improve the resilience of the force. These programs focus on substance abuse prevention, financial management, positive family relationships, physical readiness, and family support, with the goal of reducing individual stress. We continue to work toward a greater understanding of the issues surrounding suicide to ensure that our policies, training, interventions, and communication efforts are meeting their intended objectives.

Child and Youth Programs

Our Navy Child and Youth Programs, the top priority within Family Readiness Programs, provide high-quality educational and recreational programs for our Navy children. We are leveraging Military Construction funding, Recovery Act funding, commercial contracts, and military-certified in-home care expansion to increase child care spaces and to meet our goal of placing children under care within 3 months of their request. By the end of 2011, we will meet this goal and will be in compliance with OSD's direction to provide child care to at least 80 percent of our military population. While we are meeting our child care capacity goals, recapitalization of our existing infrastructure is still required. In addition to increasing child care spaces, we are also adding 25,000 additional hours of respite child care and youth services for families of deployed sailors and our wounded, ill, and injured. Our child care and youth programs are a highly valued resource by our sailors and their families, and are an investment in the Nation's future.

Bachelor Housing

Our bachelor housing program is currently focused on two goals: providing Homeport Ashore housing (at our Interim Assignment Policy) for our junior sea-duty sailors by 2016 and eliminating our substandard (Q4) bachelor housing inventory by 2020. We appreciate the assistance of Congress to commence a Homeport Ashore initiative in Coronado, CA, with an fiscal year 2009 Recovery Act bachelor housing project that will eliminate 1,056 spaces in the deficit. We are continuing this important Quality of Life initiative by requesting $75 million in new construction in fiscal year 2011 for bachelor housing in San Diego to provide an additional 772 spaces to our inventory. The PB11 Future Years Defense Plan contains 6 Military Construction projects that will provide the 4,305 spaces required to complete the Homeport Ashore initiative by 2016.

Family Housing

Our fiscal year 2011 family housing budget request includes $68.2 million for family housing construction, improvements, planning, and design. This amount includes $37.2 million for replacement construction of 71 homes for naval base personnel at Naval Base Guantanamo Bay, Cuba and $28.4 million for 116 housing units in Japan. In addition, our fiscal year 2011 budget request includes $329.7 million for the operation and maintenance of 10,000 Navy-owned homes and 3,700 leased homes.

Utilizing a combination of increased recapitalization funding and PPV authorities, the Navy met the Secretary of Defense's goal to fund by, fiscal year 2007, the elimination of all inadequate military family housing units, which Navy defined as homes requiring repairs, improvements, or replacement costing more than $50,000. To establish common standards across all four Services, the Secretary of Defense redefined family housing condition ratings in 2009 to correlate with the Facility Condition Rating system used across DOD. This system classifies any unit in a Q3 or Q4 condition as inadequate. Navy has identified those government-owned units as Q3/Q4, most of which are overseas. These units represent 6 percent of the entire Navy inventory. Navy is on target to achieve the Secretary of Defense goal that 90 percent of family housing to be at an adequate (Q1/Q2) condition by 2015.

Our portfolio management program collects and analyzes financial, occupancy, construction, and resident satisfaction data to ensure our PPV projects are optimized and performing as required and the services provided meet expectations. We regularly host PPV focus groups to assess the quality of privatized housing and housing services delivered to Navy families and make changes in Navy policies and procedures as required. We continue to receive very positive feedback from our Navy families. This enhanced oversight of our PPV partners meets required congressional reporting and ensures Navy sailors and their families continue to benefit from quality housing and services.

Individual Augmentees (IA)

Navy currently has over 11,000 sailors serving as IAs worldwide. Since last year, Navy designated Commander, U.S. Fleet Force Command (CUSFF) as the Executive Agent for Individual Augmentees, accountable to the CNO for the IA program. Through the efforts of USFF, including the creation of the Navy Preparedness Alliance to focus the efforts of our personnel assignment, medical, Reserve, ashore, and fleet leadership, the efficiency and effectiveness of the program has improved dramatically. For example, as testified to by our sailors and their families, notification to our sailors of IA assignment has improved, and our IA "family support" programs are more effective.

More than 8,000 IA sailors are on the ground in CENTCOM, serving in vital support roles across both adaptive core and temporary [1] mission areas such as provincial reconstruction teams, detainee operations, civil affairs, training teams, C–IED, intelligence, and medical support. As the focus shifts from Iraq to Afghanistan, we anticipate the demand for sailors to support the joint force in nontraditional missions to remain at or above their present levels.

To better support our IA sailors and their families, we have made significant progress in integrating the IA experience into a Navy career, ensuring IA duty enhances a sailor's career and increased predictability associated with IA deployments. IA resourcing and support is a priority, and will require vigilance by Navy leadership.

CONCLUSION

In a recent statement, Secretary Mabus clearly described the mindset of our Navy. "Our sea services are always forward-deployed, always forward-leaning. We do not rest or lie at anchor, waiting for the call. For the call is now, and unremitting—and so is our resolve." We work to refine Navy readiness processes to ensure "Forces Ready for Tasking" are delivered whenever and wherever the Nation calls. In an increasingly interconnected and multi-polar world, the nature of challenges to our Nation's interests tomorrow could be different from the nature of the challenges that we face today. We are a force ready to fight our Nation's wars, but we are also focused on deterring or containing conflict regionally or locally. To deal effectively with today's myriad challenges requires established relationships of trust and confidence with potential partners all over the globe. Our Navy plays an enduring role in meeting that requirement through the execution of our Maritime Strategy. Our presence provides the opportunities to positively influence circumstances

---

[1] Temporary—missions for which Navy does not have standard, mission-ready capabilities.

and events to protect or optimize our vital national interests. That presence also enables the Navy to respond to requests for humanitarian assistance and disaster recovery as needed.

Readiness is a matter of capable forces ready for tasking, with sufficient capacity. The return on investment in our readiness accounts is measured by the ability of the Navy to deliver required capabilities in rotational deployments and in response to emergent needs of the COCOMs. In a high demand environment with finite resources, achieving that readiness requires careful assessment of risk and consequences, a judicious balance of multiple, equally valid but competing requirements. The support of Congress and this committee in effectively maintaining that balance is most appreciated.

I ask for your strong support of our fiscal year 2011 readiness budget request and our indentified priorities. Thank you for your unwavering support and commitment to our sailors, Navy civilians, and their families, and for all you do to make our U.S. Navy an effective and enduring global force for good.

Senator BAYH. Thank you, Admiral, for your leadership. General Chandler.

STATEMENT OF GEN. CARROL H. CHANDLER, USAF, VICE CHIEF OF STAFF, U.S. AIR FORCE

General CHANDLER. Mr. Chairman, Senator Burr, and distinguished members of the subcommittee, thank you for the opportunity to represent your U.S. Air Force to the subcommittee today. I, like the rest of my joint teammates, am proud to be here to represent our Service.

Let me begin by saying that your 680,000-strong U.S. Air Force—Active Duty, Guard, Reserve, and civilians—is ready to execute its mission. Our readiness is demonstrated every day as we serve alongside our joint and coalition partners in Iraq, Afghanistan, and around the world. On any given day, there are approximately 40,000 deployed airmen providing close air support, tactile and strategic airlift, intelligence, surveillance, reconnaissance (ISR) critical medical care, and combat search and rescue, along with combat and combat support functions. Of these 40,000, there are approximately 5,300 airmen performing joint expeditionary taskings, providing combat and combat support functions within the Army and the Marine Corps in Afghanistan and Iraq.

In addition to our deployed presence, more than 131,000 airmen are performing deployed-in-place missions, supporting combatant commanders. These airmen are operating remotely piloted vehicles, maintaining satellite constellations, conducting inter-theater airlift, and maintaining our nuclear deterrence posture. Additionally, the Air Force continues to provide defense for the Homeland as the total force effort, with the Active Duty, Guard, and Reserve personnel, from locations across the United States.

Stabilizing our end strength is a critical part of maintaining personnel readiness. We're moving toward a force with approximately 332,000 Active Duty airmen, approximately 71,000 Reserve airmen, and approximately 107,000 Air National Guard personnel.

The Air Force met its goals for new accessions in retaining our current experience in nearly every area. Our retention rates are the highest that they've been in 15 years and generally exceeding our goals by about 20 percent. Only health professionals fail to meet their retention in recruiting goals, and efforts are underway to mitigate these shortfalls through bonuses.

Selective retention bonuses remain our most effective retention tool. These bonuses, along with critical skills retentions bonuses for officers, are successfully targeting 91 enlisted and 3 officer special-ties.

Last June, the Air Force initiated the Year of the Air Force Family. More than half way through this effort, we're on course to eliminate known childcare deficit in our child development centers by 2012. We're increasing spouse employment referral assistance and adding 54 school liaison officers to assist school transitions for almost 175,000 school-aged Air Force dependents. We're improving our exceptional family member program, which supports more than 15,000 airmen with special-needs family members. We're also increasing the quality of programs provided for deployment and re-integration support for our airmen and their families.

Our aircraft are well-maintained and ready. Although our air-craft inventory is seeing extensive use in contingency operations, the fleet's average age is continuing to increase, the dedicated work and professionalism of our airmen ensure that we're ready.

Our combat Air Force aircraft continue to provide global power when and where required. Our airlift fleet continues to provide strategic airlift, as well as theater and direct-support airlift mis-sions, moving a wide variety of equipment, personnel, and supplies.

The recent release of the KC–X request for proposal begins the process of recapitalizing our aerial refueling aircraft. The planned acquisition of 179 KC–X aircraft will help provide refueling capa-bility for decades to come.

The Nation's nuclear aircraft and intercontinental ballistic mis-siles (ICBM) remain the highest priority for our Service. Of all the missions the Air Force accomplishes every day, none is more crit-ical than providing strategic deterrence. ICBM crews sit nuclear alert every day, and nuclear-capable fighter and bomber crews and their weapons systems contribute to our deterrence posture.

Again, Mr. Chairman, the Air Force will continue to provide our best military advice and stewardship, delivering global vigilance, reach, and power for America. We thank you for your continued support for the U.S. Air Force, and particularly for our airmen and their families. I look forward to your questions.

[The prepared statement of General Chandler follows:]

PREPARED STATEMENT BY GEN. CARROL H. CHANDLER, USAF

INTRODUCTION

Today, the United States confronts a dynamic international environment marked by security challenges of unprecedented diversity. Along with our Joint partners, the Air Force will defend and advance the interests of the United States by providing unique capabilities to succeed in current conflicts while preparing to counter future threats to our national security. Over the last year, the Air Force made progress in strengthening not only our readiness for today's operations, but also in fostering the flexibility required for the uncertain requirements of tomorrow. Through in-creased balance, our Service can maintain its readiness to meet the obligations set forth in the Quadrennial Defense Review: prevail in today's wars, prevent and deter conflict, prepare to defeat adversaries and succeed in a wide range of contingencies, and preserve and enhance the All-Volunteer Force.

DAILY OPERATIONS AND READINESS

The Air Force is committed to readiness and ongoing operations. After 19 years of continuous deployments and 9 years of operations in Afghanistan and Iraq, these operations continue to stress both people and platforms. Since the events of Sep-tember 11, the tempo of our operations has continued to increase: we have executed more than 50,000 sorties supporting Operation Iraqi Freedom and almost 66,000 sorties supporting Operation Enduring Freedom, delivered over 1.73 million passengers and 606,000 tons of cargo, and employed almost 1,980 tons of munitions. Additionally, we have transported nearly 70,000 patients from the Central Command (CENTCOM) area of responsibility, and our combat search and rescue forces met the "golden hour" goal of transporting seriously wounded warriors to treatment facilities within 60 minutes of injury nearly 98 percent of time. Lastly, our aeromedical evacuation sorties moved critically injured warriors to regional hospitals within hours of injury, contributing to the 95 percent battlefield injury survival rate.

We are a global force that is dedicated to supporting combatant commander requirements from both the continental U.S. and overseas bases. Nearly 40,000 of America's airmen, or about 7 percent of the force, are deployed to 263 locations across the globe, including 63 locations in the Middle East. Also, deployed airmen currently fill about 5,300 Joint Expeditionary Taskings, helping the joint team with critical combat and combat support functions. In addition to those deployed, nearly 219,000 airmen—fully 43 percent of the force—support combatant commander requirements from their home stations in the continental U.S., Europe, and the Pacific each day. These airmen operate the Nation's space and missile forces, process and exploit remotely collected intelligence, surveillance, and reconnaissance (ISR), provide national intelligence support, protect American airspace, actively engage with our allies and partners, and contribute in many other ways. Finally, defense of the homeland is a total force mission with a minimum of 40 aircraft from 18 locations engaged in operations at any given time.

FISCAL YEAR 2011 BUDGET REQUEST OVERVIEW

The fiscal year 2011 Air Force budget request of $119.6 billion reflects our commitment to the Joint fight, and contributes to a refocused investment strategy emphasizing Joint force activities. This request balances providing capabilities for today's commitments and posturing for future challenges. We chose to improve existing capabilities whenever possible, and to pursue new systems when required. This approach to modernization and recapitalization keeps pace with threat developments and required capabilities, while ensuring responsible stewardship of resources. In developing this budget request, we also carefully preserved and enhanced our comprehensive approach to taking care of airmen and Air Force families. In fiscal year 2011 we will stabilize end strength at 332,200 Active Duty airmen, Reserve component end strength at 71,200, and Air National Guard end strength at 106,700.

Our fiscal year 2011 $45.8 billion operations and maintenance (O&M) budget request supports operations at 80 major installations and funds air, space, and cyber operations, as well as intelligence, logistics, nuclear deterrence, Special Operations, and search and rescue capabilities. This O&M request is 8.5 percent above the fiscal year 2010 authorization due largely to fuel price increases, growth in enabling functions such as intelligence and communications, force structure transformations such as joint basing and in-sourcing, and shifting focus toward new missions such as cyber capabilities supporting the stand-up of U.S. Cyber Command.

PERSONNEL READINESS

Our dedicated airmen are the foundation of the Air Force. Recruiting, training, and retaining an All-Volunteer Force requires significant investment. This investment drives the very effectiveness of our highly-skilled and technically proficient force.

Deployed Forces

The Air Force can, at times, support combatant commands without forward deploying personnel. Some tasks, however, require physical presence. Nearly 40,000 airmen are forward-deployed to combatant commands on any given day, 55 percent for 179 days or longer. Approximately 75 percent of deployed airmen support operations in Afghanistan and Iraq. Due to the capabilities required by current conflicts, a relatively small portion of our total force deploys more frequently than the force as a whole. Sixteen of the 132 enlisted specialties and eleven of the 125 officer specialties are considered "stressed" due to their deployment operations tempo. A number of programs are in place to bolster the manning in these career fields as well as mitigate potential negative effects on their families and personal well-being.

We will continue to provide the full range of air, space, and cyber capabilities to meet combatant commander requirements. Remotely piloted aircraft currently provide 41 continuous combat air patrols to U.S. CENTCOM. This number will grow to 50 by the end of fiscal year 2011, and to 65 by the end of fiscal year 2013. Over the last year we developed and fielded the Project Liberty program, providing additional airborne ISR capability. We are also increasing our deployed capacity in explosive ordnance disposal, intelligence, security, provincial reconstruction teams, tactical air control parties, and air liaison officers. As the surge in Afghanistan ramps up, the Air Force will not only increase its presence in Afghanistan, but also increase our strategic airlift commitment, including mobilizing 2,400 Guard and Reserve airmen.

Recruiting and Retention

We continue to meet both our recruiting and retention goals for nearly every Air Force career field. Recruiting among the Active, Guard, and Reserve components has been solid. Active duty recruiting met fiscal year 2009 goals and is on track for fiscal year 2010 in all but the medical and health specialties. Officer recruiting for health professions dropped to 70 percent of the goal, and enlisted health specialties fell to 60 percent. The Air National Guard exceeded their enlisted recruiting goals in fiscal year 2009, and they are on track to meet or exceed their desired number of accessions in fiscal year 2010. However, the Air National Guard recently initiated a new campaign to improve officer accessions which are approximately 25 percent below their target.

Both officer and enlisted retention remain strong. Enlisted retention is well above 95 percent overall, and in excess of our goals for mid-career enlisted airmen. Although retention of mid-career officers in the contracting, special tactics, and health-related specialties is challenging, efforts are underway to mitigate shortfalls through targeted accession and retention bonuses. The fiscal year 2011 budget request allocates $685 million for targeted bonuses and retention incentives in part to fund Critical Skills Retention Bonuses for the specialties critically short of officers between 8–14 years of commissioned service, and Selective Retention Bonuses (SRB) for the enlisted force in 91 specialties. Enlisted SRBs remain our most effective and targeted retention tool, and this budget will improve this program's effectiveness by increasing the maximum enlisted retention bonus to $90,000. In the short-term, however, dealing with fewer airmen exiting the force may be more challenging than meeting our recruiting and retention goals.

Total Force Integration

The Air Force is maximizing our capacity by leveraging the strength of National Guard and Reserve airmen through associations with the Active-Duty Force. We are currently executing 142 Total Force Integration (TFI) initiatives that pool Active, Guard, and Reserve personnel and equipment. Many of these associations result in new missions for total force personnel as we seek greater balance. In conjunction with the National Guard Bureau and Air Force Major Commands, we are currently conducting a top-to-bottom assessment of our TFI processes to maximize the effectiveness of current and future associations.

Year of the Air Force Family

Air Force families bear the greatest burden at home when airmen deploy. The Secretary of the Air Force and Chief of Staff established July 2009 through June 2010 as the Year of the Air Force Family. More than half way into this effort, we have completed our assessment of existing programs and are now recalibrating family support efforts. As part of this focus, we are on course to eliminate the known child care deficit at our Child Development Centers by 2012, increase spouse employment referral assistance, and add 54 school liaison officers to assist school transitions for the almost 175,000 school-age Air Force dependents. We augmented our exceptional family member program which supports more than 15,000 airmen with special-needs family members. We also increased the quality of programs providing deployment and re-integration support to our airmen and their families, and foresee adding a number of initiatives designed to enhance the resiliency of airman in the face of emotional and psychological hardships related to the stress of deployments.

Suicide Prevention

Despite our focus on resiliency, too many airmen are lost to suicide each year. There have been 24 suicides among Active, Guard, Reserve, and civilian personnel so far in calendar year 2010, 7 more than this time last year. In response, our Air Force Suicide Prevention Program is focusing on clinical and non-clinical intervention as well as leadership involvement at all levels. As part of this emphasis we fielded new training programs, improved access to mental health providers in primary care settings, and increased training for military chaplains. In the coming months we will roll out an updated clinical guide to managing suicidal behavior, tailor training for our higher risk populations, and emphasize suicide prevention in forthcoming airmen resiliency initiatives.

Wounded Warriors

The Air Force is committed to taking care of its wounded airmen. We fully support the Office of the Secretary of Defense programs designed to keep highly skilled men and women on active duty. If this is not feasible, the Air Force will ensure airmen receive enhanced assistance through the Air Force Wounded Warrior program. We have 17 Recovery Care Coordinators at 15 locations dedicated to aiding the recovery, rehabilitation, and re-integration of airmen, and we are adding 10 more care coordinators this year. This program, currently serving 651 Wounded Warrior airmen, will provide lifetime support.

AIRCRAFT READINESS

Although our aircraft inventory has seen extensive use in contingency operations and its average age continues to increase, the dedicated work and professionalism of our airmen ensures we are ready. After retiring many of our oldest and most maintenance-intensive aircraft such as all KC–135Es and a fourth of the C–130Es, less than 1 percent of Air Force aircraft are grounded and fewer than 5 percent are flying with operational restrictions. Although we continue to meet combatant commander requirements, operations tempo continues to take a toll and many of our aircraft are increasingly unavailable due to required maintenance.

Consequently, modernization and recapitalization remain priorities. By accelerating the planned retirement of 257 legacy fighter aircraft, we are committed to a smaller, but more capable fifth-generation fighter force. These retirements freed more than 4,000 personnel to operate remotely piloted aircraft and to process, exploit, and disseminate intelligence. This shift accepts a moderate amount of warfighting risk due to decreased capacity, but is necessary to move forward to more capable and survivable next generation platforms. Within our mobility fleet, the recent release of a KC–X request for proposal began the process of recapitalizing our aerial refueling aircraft. The planned acquisition of 179 KC–X aircraft will help provide refueling capability for decades to come. Similarly, the recent release of the Mobility Capabilities Requirements Study-2016 indicates that there is excess strategic airlift capacity. Consequently, the fiscal year 2011 budget request proposes the early retirement of 17 of our oldest C–5As.

Combat Air Forces

The readiness of Combat Air Forces aircraft is adequate despite challenges from accumulating hours on our fleet faster than envisioned when these aircraft were fielded. The B–1, B–52, and F–15E did not meet aircraft availability standards due to maintenance and depot-related issues, and the F–22 fell short of the projected availability due to low observable maintenance requirements. Recent improvements in many F–22 system components and increased durability of low observable materials resulted in a 32-percent reduction in maintenance man-hours per flying hour.

Mobility Air Forces

The readiness of the Mobility Air Forces remains high while meeting robust and dynamic operational requirements. Our airlift fleet continues to provide strategic airlift as well as theater and direct support airlift missions moving personnel and a wide variety of equipment and supplies. We recently concluded a successful demonstration of direct support for the Army in Iraq, validating both the operating concept and the use of C–130s and C–27Js for that mission. The direct support mission is a matter of trust for the Air Force, and we are committed to providing this capability for the Joint Force. In addition, we will continue direct support through aerial delivery—a mission that airdrops supplies to isolated locations and is essential to the success of the Afghanistan strategy. Our airdrop requirements increased sevenfold in the last year.

Exercises

Green Flag and Red Flag are the primary predeployment close air support and large force composite training opportunities for most units deploying to contingency operations. These exercises continuously incorporate lessons learned from ongoing operations. Both exercises include other services and more than 20 partner nations, contributing to Joint and Coalition interoperability.

Flying hour program

This is the first year the Air Force recalibrated our annual flying hour submission to reflect the amount of executable flying hours in light of deployment-related pilot availability. This change decreased the flying hour request by 162,000 hours, and is consistent with recent under-execution of peacetime flying hours and over-execution of overseas contingency operations hours. The revised request for 1.2 million flying hours is fully funded within our budget request.

NUCLEAR DETERRENCE

Today we continue to strengthen the nuclear enterprise, which remains the number one priority of our Service. Air Force Global Strike Command, established in August 2009, provides a renewed vigor and energy to the operation, training, and equipping of Intercontinental Ballistic Missile (ICBM) and nuclear-capable bomber forces. The stand up of a fourth operational squadron of B–52s in October 2009 enhances our readiness to perform nuclear deterrence missions, as well as support conventional mission requirements.

The sustainment of nuclear weapons was consolidated in the Air Force Nuclear Weapons Center (AFNWC), which manages nuclear weapons system life cycle sustainment. AFNWC is instituting a positive inventory control methodology for weapon system components and 100% accountability of all nuclear weapons related material. Finally, Air Force leadership instituted a more robust, standardized inspection capability that increased the rigor and intensity of the inspection and verification process to ensure our Air Force maintains the high standards required by the critical nuclear mission.

Of all the missions the Air Force ably accomplishes every day, none is more critical than providing strategic deterrence. ICBM crews sit nuclear alert everyday in underground facilities, just as they have for the last 50 years, and nuclear-capable fighter and bomber crews and their highly-capable weapon systems contribute to our deterrence posture.

CONCLUSION

Despite 19 years of sustained Air Force deployments, the personnel and aircraft of the U.S. Air Force are ready to face any challenge with precision and reliability. Although ongoing operations affect a portion of our readiness, we are balancing our force to ensure our personnel, weapon systems, equipment, and organizations are prepared for today's operations and tomorrow's uncertain challenges.

Senator BAYH. Thank you, General Chandler.

I note the presence of Senator Chambliss.

Senator Chambliss, thank you. I appreciate your service on this subcommittee, and your leadership.

We're going to have 7 minutes per round. So, I'll try and be brief, and then turn to Senator Burr, and we'll then proceed in order of arrival at the subcommittee hearing.

Admiral Greenert, let me begin with you. First, a little background, then I'll get to my question.

Last year, the Chief of Naval Operations (CNO) submitted only two unfunded priorities—ship and aircraft depot maintenance—to the amount of about $395 million. This committee, on both sides of the aisle, supported that request. Unfortunately, those amounts were not supported by the Appropriations Committees. As a result, a 1-year backlog of critical maintenance was not executed and deferred, which places unnecessary risk on fleet readiness, reduces the service life of the fleet, drives up long-term sustainment costs, and increases strategic risk for the Nation. While I am encouraged that the fiscal year 2011 budget request, including OCO, resources the ship maintenance to 99 percent of the requirement, we still have the 1-year backlog to confront. To the Navy's credit, once again you have submitted only three unfunded priorities for ship and aircraft depot maintenance and spare parts.

So, my questions, Admiral, are, what was the impact of not getting the $395 million in fiscal year 2010? What happens if we do not support your unfunded maintenance priorities again in this fiscal year? What is the risk and impact to readiness?

Admiral GREENERT. Senator, thank you for the question. The most difficult portion of dealing with the shortfall in the year of execution is, frankly, determining where you have to mitigate that lack of funding, if you will. What we've determined—in the past, we used to take the ploy that surface ship maintenance, being a predominantly privately contracted entity was where we would mitigate that shortfall. But, you also hit the nail on the head when you said "mean expected service life for our ships." That is a primary concern of ours.

Without the additional funds, and to mitigate $395 million in unfunded requirements, on top of a growing requirement that we have in fiscal year 2010 of about $450 million in CENTCOM operations due to the shift from Operation Iraqi Freedom to Operation Enduring Freedom, on top of $250 million in fuel price increases, and on top of another $150 million in requests for forces, which are emergent requests from our combatant commanders, we find that, among our operating accounts, we have to take actions, such as to defer some port visits, defer some exercises, reduce flying for those that are nondeployed or for airwings that return. But, what I'd like to assure you of is that one of our focuses is to make sure that our ships meet their expected service life.

So, we are honing the line as much as feasible on ship maintenance. However, when we don't receive the unfunded priority list, that puts more pressure on that. It can be debilitating as it rolls over into the next year.

The risk is the long-term health of the ships. It tends to manifest itself, sometimes, in that year, but, too often, later down the road, when we need to reset our forces.

So, in summary, it really becomes a matter of mitigating among the operating accounts. That's the problem that we have to deal with, sir.

Senator BAYH. Admiral, what does fiscal year 2011's unfunded maintenance request buy back?

Admiral GREENERT. Fiscal year 2011's maintenance request for aircraft spares is $423 million. We've found that we have introduced some type model series aircraft, the MV–22. It has been in service for some time, but as we get to understand the needs, that cost has gone up and we're using more spares. We're using the aircraft more. The increased operations in CENTCOM, in our Hornets, in our helicopters, and in some of our P–3s, have added to an increased use of spares, so that describes that piece.

$75 million is for aircraft depot maintenance, and that would buy down our backlog of airframes and engines to no more than 1 year's backlog, which we find to be a risk that we can deal with without too much——

Senator BAYH. Do you have the capacity to execute, here, if your requests are authorized and appropriated?

Admiral GREENERT. We do have the capacity to execute, yes, sir. Lastly, $35 million is——

Senator BAYH. Make sure the Appropriations Committee has the benefit of your testimony here today. Hopefully, they'll make sure.

Admiral GREENERT. I will do that, sir, you can be sure of it.

Senator BAYH. Let's see. We don't have the light system in effect here today so someone is going to let me know when my 7 minutes is up. I don't want to have a mini-filibuster here.

This question is for all the witnesses. Are we budgeting to restore readiness in the fiscal year and the years beyond? Specifically, when can we expect to reach our dwell-time goals and to increase or restore the restoration of our strategic depth? Anybody want to take a stab at that one? Any volunteers from the committee?

General Chiarelli? You're a brave man, General. [Laughter]

General CHIARELLI. Senator, we expect to reach our dwell goals in most military occupational specialties (MOS). I talk in individual dwell goals, where an individual will see he or she is going to be home for 2 years in 2012. But, I think it's important to note that, although in 2012, you will be in a position where you will have 2 years of dwell, you really don't have the dwell until you have the dwell. It is like Ranking Member Burr talked about when he talked about the 82nd. The 82nd was supposed to be home for 2 years, but took a detour down to Haiti. So, that creates issues, when we see these unforecasted contingencies.

The second part of the question, Senator?

Senator BAYH. I think that pretty adequately covers it.

General CHIARELLI. Okay.

Senator BAYH. Let me follow up, though, with you on something else, if I can shift gears a little bit, General. Last week, DOD sent Congress a reprogramming request for fiscal year 2010. Included in that request was a $573 million reduction in the $1.3 billion Humvee procurement funding Congress approved for the Army. Can you confirm that the Army plans to buy new Humvees with the remaining $770 million?

General CHIARELLI. We plan to buy 2,662 additional Humvees. We have reached our acquisition objective for Humvees—in fact, gone over it—and will begin a recap program for other Humvee requirements.

Senator BAYH. That's about $560 million for recapitalization, I think.

General CHIARELLI. I believe so.

Senator BAYH. Can you explain the difference—Humvee recap programs and the number of each type of vehicle you intend to recap, and the cost per vehicle for each?

General CHIARELLI. Currently, we are recapping 5,046 unarmored Humvees at about $55,000 per vehicle, and 4,270 uparmored Humvees in fiscal year 2011, at a cost of $105,000 to $130,000 apiece, depending on the Humvee.

Senator BAYH. Thank you very much, General.

My time is expired in this round. I will now turn to my colleague, Senator Burr.

Senator BURR. Thank you, Mr. Chairman.

General Chiarelli and General Amos, given the surge of 30,000 forces that are currently being deployed to Afghanistan, do you have the right type of equipment in sufficient quantities to fully equip the surged forces for the mission in Afghanistan?

Let me go to you first, General Chiarelli.

General CHIARELLI. We do. As the mine resistant ambush protected (MRAP) all-terrain vehicles (ATV) arrive in Afghanistan, it will not be too long before, I believe, we'll be able to get everybody who can be out of them, out of the uparmored Humvee and into the MRAP ATV. But, we have had great success in getting equipment into Afghanistan, thanks to the great work of 3rd Army as they took equipment coming out of Iraq, ran it through maintenance, and we were able to get that equipment into Afghanistan. In fact, we have equipment in Afghanistan ahead of forces right now.

Senator BURR. General Amos?

General AMOS. Senator, we do. We have everything we need in Afghanistan. There's a little bit flowing in, but not much. The last time I checked, we had about 2 percent left to flow in for that 19,400 marine and sailor force that you talked about in your opening statement. We are good in Afghanistan. Of note, though, about 42 percent of the equipment that ended up fleshing out—it's a total of about 75,000, what we call, principal end items—now, that doesn't mean 75,000 vehicles, but a vehicle is a principal end item; it could be a radio that's a principal end item—but 75,000 principal end items to flesh out and get that command the equipment that it needs in Afghanistan. About 40 percent of that came from Iraq.

So, I think the key piece is—the answer is yes, we do. They are fully equipped. They are reporting the highest levels of readiness in Afghanistan. So, our young men and women that are forward deployed have everything that they need. It works, and it's up. But, to get that, we ended up taking equipment that we had planned on—this responsible drawdown that I referred to in my opening statement. We've been going through there, for the last year in Iraq, to get ourselves out, get positioned in Kuwait, get it on ships, and get it back to Albany and get it back to Barstow, to depots. About 42 percent of that gear, or 40 percent of it, is not going to make it back this year. It's probably not going to make it back next year. So that's the kind of strain on the force, but we have everything that we need over there, Senator. You can rest assured of that.

Senator BURR. Thank you. Thank you, General.

Admiral, in your written testimony you said, "The cost to operate and maintain our fleet has outpaced inflation by almost 2 percent each year. The need to balance between future fleet readiness and current readiness for the operational requirements has resulted in risk." In what areas of readiness are we at risk?

Admiral GREENERT. My concern, readiness at risk, is in surface ship maintenance, predominantly, to be most specific. We have to do a few things. One, we have to make sure we understand the requirement to make sure that when a ship goes in for long-term maintenance, we know what needs to get done in order to assure that it will reach its expected service life. Two, then we have to fund it to that level and ensure that that gets executed. Then, three, in the operations—when the ship is operating, we need to understand the impact of what the additional—we're riding them pretty hard—roll that into that next maintenance package. That's what I called "reset in stride." We have to keep up with that, Senator.

Senator BURR. Is the risk reflected, in the underfunding of certain readiness activities, in the fiscal year 2011 base budget, or is it OCO requests?

Admiral GREENERT. The risk is that we are at 99 percent of our known maintenance requirement in fiscal year 2011. So, that's not much risk. That 1 percent is manageable.

My concern is carryover from the fiscal year 2010 execution, and I described some of that risk at a previous question. We have shortfalls in the year of execution. To your point, if we do not receive the OCO request, then we are operating these ships in contingency manner, and that's taking away from their service life. That's risk we'll carry forward.

Senator BURR. Thank you, Admiral.

General Chiarelli, as I stated in my opening statement, I'm concerned about the long-term cost of resetting the resources of the Army units, that they may not be supported amidst other Federal budget decisions we still need to make in the next 2 years. You stated in our readiness hearings last year, and I quote, "The Army expects our reset requirements will be in the range of $13 to $14 billion per year, as long as we have forces deployed in for 2 to 3 years thereafter to ensure readiness for the future." Is that number still an accurate number, or would you like the opportunity to update it in any way?

General CHIARELLI. If I look forward to the next 3 years, we're looking at anywhere between $30 billion and $36 billion, total, for reset. For fiscal year 2010 and fiscal year 2011, our numbers are almost identical—close to $11 billion in each year, and that includes procurement money.

Senator BURR. That's in your budget request?

General CHIARELLI. That is in the OCO request. It is, sir. We expect—and that is in fiscal year 2011, too, just—almost identical.

Senator BURR. Does that amount include the cost required to restore prepositioned equipment?

General CHIARELLI. It does not, I believe, include that cost.

Senator BURR. Okay. Again, in your written testimony you state that, "In order to restore the Army's full operational depth by fiscal year 2012, the Reserve component—that is, our National Guard and Reserve Forces—must continue a transition from a Strategic Reserve to an Operational Force, thus allowing the Army recurrent, assured, and predictable access to the Reserve components to meet operational requirements." How would you characterize the availability of equipment and resources for nondeployed Guard units, as compared to nondeployed Active Duty units?

General CHIARELLI. Active component units are reaching an equipment level of about 80 percent, and National Guard units, in all equipment, 75 percent. However, the critical dual-use equipment is at 83 percent, and expected to make it to 87 percent, here, in the next 6 months.

Senator BURR. General Chandler, if I could turn to you with the same question, relative to the nondeployed Active-Duty Force, versus the Guard and Reserve nondeployed.

General CHANDLER. Sir, I would say exactly what General Amos said earlier. We have, in some ways, taken from some of our non-deploying units to make sure some of our deploying units have exactly what they need to do the job. That's reflected in a lot of Status of Resources and Training System ratings that you see, both in flying units as well as support units.

Senator BURR. I've heard information that the Air Force intends to draw down a disproportionate number of C–130s from service in the Air National Guard. One, is it true? Two, can you elaborate on the pros and cons of maintaining aircraft in the Active component, as opposed to the Air National Guard?

General CHANDLER. Sir, I understand your question. I will tell you, I've spent a lot of time over the last week with the director of the Guard as well as the Reserve. Just as a point of background, I will tell you that what you saw in that budget was an effort to react to what we saw coming in the military capabilities assessment; in other words, the C–130 fleet getting smaller. We took that opportunity to retire some of the older aircraft. Exactly how we get at the distribution, and how we'll do that, realizing that we have a Federal mission, and the States have a mission as well, and how we balance that, is what we're discussing with the Chief and the Secretary. We should have an answer shortly.

Senator BURR. I appreciate your consideration under that, especially given the fact that we drew down that Guard contingent some time ago, and the further drawdown would deplete their resources to carry out their mission.

My time's expired. Thank you, Mr. Chairman.

Senator BAYH. Thank you very much, Senator Burr.

It's good to note Senator Udall's attendance today.

Thank you for your good work on the committee.

Senator Burris, I think you're next.

Senator BURRIS. Thank you, Mr. Chairman.

I'd like to add my thanks to these four distinguished Americans for your committed service to this country and to the world. So, my hat's off to you, Generals and Admiral. Job well done.

Recently completed Joint Staff studies show that in Iraq, DOD was highly dependent on contractors in four of the nine joint capacity areas. Furthermore, the Government Accountability Office has recently reported that planning operations planned for future operations include little or no information on contractors. Given DOD's high dependency on contractors to meet its mission, how do the Services assure themselves that the needed contractors will be available when needed? General Chiarelli, do you want to try that one?

General CHIARELLI. As far as I know, Senator, we have not had issues in getting the contractors that we need. That has not been reported to me as an issue. I think you know that, currently, we have about 1-to-1 contractor for every soldier who is deployed, so the numbers are high. However, I do not know of any issues in getting contractors.

Senator BURRIS. General Amos, any word on Marine Corps' contracting?

General AMOS. Senator, ours is a little bit easier. Because we nest under the Army, as executive agent for things like logistics and a lot of the logistics hauling and that kind of stuff, we don't really hire contractors. We have brought some contractors forward, for instance, from our depot in Albany, GA, and brought them forward. We had them in Iraq working, doing some less-than-depot-level work to keep our equipment up to speed. We're in the process of transitioning that same kind of capability into Afghanistan right now. But, we don't really do much contracting in the way that I think your question leads us to.

Senator BURRIS. Admiral, does the Navy do any contracting?

Admiral GREENERT. Not much, Senator. We come self-contained; our Seabees, self-contained, don't use contractors. Same story with our explosive ordinance detachments. Otherwise, we are embedded in a ground unit in their support, so we would depend on their support, to the degree they use contractors, sir.

Senator BURRIS. Just to change the subject a little bit, Admiral, I just left Djibouti, down at Camp "Lemonyar" or however you say it, "Lemonyon".

Admiral GREENERT. "Lemonier" sir.

Senator BURRIS. Lemonier?

Admiral GREENERT. Lemonier. Yes, sir.

Senator BURRIS. My French is not very good, my German is better. I see our people are living down there, I talked to the Seabees, and the captain there was very excited, but they're living in containers and tents. Can we at least get them in some containers or some decent facilities? Has that been budgeted, Admiral?

Admiral GREENERT. Senator, I can assure you, what they are living in has been budgeted.

Senator BURRIS. In some new facilities?

Admiral GREENERT. Some new facilities. These containers are, frankly—did you have the opportunity, by chance, to get inside one?

Senator BURRIS. Oh, yes, I did.

Admiral GREENERT. You did? Okay.

Senator BURRIS. I was there.

Admiral GREENERT. The reports that I get—and I was there about 6 weeks ago—was that those were satisfactory. The tents were not. The tents are very hot and they use massive amounts of energy.

Senator BURRIS. Yes.

Admiral GREENERT. We're getting out of the tents. That will be before the year ends.

Senator BURRIS. But, that is the plan, to get out of the tents.

Admiral GREENERT. Get out of the tents, yes, sir. Two reasons. One, they're not good quality-of-life for support, but also two, they are extremely energy depleting.

Senator BURRIS. I'm sure Captain Flynn will be glad to hear that, because he made a special remark on that.

General, how about the Air Force, you all doing any contracting there?

General CHANDLER. Sir, we have a certain amount of expeditionary integral support in the Air Force, in terms of Red Horse Civil Engineering, for example, and services to take care of the folks. Based on what I've seen, and if my numbers are right, the Air Force does about 70 percent of the contracting work, in terms of officers and noncomissioned officers, for contracting in that part of the world.

Senator BURRIS. So, General, if you were to do some work at Scott Air Force Base—say, that you were to expand housing or do something for those four commands down there in my territory—who would do the work? Would we contract it out to private contractors, or how would that be done at Scott?

General CHANDLER. There would typically be a contracting officer that would work the contract, in whatever arrangement—and particularly in terms of housing in the privatized scheme that we're doing now.

Senator BURRIS. Yes.

General CHANDLER. That would be work by a contracting officer in the Air Force civil engineering organization that handles those contracts.

Senator BURRIS. By the way, I want you to know I was born and raised down in that area. I remember when we used to call it Scott Field, and there were maybe two or three planes flying out of there. You all have really expanded that area, General.

General CHANDLER. It's a great installation, Senator.

Senator BURRIS. It's really good for our southern Illinois community, and we appreciate what those commands are doing down there.

Now, do the Services need a readiness reporting system for contractors—and maybe the Army can answer—do you need a readiness reporting system for contractors?

General CHIARELLI. I don't believe we do. We have contracting officers representatives (COR), who are watching our contractors to make sure that they're fulfilling their portion of the contract. That's become a priority in the Army as we both increase the number of folks that we have in contracting command, and commanders realize the absolute necessity of ensuring that they have good, qualified CORs to ensure that the terms of contracts are being met.

Senator BURRIS. Okay. General Chiarelli, the Army Chief of Staff recently directed that units preparing to deployed to Iraq or Afghanistan identify and train CORs prior to deploying. How does the Army track this information?

General CHIARELLI. We have requirements for CORs. I do not know how we track the total numbers, but commanders have been told to train the necessary number that they need for the area that they're going into. I have not received any reports that they are not doing that. In fact, I've heard that the quality of the CORs has gone up considerably since the beginning of the war.

Senator BURRIS. Thank you, General.

My time is expired, Mr. Chairman. Thank you very much.

Senator BAYH. Thank you, Senator Burris.

Senator Chambliss.

Senator CHAMBLISS. Thank you very much, Mr. Chairman.

Gentlemen, as always it's a pleasure to have you here. Thanks for your service. Be sure and convey to all those men and women that serve under you how much we appreciate their great service.

Just this past week, I was informed that one of my Academy nominees to West Point, 1st Lieutenant Robert Collins, class of 2008, was killed by an improvised explosive device in Mosul. It certainly hits home when those tragic events occur, and it emphasizes more the importance of your testimony here today. I'd like to thank each of you again and to recognize Lieutenant Collins' family for their sacrifice and for their son's service to our Nation. When I talked to his mother yesterday—both his mother and his father are retired Army lieutenant colonels—she said, "You know, we knew and he knew that when he joined the family business, there were risks involved," but it doesn't make it any easier when you lose a top young man like that, General Chiarelli.

I want to start with you, General Chandler. You note in your written statement that Air Force has been operating under continuous stress in deployments for 19 years, including 9 years of operations, obviously, in Iraq and Afghanistan. I know this has taken a toll on your airmen, but also on your aircraft. I understand that your air logistics centers have a backlog of work and have been challenged to deliver aircraft on schedule, back to warfighters, due in part to aircraft coming into the depots requiring more work than they have previously had, based on the near continuous use that you referred to. I assume that you agree this is extremely important, that the Air Force receive every dollar that you requested in the fiscal year 2011 budget to support aircraft maintenance and depot activities. Is that correct?

General CHANDLER. Yes, sir, it is.

Senator CHAMBLISS. I note that the number-one priority of the Air Force's unfunded requirements is $337 million for weapon system sustainment, which will go towards a variety of depot maintenance and service life extension programs that you had deemed to be high priorities. Could you elaborate on how you would use those funds and how important they are to the Air Force?

General CHANDLER. Sir, they are extremely important, because it takes us from about an 82 percent dial to an 85 percent dial on weapon system sustainment of at least known requirements. Like the other Services, our requirements continue to grow, and we continue to chase that, hence the unfunded priority. That represents about 16 aircraft through depot maintenance and about six to seven engines that would go through depot maintenance, as the vast majority of the money.

Senator CHAMBLISS. Thank you.

General Chiarelli, General Amos, from your testimony we've heard that our soldiers and marines are stressed, particularly our ground forces, and that you've had challenges in fulfilling your manning requirements for deploying units. I'm also told that in some of our deploying units, mainly Army BCTs and Marine regiments, that we have almost battalion-sized elements remaining back in the rear as nondeployables. More importantly, I've also been told that these nondeployable numbers have been rising over the past few years.

Now, it seems to me if we were to take efforts to reduce these nondeployables, that it should invariably increase the amount of available personnel for deployed units. Are the Army and Marine Corps taking steps to reduce these nondeployable soldiers and marines and replace them or turn them into individuals that we are able to deploy?

General Chiarelli?

General CHIARELLI. We're doing our best to do that, but our numbers continue to go up. One reason they've continued to go up, we are averaging between 12 and 14 percent nondeployable in our BCTs at this time. One of the reasons why we've seen it go up is because the Army has taken units off stop-loss since the first of the year. That alone, given the fact we can only give them a 90-day drop on their contract, means that we have to hold onto them until we reach that point, which drives up the nondeployable rate. Other nondeployables we've seen increase are medical nondeployables. But, we have young men and women, who, after three rotations— the knee operation that they needed after the first rotation won't wait for the fourth rotation. We owe it to them to make sure they have the opportunity to be taken care of, and that's what we're doing. Our largest increase has been in medical nondeployables, and it is because of many of those muscular-skeletal kinds of issues that arise.

Senator CHAMBLISS. General Amos.

General AMOS. Senator, right now, of a force of 202,000 reported as of just a couple days ago, we had 31,602 that we would classify as nondeployables. That sounds like an awful lot, but, of note in there, just about 29,000 of those are what we call trainees—marines that are in boot camp, marines that are in advance infantry skill training, marines that are in pilot training and going through their military occupation specialties training—22,000 of that 31,600 are in training right now, so they are nondeployable. Another almost 4,000 are in transit; at any given time, they're moving from the east coast to the west coast or coming out of schools or moving into their new units, and they're in what we call transit. Then we have about 3,400 of them that are medical, that are not expected to recover. We track those very carefully. So, while the number 31,000 sounds high, it actually makes sense. Then there's some other small or very small numbers in there.

But, we have not had any trouble fleshing out our combat units, Senator. We have marines reenlisting and extending contracts, their 4-year enlistment, to extend for 6 months so that they could go back with the unit that they deployed with, in some cases already twice. So, we have not had a problem with fleshing out our units. We track the nondeployables very, very closely.

Senator CHAMBLISS. General Chiarelli, is this a funding issue, that these folks are having these medical problems, or what's the reason?

General CHIARELLI. It's the time between deployment, Senator. We have aviation units that are going 1-to-1 right now. They are 1 year deployed, 1 year back home. It is that. We have instances where, as I indicated earlier, the only thing that counts is individual dwell. Keeping track of the dwell of an inanimate object, like a flag, means nothing; it's the individual that's key and critical. We do not allow anybody to redeploy that doesn't have 12 months of dwell time. One of the increases I've seen in our nondeployables are individuals we have to leave behind for a month or 2 in order to get them 12 months of dwell time back home, because they've transferred from another unit. With the MOSs we have, some are just more stressed than others are. Those things are driving it up. It's not a money issue, Senator.

Senator CHAMBLISS. Let me go back to that dwell time. As far as training is concerned, I know there are efforts underway to increase that dwell time for all of our service men and women once they return from deployment, and I think that, once we get to where we can have a 1-to-3 ratio, it'll make things much better for you. But, as it now stands, are units, particularly our tactical units, able to train in their traditional core competencies while still preparing for full-spectrum operations and counterinsurgency?

General CHIARELLI. They're doing more today than they were doing yesterday. The mere fact that we're focusing on Afghanistan, which I believe is a different fight, has caused us to move into more full-spectrum type of training. But, as we approach at least 1-to-2, we're going to see the amount of that training be able to increase over time.

Senator CHAMBLISS. Okay. Thank you very much.

General Amos, just be sure when you go to Albany, that you don't say "ALL ben ny," it's "All BEN ny." [Laughter.]

General AMOS. Sir, I'll take that under advisement. When I do go to "All BEN ny," I'll be happy to pronounce it correctly. Thank you, sir.

Senator CHAMBLISS. It's a great base, too, but—you can bring that depot to North Carolina. We'll let you call it whatever you want to. [Laughter.]

Senator BAYH. All politics is local. [Laughter.]

Thank you, Senator Chambliss.

Senator Udall.

Senator UDALL. Thank you, Mr. Chairman.

Good afternoon, gentlemen. As an old expedition mountain climber, I'm reminded of the adage that I think I heard first applied to the military, which is in—with all due respect to those in the military of other responsibilities, that—if I can get this right—tactics are for amateurs; strategies are for rank amateurs; logistics are the responsibility of the true professionals. So, thank you for the work you do in this important area that often is taken for granted.

General Chiarelli, great to see you again. I have fond memories—and again, I don't want to cast dispersions on anybody else who was in Iraq at the time I first met you, but you were serving as the "Mayor of Baghdad" and, I think, were on the cutting edge of helping us understand this concept of counterinsurgency and how we best help these countries in which we're forced to operate, rebuild themselves, and take responsibility for their own future. So, again, it's good to see you.

Gentlemen, if I might, I want to be slightly parochial before I move to some broader questions, although I think the parochial nature of my concerns apply across the Service branches, and certainly in theater. We're about to begin the latest round of a fighting season in Afghanistan. Rotary-wing capabilities are really important. In Colorado, we have the High Altitude Army Aviation Training Site (HAATS) in Eagle, which is near Vail. What it does is, it captures the expertise and institutional knowledge of cadre of the experienced Colorado National Guard pilots, and leverages that to save lives in battlespace. It appears that the high altitude mountain environment training that the Active component is offering at Fort Carson, based on the train-the-trainer course that HAATS offers, is also trying to address the need for high altitude training. I'm concerned that the nature of the Active component means that those trainers, after doing their good work, will then move on in their careers. In addition, Fort Carson, I believe, doesn't have the varied terrain and consistent environmental conditions that are found in the mountains around Eagle.

So, my question to General Chiarelli is, can we institute multi-component training at HAATS, following the successful multi-component warrior leader course that the Colorado National Guard runs at Fort Carson?

General CHIARELLI. HAATS is a national treasure. My executive officer happens to be an aviator. Aviators are always telling stories, and he told me, in preparing his brigade to go to Afghanistan, he sent about 200 of his pilots in command and instructor pilots to HAATS for training, but he, too, deployed his brigades by battalion to Denver, and they did individual training as part of HAATS, brought those instructors down, because of the throughput issues at HAATS, and had them do train-the-trainer on their battalions, doing collective training in the Denver area. It was much less expensive. At the same time, he was able to give everybody the benefit of that fantastic training by using a train-the-trainer model for pilots in command and instructor pilots.

I believe that is what a majority of our brigades are doing. There's no doubt, HAATS is saving lives today in Afghanistan, because of our ability to get that key and critical training. It is a fantastic course.

Senator UDALL. General, I think you're aware, too, of the recent tragedy that occurred on Mount Massive, which is the second highest peak in Colorado, at 14,400 feet. A rotary-wing exercise took place on Mount Massive. The bird was piloted by those that hadn't had that kind of training, and there was a tragic fatal accident that occurred. I know we're learning a lot of lessons from that, but I hope we'll continue to use HAATS and think about how we keep that training capability as broadly available as possible.

I know you've had this invitation before, we'd love to get you out to Colorado. I know your executive officer has spoken, but we'd be happy to accompany you and do some flying with you, if you're able to come out at some point.

General CHIARELLI. Appreciate it, Senator.

Senator UDALL. I'll leave that as an open-ended invitation to you.

General CHIARELLI. Thank you, Senator.

Senator UDALL. If I might, I'd like to follow up on a question I think the Senator from Georgia—who's also trying to teach me how to speak Georgian, by the way. He was talking about dwell time, and you've talked about musculoskeletal situations and the need for knee surgery and rehabilitation. We're learning more and more about this marvelous organ we have, called the brain, and we have hidden wounds that occur in combat, we increasingly understand. Could you talk a little about what you've learned—and perhaps the other general officers that are here might want to chime in—and, when it comes to dwell time, the need for our men and women in uniform to recuperate, mentally, emotionally, spiritually, as well.

General CHIARELLI. I have, currently, 6,200 soldiers that are most seriously wounded. We categorize anyone who has a single disqualifying injury of 30 percent or greater, and put them in what we call the Army Wounded Warrior (AW2) program. Of that population, 56 percent have either post-traumatic stress (PTS) or traumatic brain injury (TBI); 18 percent, TBI, and the remainder is PTS. We are instituting now protocols in theater that require soldiers, that are either in a vehicle that is damaged within 50 meters of a blast or in a building with an explosion, to go through an evaluation for a concussion as soon after the event as possible and 24 hours later. If they pass both those evaluations, they'll return to duty; if they don't, they are treated by a doctor until their brain has had an opportunity—the concussion has had an opportunity to repair itself.

PTS is a concern for soldiers back here, and we are working to both inform our medics so they can better identify PTS when it occurs down range, and we're using telemedicine to give a 30- to 40-minute evaluation of every soldier that comes back to the States. We've done two units now, one battalion in Hawaii and a brigade in Alaska, so we can get a good evaluation. The results, using this telemedicine, are very, very encouraging.

Senator UDALL. Thank you for that update. I know my time's expired, but would anybody else want to comment briefly?

General Amos?

General AMOS. Senator, we share the same battlefield with our Army brothers, and have experienced the same levels of TBI and PTS. General Chiarelli and I worked on that pretty hard last fall to develop this protocol that he just described. That is in use right now in the Marine zone as well in the Helmand Province. The idea is recognition that you get that wonderful thing between your ears rung really hard and there is a propensity—if it's not treated, if the brain is not put at rest immediately, the propensity, they've found, for PTS down the road is there. It doesn't mean you're going to have it, but it does mean that there's a propensity towards that. So, there's a recognition, both in the Army and the Marine Corps, that this is serious problem. This effort, this concussive protocol that General Chairelli described, is in effort to say, Okay, 100 percent of those marines and soldiers that have been either knocked out, had what we call a grade-three concussion—which is, you are knocked unconscious or something less—you are done. You're going to go back into the wire, you're going to get evaluated, we're going to put your brain at rest. Then, depending on how you look and what the doctors are saying, we'll determine whether you ever even leave the wire again. In fact, the way we do it is, it's called "three strikes, you're in." If you just get three grade-one concussions, you're done. You're going to stay inside the wire, you'll perform a function; you're not going to go back out again. So, it's a recognition for that, sir.

We've had—I'm just looking at—since January 2003 to September 2009, there have been 7,746 mild TBI cases reported within the Marine Corps. So a mild TBI case would be something that, "Okay, I took a pretty hard blow—I may not have been knocked out, but I took a pretty hard blow to the head." So, there is great recognition of that problem, Senator, and I just want you to know we're working as fast as we can to try to ameliorate that.

Senator UDALL. Thank for that. I test the patience of the Chairman, but I certainly would welcome the Navy and the Air Force, as well, to weigh in.

Admiral GREENERT. Senator, given we deploy embedded in the ground units, our folks are susceptible to the same thing. I think overarching the program, the factor is, our work is not done when folks return from deployment. That's a cultural change. A lot of our sailors, that's something new to them. "What do you mean, you need to do a post-deployment health assessment?" We need to look at folks, not just when they come back—30 days, 90 days—sometimes it takes 120 days for this to manifest itself and their personalities to change.

The other factor I would just mention to you is, their support group is the family. They're back here worrying all this time. There's a lot of stress. It's almost the boiling frog concept—just a little bit more, a little bit more, a little bit more—and we're finding it manifests itself in what we call the tone of the force—things from divorces, to drinking, to behavioral changes around the force, within our families. We need to watch them, as well.

Thanks.

Senator BAYH. Thank you.

General, my patience is infinite, but Senator Thune is being very patient, as well. This is a very important subject. If you have some thoughts, could you make them brief?

General CHANDLER. Sir, I would just say, we have approximately 650 airmen in the AW2 program; that's out of about 1,100 airmen that have been wounded in combat, some of which suffer the same consequences, in terms of TBI. We've put a lot of effort and, frankly, learned a lot from the Marine Corps and from the Army, in terms of resiliency, what it takes, not just for the member, but their family, as well.

One other aspect of this, of course, is the remotely-piloted business, where you can find yourself in combat part of the day, and then home the rest of the day, which is something that we also watch very carefully.

The only thing that I would add is, we've actually had some— "success" is not what I would call it, but—in the early stages of experimentation with hyperbaric chamber treatment for TBI, which I know is something that our surgeons general share amongst themselves.

Senator BAYH. Thank you very much, General.

Thank you, Senator Udall, for asking about that, a very important signature of challenges from the conflicts we find ourselves in.

Senator Thune?

Senator THUNE. Thank you, Mr. Chairman.

Thank you, gentlemen, for your great service to our country.

General Chandler, in your prepared statement, you said that, "The B–1, B–52, and 15E did not meet aircraft availability standards, due to maintenance- and depot-related issues, and the F–22 fell short of the projected availability, due to low observable maintenance requirements." Yet, this year the Air Force's number-one unfunded priority was for depot-level maintenance on several aircraft, including the B–1. Can you explain what maintenance standards the B–1 and the B–52 failed to meet, and what depot-related maintenance issues the Air Force is having with these aircraft?

General CHANDLER. Yes, sir. What you're seeing is a manifestation of trying to balance the requirements for today with being prepared for tomorrow on the throughput, obviously, in depot maintenance and the things that we need to do there.

Let me address, if I may, the F–22 first. I would tell you, we're still learning a lot about that aircraft. Eighty percent of the low observable maintenance that we're required to do on the aircraft is caused by having to do maintenance on something that really had nothing to do with low observable. Said another way, we had to remove a panel to repair a part or replace something underneath that panel that subsequently led to low observable maintenance requirements.

Over the last 2 years, we've been able to lower maintenance man-hours per flying hour by 30 percent each year—frankly, by getting smarter and by replacing things under those panels, to give them a longer service life. We're sitting somewhere between 65 and 70 percent—66, 67, typically, on a daily basis—of mission-capable rates in the F–22 today; that's against an Air Force standard of about 75, and we project that that will continue to improve.

I would tell you, as far as the F–15E and the B–1, and even the B–52 for that matter, some of this reduction in mission-capable status is goodness, from the standpoint of taking those aircraft down and working on them, primarily in the areas of avionics. The B–1, for example, replacing the front cockpit, if you will, the pilot and co-pilot avionics displays. Also, we've podded that aircraft to give it situational awareness and to be able to do precision targeting and part of the maintenance that's being performed is moving that display into the cockpit so we can not only control the pod, but display the pod the way we want to do it.

So, there are some things that are going on, in terms of driving the rates down. We have the aircraft we need to do the job. Now's the time, we feel, as long as we can get the money, to continue those kinds of improvements on the legacy fleet that will then allow us to transition to the fleets of the future, whether it be the F–35, in the fighter world, or looking down the road at the next-generation long-range platform.

Senator THUNE. If these particular aircraft didn't meet the projected availabilities, why were there depot-level maintenance initiatives unfunded in this year's requests?

General CHANDLER. Again, sir, I would tell, that's simply a matter of trying to balance what we do with what we're being required to do today, and then maintaining the depot maintenance. There's no doubt in our mind—and we understand that it's taking OCO funding to get us to 82 percent, and then the $337 million unfunded requirement to get to 85 percent, of weapon systems sustainment. That is one of those big issues that we're going to have to watch closely, not only with the amount of money that we're finding and asking in OCO funding, but how we transition that to the base budget, so we can get at the issue that you're pointing out.

Senator THUNE. Okay. In your prepared statement, you also said that the standup of a fourth operational squadron of B–52s in October 2009 enhances our readiness to perform nuclear deterrence missions as well as support conventional mission requirements. It's my understanding that one of the reasons that the standup was ordered was to help the Air Force focus specifically on nuclear training issues in the midst of constant deployments, and yet the recently published Nuclear Posture Review (NPR) states that it will convert some B–52Hs to a conventional-only role. The question is, what is the thinking behind standing up a new squadron of B–52s in order to help focus that community on the nuclear mission and, less than 5 months later, having the administration announce it will convert the number of nuclear-capable B–52s to conventional-only aircraft?

General CHANDLER. Sir, the fourth squadron, as you describe, allows the units to not only concentrate on the nuclear mission, but have a constant and sustainable rotation of units through the nuclear mission and the conventional mission, which we asked them, obviously, to do both of. We know that the triad will be supported by the new NPR. The analysis of that force structure, I would say, is still ongoing. Exactly how we adjust, in terms of nuclear and conventional bombers, remains to be seen.

Senator THUNE. I want to come back, General, you mentioned the sniper advanced targeting pod, and the integration of that into the B–1 bomber and other Air Force aircraft, and how I think that's had a great impact on effective close air support in Afghanistan. However, there seems to be a lack of these advanced targeting pods for training use, because they're in such high demand in theater. So crews are using these advanced targeting pods overseas in combat; however, they have very limited ability to train with these advanced pods at home. Does the Air Force have a need for additional advanced targeting pods for training use? If so, how would additional pods affect combat readiness?

General CHANDLER. Sir, the overall requirement is approximately 835 pods. We find ourselves programmed through fiscal year 2012 to get up to about 625 or 35. Through 2012, we anticipate we'll be able to get away from the just-in-time training scenario that you describe, and then we'll have to follow on with 200 additional pods to do that.

Senator THUNE. Okay.

Thank you. I think that's all I have, Mr. Chairman.

Thank you all very much.

Senator BAYH. Thank you very much, Senator Thune.

Out of respect for the time of our witnesses today, and in the interest of moving things along, I think we'll now move to 5-minute rounds of questioning. I just have two.

General Chandler, I'd like to follow up on some of your remarks to Senator Thune. As you say, it is an important issue. Just a little preamble before the question.

In your prepared statement, you say, "Modernization and recapitalization remain priorities." However, the fiscal year 2011 budget request only funds weapon system requirements at 65 percent, as you mentioned, of your requirement, and that increases to only 83 percent with OCO funding. While I admire the Air Force for making weapon system sustainment your top unfunded priority, even if we authorized the maximum amount, which I support—and I hope my colleagues in the Appropriations Committees support, as well—you will still only be at 85 percent of your requirement.

I understand we operate in tough economic times, but if we do not fully fund weapon system sustainment, we will always have a maintenance backlog. So, my question is, what does the Air Force risk by not fully funding weapons system sustainment?

General CHANDLER. Sir, the majority of the risk that you see, that 15 percent that's not funded, will be reflected in aircraft and engines that go through depots. That's about a $2 billion deficit. We understand that that is no small thing to try to get our arms around. That will continue to build in bow wave that someday we will pay the price for. So, we're looking next year at how we continue to move things out of OCO into the baseline budget and produce a more sustainable, if you will, weapon system support plan.

Senator BAYH. Thank you, General.

General Amos, this is for you. It came to the attention of some on the committee—I'd like to kind of cut to the chase—I'd like to ask you—there's apparently a small brouhaha about uniforms, which, in the great scheme of things, isn't the most important issue out there, but it was requested that I ask you about this. I understand the Marine Corps objected to the Navy fielding a ground combat uniform, and that if it were fielded, it be restricted to, basically, the SEALs, because it was too similar to the Marine Corps camouflage pattern. I wanted to ask you if that was correct; and if so, what was the rationale for objecting to the uniform being used more broadly? I understand the unique character of the Corps, and maybe some rivalry with the Navy, that kind of thing, but what's the rationale for that?

General AMOS. Sir, what you described is true. Two commandants ago, when General Jim Jones became the Commandant, he set on a course to put the Marine Corps in a unique uniform and get something that was more practical, something that didn't require having to go through the laundry and get starched and all the things we've been living with for years and years and years and years and years. We even went away from the old spit-shine boots, and went to the rough-out boot, and it just all made sense. So, 10 years ago, he was successful in doing that. It was an enormous effort, and that single uniform effort generated an enormous amount of pride inside an organization that is steeped in tradition.

So we have had that now for 10 years, and it's served us well. In fact, you talk to any marine out there, they love them. They're comfortable, and they wear well.

Other Services have come online over the last several years and developed their own Service-particular uniform, but—I think all our Services have done that—there was an effort.

Senator BAYH. I think the Corps actually patented this uniform, didn't they?

General AMOS. They did, sir.

Senator BAYH. Is that correct? That's interesting.

General AMOS. There's little eagle, globes, and anchor in the pattern, and it was put in there for a purpose. The purpose is that this would be a Marine Corps-unique uniform. We're not saying that other Services can't have additional uniforms. In fact, all the Services have them now. But, it came to our attention last fall that there had been an effort underway, down in U.S. Special Operations Command (SOCOM), to use a pattern that was so close that, from 5 or 10 feet away, it looked absolutely identical, and we ob-

52

jected to that. We just said, "Look, there are plenty of patterns that are out there that are effective. There are patterns out there that can provide your Service whatever unique uniform you want. But, in this case, we'd appreciate it if your Service would pick—or your effort would pick—a uniform that was significantly or enough different from ours that you could determine a marine on the ground versus somebody else on the ground." It became a point of internal pride within the Marine Corps.

Senator BAYH. Boy, my time is expired, but how did they respond to your response? I take it they brought it to somebody's attention around here, so they must not have been completely thrilled.

General AMOS. Sir, I think it's settled down now, and there is an agreement with the SEALs, forward deployed, to wear that pattern. It is a very good camouflage pattern. Tactically, it does what they hoped would happen. So, the agreement between the CNO and the Commandant of the Marine Corps is that those forward-deployed SEALs and those types of folks can use that uniform over there. Even though it is not using the patented pattern—like I said, it's so very, very close—and it's a point of pride, sir. It's internal pride. It actually transcends all the general officers. It's down to the young lance corporals and privates first class, the young 18-year-olds, who go, "No, wait a minute, this is my uniform, and I'm a U.S. Marine." So, it's probably hard to understand outside the Corps, but that's the inertia generated inside the institution.

Senator BAYH. Pride and unit elan are certainly important factors, so I appreciate your response.

Senator, I think it's down to you and me. Senator Burr.

Senator BURR. Thank you, Mr. Chairman.

General Amos, in view of the limitations on the legacy Marine Corps helicopter assets, such as the CH–46 and C–53, which have been deployed in Afghanistan, what other aviation assets do you believe will be in high demand?

General AMOS. Sir, we are in a transition from your time down at New River and Camp Lejeune, and what we transitioned from—almost 10 years ago—about 13 type model series down to what we're going to end up with, something around, I think, five or six. 53 Echo, there's no question that that airplane has been a workhorse. I'm just looking at—for the last 10 months, from February 2009 to January 2010, readiness, the average mission-capable rate across the 53 Echo community is 65 percent. That is a heavy, heavy maintenance-intensive airplane, probably the most maintenance man-hours per flight hour. I don't know what that is, but it is significant. So, that airplane is—we'll continue to maintain until we get its replacement, the 53 Kilo.

But, most of the rest of our stuff, our legacy platforms—the CH–46, the 40-plus-year-old helicopter that we dearly love and have been flying—is transitioning to the MV–22. We've done it back in your State, in North Carolina; it's completely done. We have one squadron standing up on the west coast right now, and we have one foot in the 46 and one foot in the V–22 and we will have completed that in the next several years.

So, our Hueys and Cobras, the older versions have been under an enormous amount of strain. But, we have fielded the new replacement for the Huey, the Yankee version of that airplane—four blades, new engines, new rotor head, glass cockpit—and the readiness on that airplane is high, and it is significantly more capable than the older ones.

So, we have lived with these legacy airplanes now for a long time, tried to be good stewards. But, we are in that transition right now, Senator, leaving the old and going to the new, and so, we're going to sustain the old, while we have to. We have 53 Deltas in Afghanistan right now, the old two-engine version that was a predecessor to the Echo. So, we are flying and trying to maintain them as best we can. I don't know whether that answers your question.

Senator BURR. General, have I asked you if you have adequate airlift capabilities?

General AMOS. Do we have what, now?

Senator BURR. Do you have adequate airlift capabilities?

General AMOS. We do, sir, we do.

Senator BURR. Okay.

General AMOS. In fact, it's interesting you ask that, because the Secretary of Defense, one of his highest priorities in really the last year has been ISR—increase the amount of ISR, and then rotary-wing lift. The ISR is a combination of everybody sitting at this table and their assets; and rotary-wing lift is predominantly the Army and the Marine Corps. But, I will also tell you, the Air Force—for instance, down in Helmand Province, the boys flying those medevac airplanes that are down there have saved an enormous amount of lives for us. But, lift capacity, as far as moving around the theater, we absolutely do. We have what we need for that, sir. We're not wanting in that.

Senator BURR. Good.

Just as a general note—and I shared this with the Chairman—I looked at new technology over the Easter break that's designed for rotary aircraft, to balance that engine and the propeller when it's revved up, which eliminates the shaking in a helicopter. It was an amazing simulator to sit in and see one with and without. It made me really question how that would change the depot hours and intervals for some of the rotary aircraft. I know across DOD that technology is being looked at. I'm sure I didn't see a single technology. There are probably others out there. But, clearly we're going to bring some things that provide us longer life, based upon how we change what, historically, we've used, because we've used technology to extend its life and to have a lesser impact on the platform itself over time.

Last question. Again, General Amos, the establishment of a Marine Corps component of Special Operations Forces was a relatively recent force structure development. From my time down at Camp Lejeune, I can report that the marines assigned to Marine Corps Forces Special Operations Command are training well, they're ready to be deployed worldwide with their brethren of the other Services. How do you assess their readiness?

General AMOS. Sir, I don't have the precise readiness figure in front of me where I could tell that this Special Operations Battalion is—on average because they don't report their readiness through us, they report it through the SOCOM. But, absolutely no question, we put our arms around them. They're marines. Those marines came out of our Force Reconnaissance Units and our

standard Marine Reconnaissance Units and then across the Marine
Corps, when we stood them up. It sits about 2,500 marines and
sailors right now. What we're doing now is, we are rebalancing
within that number of 2,500, with lessons learned. We found out
that we needed one less Special Operations battalion, but we needed more combat service support integrated within those battalions,
that would deploy with them. So, inside that number, that box, we
are shifting around the deck chairs, so to speak, to make sure we
have the right balance. But, I'll tell you, my sense is, having seen
it—I was there when we stood it up at Camp Lejeune, and I just
visited, with some of our marines—Special Operations lads—out in
the western part of Helmand Province and out there towards the
Iranian border—they are highly trained. They are incredible young
men. I think the testimony for me is, when you see them, and
they're wounded—in Bethesda or Walter Reed or Brooke—they're
the ones that are getting out of the beds. They're severely wounded. They're the ones that leave the hospital first. They're the ones
that are determined to get back on their feet and get back with
their brothers again. So, it's a special breed, and they're well
trained, and their morale is enormously high. I think it's a huge
success story, sir.

Senator BURR. Thank you. I'm impressed with what I've seen
when I've been there.

Let me conclude—by once again stating to all of you, thank you
for your service. More importantly, please share those thanks with
the men and women that serve under you. We can't thank you
enough for the insight that you're able to provide this committee.
More importantly—I think I can speak for the chairman—our door
is open. When there is a need, let us know what the need is. We
want to make sure that every warrior has the equipment that they
need, that they don't fall short, that our mission is one we intend
to win, and not one just to be there.

Thanks.

Senator BAYH. Those are my sentiments exactly, Senator. Thank
you for your comments.

This is a collaborative process. Let us know what you need. We're
here to make sure that our military men and women have the
equipment that they need to perform the services that they so gal-
lantly do on our behalf.

So, gentlemen, thanks to each of you for your service. Please convey our respect and appreciation to the men and women who work
with you. I look forward to working with you the rest of this fiscal
year to make sure you get what you need.

Thanks very much.

This hearing is adjourned.

[Questions for the record with answers supplied follow:]

QUESTIONS SUBMITTED BY SENATOR EVAN BAYH

ARMY EQUIPPING AND MANNING

1. Senator BAYH. General Chiarelli, I'm concerned about the current process in
which we man and equip units just in time for deployment. I understand you must
accomplish your mission under many constraints, and high operational tempo continues to severely stress the force. Your hard work in these challenging times is to
be commended. What is the risk in building unit readiness just in time for deploy-

ment and where is there room for improvement in the predeployment process with respect to manning, equipping, and training?

General CHIARELLI. The risk is that some Army units may not deploy with the desired combination of soldiers and equipment with enough time to train collectively before deployment. As long as demand for forces exceeds the available supply of Army units, the Army will continue to be forced to shift the elements of readiness (soldiers and equipment) to units that have pending deployments. The Army Force Generation (ARFORGEN) model provides the Army a mechanism to synchronize soldiers and equipment in a predictable manner in order to provide trained and ready units to combatant commanders.

To improve this process, the Army is refining its force generation model to build provisions for a contingency force consisting of 1 corps headquarters, 3 division headquarters, 10 brigade combat teams (BCT), and the 45,000 enablers required to support these formations. The Army will use fiscal year 2011 as a transition year to begin to build operational depth; by 2012, the Army will have achieved operational depth by resourcing the contingency force; by 2013, the Army will have sustained operational depth. Of course, this is contingent upon predicted levels of demand for forces decreasing to sustainable levels.

2. Senator BAYH. General Chiarelli, what is the readiness impact, we leave equipment in Afghanistan and Iraq, on deploying and nondeploying units as well as our National Guard and Reserve units?

General CHIARELLI. The Army leaves equipment in theater for the specific purpose of providing deploying units with the equipment necessary to meet mission requirements. This process achieves readiness for the deploying unit, while degrading the readiness of the nondeployed units. Army equipment on hand (EOH) as of 30 March 2010 is 78 percent for the entire Army, 80 percent for the Active component, 80 percent for the Reserves, and 77 percent for the Guard. We are intensively managing our EOH to ensure that next deploying units from all components have sufficient equipment for training and deployment. Specific examples of our most critical shortages are Prophet Systems, Self-Protection Adaptive Roller Kit mine roller, Route Clearance Vehicles and associated Ground Penetrating Radar, Family of Unmanned Aircraft Systems, and Tactical Satellite Radios. We are mitigating these shortages using theater provided equipment and other strategies.

3. Senator BAYH. General Chiarelli, how long can we expect nondeploying units to be the bill payers for deploying units, and what impact will that have on long-term readiness?

General CHIARELLI. To some extent, a portion of the nondeploying force will remain the billpayers for our deploying forces in the future. Since the implementation of the ARFORGEN, we have migrated from a tiered-readiness system to a cyclical readiness system by instituting periods of degraded readiness into a unit's deployment cycle (Reset, Train/Ready, and Available phases). So, naturally, some of the low readiness levels reported by nondeployed Army units are expected as part of this ARFORGEN process. Both Active and Reserve component units move through a Reset phase of ARFORGEN where readiness is expected to be low.

Over the long term, however, the critical area for the Army to improve readiness in nondeployed units is in the Train/Ready phase of ARFORGEN. Here, units should be resourced to begin collective training. As the demand for forces decreases to sustainable levels and the Army is able to restore balance, the ARFORGEN model will enable the Army to better manage unit readiness.

4. Senator BAYH. General Chiarelli, how can we help you alleviate some of the constraints such as time, funding, and planning?

General CHIARELLI. Continued support from Congress for fully funding our budget request on time remains a critical element to achieving stability for our Army. Assuming the drawdown in Iraq continues on schedule and no further troop requirements are needed in Afghanistan, we will achieve our intermediate goal of Boots-on-the-Ground (BOG): Dwell ratio of 1:2 for the Active component and 1:4 for the Reserve component beginning in fiscal year 2012. These combined factors will help alleviate constraints affecting unit readiness levels.

RETURN TO FULL SPECTRUM OPERATIONS

5. Senator BAYH. General Chiarelli, the way in which we train our soldiers according to their mission essential task lists (METL) has changed recently. My concern is that in compacting our METLs we may be changing what we have to do in accord-

ance with our National Military Strategy (NMS), to what we can do because of current global commitments in Iraq and Afghanistan. In the process we are not truly prepared for full spectrum operations (FSO). Are our METLs truly capturing FSO and in what areas of training are we currently accepting risk?

General CHIARELLI. Our recent doctrinal shift to a FSO METL more closely represents the full spectrum operations requirements of the NMS. The last few years of frequent deployments and short dwell periods left our units focused either on their current deployment, or in preparation for specific mission requirements of their next deployment. This has created risk in our proficiency to conduct operations in other mission environments. With increasing dwell anticipated beginning in fiscal year 2012, our forces will finally be able to expand their training focus across the spectrum of conflict, thus, reducing strategic risk. As an example, a number of BCTs currently scheduled to participate in Army Combat Training Center rotations in fiscal year 2011 will undergo full spectrum scenarios, rather than being solely focused on Afghanistan scenarios.

6. Senator BAYH. General Chiarelli, to what extent did the Army validate and coordinate the reorganizing of METL with U.S. Joint Forces Command (JFCOM)?

General CHIARELLI. The Army METL is focused on tasks performed by Army tactical formations and is based on Army doctrine that is nested entirely within joint doctrinal concepts and constructs. Therefore, Army METL directly supports the joint METL developed by JFCOM.

7. Senator BAYH. General Chiarelli, given the commitments to ongoing operations, to what extent will the Army and/or Marine Corps have sufficiently trained and ready forces among its nondeployed units to respond to a Homeland defense scenario or another contingency elsewhere in the world?

General CHIARELLI. The Army currently has limited capacity to respond to unforeseen contingencies. The ARFORGEN model provides the Army a mechanism to synchronize soldiers and equipment in a predictable manner in order to provide trained and ready units to combatant commanders and respond to contingencies. The Army is improving its force generation model to build provisions for a contingency force consisting of 1 corps headquarters, 3 division headquarters, 10 BCTs, and 45,000 enablers. Likewise, redistribution of Active-Duty Forces across a 3-year lifecycle, and Reserve component units across a 5-year lifecycle, will allow the Army to generate consistent contingency force pools at a predictable rate. Together, these initiatives will restore operational depth and our capacity to respond to unforeseen contingencies.

Providing timely and appropriate response to incidents remains one of the Army's key operational concepts and the Army will continue providing military support to Federal, State, local, and tribal governments during Homeland defense operations. The Army will continue ongoing efforts to properly organize, equip, and train chemical, biological, radioactive nuclear high-yield explosives (CBRNE) Consequence Management Response Forces to enable rapid, effective responses to any CBRNE-related incident. Additionally, the Army continues to support planning efforts for a rapid and effective response to an influenza pandemic with focus on regionalized support to save lives, reduce suffering, and slow the spread of infection while preserving mission assurance and combat readiness. In the future, the Army will identify ways to streamline support provided to civil authorities in accordance with the rules and regulations established by the Department of Defense (DOD). One initiative is producing a yearly standing execution order, which will cover natural and manmade disasters. The Army has identified organizations to provide the required support outlined in the order.

8. Senator BAYH. General Chiarelli, does the Army's current budget request reflect the funds required to return to FSOs training while training forces preparing to deploy to ongoing operations?

General CHIARELLI. The fiscal year 2011 budget request asks for resources to prepare the Army for offense, defense, and stability operations in the current counterinsurgency environment. In fiscal year 2012, further implementation of the ARFORGEN model and the increased dwell time will support a FSO training strategy. This will enable the Army to train the force to combat hybrid threats in complex operating environments across the full spectrum of conflict.

9. Senator BAYH. General Chiarelli, given that training has been focused on preparing forces for ongoing operations for several years, has the Army/Marine Corps assessed the impact on the ability of its units to perform the core missions for which they were organized and trained?

General CHIARELLI. The Army continues to assess the impact that ongoing operations have on the ability of units to perform their core functions. This assessment involves analysis of pre-deployment and post-deployment readiness trends and the performance of units at key training events. Monthly, unit commanders are required to report how well their units are resourced and trained to perform the core functions for which they were designed. The Army has achieved limited success training on FSOs with units having greater than 9 months in the Train-Ready pool. We expect to see improvement as the demand for forces decreases and dwell time increases. In fiscal year 2011, up to four brigades are scheduled to conduct rotations at the Army Combat Training Centers and train on FSOs.

10. Senator BAYH. General Chiarelli, to what extent have individuals and units experienced a degradation in skills given that a large portion of the force has not been training on FSOs for several years?

General CHIARELLI. It is true that as units approach their deployment dates, they focus primarily on building proficiency for the predominantly counter-insurgency mission environment to which they are deploying. While commanders report that the current demand for forces and limited dwell are not allowing units sufficient time to develop and train on all their core competencies, training concerns fall well behind personnel and equipment issues as the primary drivers of readiness impacts. Additionally, to a degree, Army units have been and are able to train on some core competencies. The Army's current doctrine requires units to execute some mix of offense, defense, and stability operations during any mission, so preparing to execute these operations for a counterinsurgency environment prepares them, to some extent, to execute these operations in a more traditional operational environment. As time at home station between deployments increases, units will be able to train on a broader range of mission environments that includes more conventional threats and different situational complexities.

11. Senator BAYH. General Chiarelli, how does the Army/Marine Corps intend to address any skill degradation?

General CHIARELLI. Whether preparing to deploy for a specific mission or to remain ready for contingencies, Army units have maintained the fundamentals of FSOs which include offense, defense, and stability operations. The combat experience the Army gained in Iraq and Afghanistan has prepared us to serve elsewhere if required. Additionally, the Army relies on continuing professional military education to address skill degradation. Progressive educational opportunities throughout a leader's career exposes him/her to warfighting knowledge and skills required for operations across the spectrum of conflict. The Army will address skill degradation for major combat operations (MCO) by redesigning rotations undertaken by contingency forces at our Combat Training Centers. In fiscal year 2011, up to four brigades are scheduled to conduct FSO rotations which will prepare contingency forces for operations against hybrid threats under complex conditions.

12. Senator BAYH. General Chiarelli, has the Army developed a plan to ensure that sufficient knowledgeable trainers are available for its forces, in light of the recent memo from General Dempsey, U.S. Army Training and Doctrine Command (TRADOC) commander, regarding the increased reliance on contractors to conduct training?

General CHIARELLI. Yes, the Army does have a plan to ensure training requirements are sufficiently resourced with the appropriate skill set. In a time of high demands on the Army, TRADOC and the Army staff must intensively manage our instructors to ensure quality training. In some areas, the most knowledgeable trainers are not soldiers. For example, new equipment training for unmanned aerial systems (UAS) require contractors because there are no qualified soldiers who can train this skill. Culture and language training is similar. The best instructors come from academia for complex languages such as Pashtu, Urdu, and Mandarin Chinese. In other areas, trainers with current experience from Iraq and Afghanistan are desirable but not critical. For example, training mechanics how to maintain and repair vehicles can be taught by a contractor or an Army soldier. The outcome in either case will be the same. Finally, there are areas that require a soldier as the trainer—initial military training, leader development training for junior officers, NCOs, and soldiers, and the Battle Command Training Program. As a result of General Dempsey's memo, the DA Staff and TRADOC leadership work closely to intensively manage instructors to ensure we have the most knowledgeable trainers at our training posts.

PREPOSITIONED STOCK

13. Senator BAYH. General Chiarelli and General Amos, the current date to restore our prepositioned stocks of equipment around the globe is 2015. Not only have we had to draw equipment from our stocks to equip deploying units, new challenges have emerged as we field units with new types of equipment like the mine resistant ambush protected (MRAP) all terrain vehicle (M–ATV) and other urgent operational need items that are requested from the field commanders on the ground. Are we going to meet the 2015 goal to restore prepositioned stocks of equipment with our current levels of funding, and how are we modifying our inventory and lifecycle logistical management processes to accommodate these new items, such as the MRAP vehicle and the M–ATV?

General CHIARELLI. If the Army prepositioned stocks (APS) fiscal years 2011–2015 base budget and Overseas Contingency Operation (OCO) funding requests are fully funded, we feel confident that we will restore our APS capability by fiscal year 2015. We are constantly assessing our APS strategy and equipment to ensure we maintain the right capabilities based on current and future operations and contingencies. These assessments will continue to influence the equipment we place in APS, as well as our APS facilities, vessels, and maintenance requirements. In addition, these assessments include the future integration of MRAP vehicles, to include the M–ATV, into our APS sets. The Army, in preparation for the transition of the MRAP program from the Joint Program Office to the Army, will establish an Army Program Management Office responsible for the fleet management and life cycle sustainment of these systems. Tank-Automotive and Armaments Command, in coordination with Defense Logistics Agency (DLA), is reviewing parts inventories while Army Materiel Command is establishing the necessary repair program to sustain these critical assets.

General AMOS. The Marine Corps will meet the reset goal early. Our Maritime Prepositioning Ships Squadrons (MPSRON) will be fully reset in 2012 and the Marine Corps Prepositioning Program-Norway (MCPP–N) will be reset in 2013. Both Maritime Prepositioning Force (MPF) and MCPP–N will be reset within Marine Corps priorities as assets become available. With new inventory come attendant issues in lifecycle management. MRAPs and M–ATVs, for instance, were procured and deployed into Iraq and Afghanistan at a very rapid rate—resulting in numerous variants within the MRAP family inventory. With so many variants, the Marine Corps has had a tougher time procuring common spare parts, training mechanics on common systems, and resetting the vehicles as they return from Iraq as part of the drawdown.

Nevertheless, we have adjusted our practices accordingly to modernize the equipment aboard the MPSRONs. We have begun loading the MPF with capabilities that are applicable across the full range of military operations—retaining the ability to generate Marine Expeditionary Brigades (MEB) capable of conducting MCOs while also providing assets that can support missions at the lower end of the spectrum.

14. Senator BAYH. General Chiarelli and General Amos, currently we rely heavily on contractors for MRAP and M–ATV maintenance. What is the plan for the future and how are we ensuring we have an organic industrial capability to repair these combat vehicles and are we budgeting for such actions?

General CHIARELLI. Currently MRAP maintenance in theater is performed by a combination of both soldier-mechanics and contractor-mechanics. The depot-level MRAP sustainment strategy has recently been approved. This strategy developed by the Joint Depot Maintenance Activities Group (consisting of all four Services within the DOD) designated Red River Army Depot and U.S. Marine Corps Logistics Command in Albany, GA and Barstow, CA as maintenance facilities responsible for MRAP depot level repair. The Army initiated a pilot repair program at Red River Army Depot in fiscal year 2010, and plans a pilot overhaul program for fiscal year 2014. The MRAP JPO is currently funding MRAP sustainment. The Army will program funding in the Program Objective Memorandum (POM) for fiscal years 2012–2016.

General AMOS. Currently, the MRAP JPO employs a hybrid support strategy consisting of organic (military and government personnel) and contractor assets for the maintenance, fielding, and sustainment of the MRAP family of vehicles. The hybrid strategy embeds JPO Field Service Representatives in units abroad as well as within domestically located Home Station Training facilities. While contractors are a key part of initial MRAP vehicle maintenance, fielding, and sustainment, the JPO is working towards a fully organic sustainment strategy within all the Services.

Along with the above strategy, the Joint Depot Maintenance Activities Group designated Red River Army Depot and U.S. Marine Corps Logistics Command

59

(LOGCOM) (Albany, GA and Barstow, CA) as depot maintenance facilities responsible for depot level repair of MRAPs in January 2009. The Army initiated a reset pilot program at Red River Army Depot in 3rd quarter fiscal year 2010 and a pilot overhaul program planned for fiscal year 2014. The Marine Corps has already initiated Proof of Principle actions at Maintenance Center, Albany, GA. These pilot programs will provide an initial national repair capability until a full depot sustainment program is established.

The MRAP JPO is currently funding MRAP sustainment and the Services will program funding in POM 12–16. OCOs dollars will fund a level of reset for vehicles returning from Operation Enduring Freedom (OEF)/Operation New Dawn (a.k.a. Iraqi Freedom) (OIF). The program's appropriated budget through fiscal year 2010 is $40 billion including $12.0 billion in OCO funding in fiscal year 2010. A total of $1.1 billion to complete fiscal year 2010 requirements was received in the most recent OCO to address increase in vehicle procurement quantities. A total of $3.415 billion is requested in the fiscal year 2011 OCO for sustainment, retrofits, and reset requirements. Fiscal year 2012 and out-year requirements are under review to reflect decisions and assumptions regarding OIF drawdown and OEF demands, quantities planned for long- and short-term storage, and home station training.

ARMY AND MARINE CORPS RESET CONCERNS

15. Senator BAYH. General Chiarelli and General Amos, as we draw down forces in Iraq, will you meet the timelines that have been set by the President, and what are the key challenges you face while increasing forces in Afghanistan?

General CHIARELLI. Yes. The drawdown of forces in support of OIF and the increase of forces in support of OEF will meet the required timelines. There is no direct competition for the resources needed to accomplish the force drawdown and force increase, because the Army synchronized both major tasks and de-conflicted resources accordingly. The plan supporting the drawdown of OIF forces is detailed and sufficient time is available to accomplish the mission. The execution of the drawdown is on track and going according to plan. The tasks associated with the increase in forces in support of OEF are well-defined and being closely managed. Key challenges identified by the Army include the repositioning of selected units with sufficient deployment tour length remaining, from Iraq to Afghanistan. As forces drawdown in OIF, equipment to support the increased requirement in OEF has been identified and will be shipped to Afghanistan and configured for issue to units. OEF has some unique equipment requirements, such as the M–ATV, and the additional requirements have been identified in sufficient time to ensure the equipment is produced and shipped in advance of the unit arrival. The preparation of units identified to support the force increase have been given priority by the Army. The execution of the force increase is on track and going according to plan.

General AMOS. The Marine Corps met its portion of the 30,000 force increase in March of this year. We are now at a steady state of 19,401 OEF Marine Air Ground Task Force in Afghanistan and can sustain that requirement as long as the Nation requires while meeting other combatant commander requirements.

16. Senator BAYH. General Chiarelli and General Amos, to what extent has the Army and Marine Corps assessed the risks and developed mitigation strategies in the event the plans for the draw down and the surge in Afghanistan do not go as planned?

General CHIARELLI. The Army is on track to provide manned, trained, and equipped forces of the type and quantity requested by the Central Command (CENTCOM) commander. The lead brigade and enabling capabilities are already on their way to theater. If necessary, the Army will accelerate deploying units if requested by CENTCOM. While doing so, we continue to move toward our goal of restoring balance to soldiers and their families.

General AMOS. With a current force manning structure of 202,000, the Marine Corps will be able to sustain the current Afghanistan MAGTF requirement of 19,401 personnel for as long as necessary. In addition, the Marine Corps will continue to source a 3.0 Marine Expeditionary Unit (MEU) presence globally while fulfilling security cooperation (SC) foundation activities to the maximum extent possible.

EQUIPMENT RESET

17. Senator BAYH. General Chiarelli and General Amos, you have expressed some concerns about the ability to adequately reset equipment returning from Iraq, while increasing operational support in Afghanistan, and preparing troops to respond to

future contingency operations around the world. As the drawdown in Iraq continues, DOD and the Services can expect to see an increase in reset requirements as a result of force reductions in Iraq and a growing presence in Afghanistan. In addition, DOD industrial facilities and contractors will be depending on accurate demand signals to effectively and efficiently reset the right equipment, at the right time, according to the right priorities. Also, the Services maintain that U.S. forces can expect to participate in a long war that will require an enduring reset that will surpass OIF and OEF. Given these enormous challenges with resetting equipment to enhance the overall capability and readiness of forces, to what extent are equipping strategies and force generation models identifying the mix of numbers of equipment to be reset to support operations in Afghanistan or future threats, or is the demand for reset, as a practical matter, being driven by the type and numbers of equipment returning to the United States from Iraq?

General CHIARELLI. The ARFORGEN integrates units scheduled for deployment with units being replaced. We forecast our equipment reset requirements based on the ARFORGEN model, which depicts the unit relief in place, transfer of authority dates, and, consequently, equipment forecasted for retrograde. The order of induction for equipment into reset activities is prioritized based on demand. Our forecasting method is initially based on historical trends and then revised based on actual equipment returning from theater.

General AMOS. Operational needs in Afghanistan were a main driver in what was initially retrograded from Iraq. For example, approximately 40 percent of the equipment in Afghanistan came from within theater, mainly from Iraq. Maintenance was conducted in Kuwait and then the required equipment was sent from Kuwait to Afghanistan. Because so much of the OIF equipment was sent to OEF, total reset actions have been deferred until we begin to drawdown our presence in Afghanistan.

All equipment not diverted to support OEF has been retrograded to the continental United States (CONUS), and we are in the process of resetting that equipment. To help develop the requirements for OIF reset, and project costs for reset execution, the Marine Corps created the ground equipment reset cost model to estimate total reset cost. The model is a collection of ground equipment reset strategies for each equipment type deployed to the MARCENT theater. These strategies include: depot maintenance; field maintenance; new procurement; and no reset required. Reset strategies are tailored to individual equipment types based on a range of factors including relative age, density in theater, usage rates in theater, and other criteria. These reset strategies are routinely updated and validated though a comprehensive process. Managing this information for all deployed ground equipment enables more detailed maintenance, procurement, and disposal planning during reset execution.

18. Senator BAYH. General Chiarelli and General Amos, how will force modernization or modularity priorities be weighed against short-term Afghanistan specific needs when resetting equipment?

General CHIARELLI. Afghanistan is our number 1 priority. We anticipate being able to fill the vast majority of our equipment requirements for OEF with: (1) equipment retrograded from Iraq; (2) new procurement/production currently being received; (3) unit provided/deployed equipment; and (4) equipment available from national level (depot) reset. New demands from Afghanistan, however, have not significantly impacted Army modernization or modular transformation efforts. We continue to modernize and transform to sustain our soldiers and provide the necessary capabilities to guarantee success in any mission or environment.

General AMOS. New procurement must play a major part in force modernization. For the last 9 years, the Marine Corps has been engaged in a land war and we have adapted. However, as we reconstitute our force to the future, we must focus on our roots of amphibious and expeditionary capabilities. Force modernization will thus focus on those capabilities that will prepare us for the next challenge.

Afghanistan specific needs determined what equipment was sent directly from OIF to OEF. Now that the equipment has returned to CONUS, the Marine Corps continues to determine reset priorities according to several comprehensive processes. These processes will identify ground equipment challenges and recommend policies, actions, and equipment sourcing solutions to ensure ground equipment allocation aligns with prioritizations established by the Commandant.

19. Senator BAYH. General Chiarelli and General Amos, to what extent do the Services expect reset to become an enduring component in the base budget to support long-term contingency operations?

General CHIARELLI. Reset is a cost of war, and therefore has historically been funded through supplemental appropriations. The Army is not planning for reset to become an enduring component in the base budget to support long-term named contingency operations. However, the Army will continue to require reset funding for equipment deployed to OIF and OEF as long as forces are deployed plus 2 to 3 years to ensure equipment serviceability and readiness is restored and equipment is ready for the next contingency.

For other than named contingency operations, such as routine training or engagement exercises, equipment reset will be funded through the base budget.

General AMOS. Reset by definition is the cost to repair and replace equipment directly used in combat operations, thus it is not an enduring requirement and should not become a component of the base budget. Once OCO cease, a reset period of 2 to 4 years will commence to restore warfighting capabilities but will not remain a permanent baseline requirement.

AFGHANISTAN SUPPLY AND EQUIPMENT SUPPORT

20. Senator BAYH. General Chiarelli and General Amos, the difficulties in transporting supplies and equipment to Afghanistan will be a challenge as DOD implements its plans to increase U.S. forces by 30,000. Additionally, DOD must manage both the Afghanistan increase and Iraq drawdown at the same time, and the troop increase in Afghanistan will be dependent to some extent on equipment being retrograded from Iraq. Are you confident that you will be able to provide all the necessary supplies and equipment to deployed forces operating in Afghanistan when they need them?

General CHIARELLI. The plus-up of forces in Afghanistan and the drawdown of forces in Iraq are indeed challenges; however, I am confident that we will accomplish this mission. The Army works very closely with the CENTCOM, U.S. Transportation Command (TRANSCOM), the DLA, and multiple other supporting organizations to overcome the myriad of challenges.

In doing so, we establish clear standards and have included enforceable metrics for our commercial carriers to ensure that required delivery times are met, that we maintain in-transit visibility of supplies and equipment, and that equipment and sustainment cargo is delivered in good order and condition.

To optimize airlift capability, TRANSCOM and CENTCOM worked hard to maximize multi-modal operations (movement of cargo initially by sea and then by air from an airfield closer to Afghanistan), to minimize delays leading up to our required delivery dates, and to aggregate airlift requirements so as to produce more efficient and effective loads.

Additionally, advancements in property accountability processes ensure that equipment no longer needed in Iraq is readily identified and offered for use in Afghanistan. This equipment is being sent through maintenance in Kuwait before being onward moved to Afghanistan. Furthermore, units redeploying from Afghanistan have been instructed to leave behind much of their equipment for follow on units in order to minimize the burden on the ground lines of communication leading into and out of Afghanistan.

General AMOS. Yes, we were successful in deploying equipment and supplies to meet the required timelines for the OEF surge and we continue to equip and sustain our forces deployed in Afghanistan. The Marine Corps units, personnel, and equipment tied to MAGTFs that are assigned to the CENTCOM commander are moved in accordance with the Time-Phased Force Deployment Document (TPFDD) within the Joint Operational Planning and Execution System (JOPES) as validated by CENTCOM and executed by TRANSCOM's organic and contracted commercial transportation assets. The Marine Corps sourced equipment for the surge using the TPFDD and JOPES procedures to ensure equipment was provided in accordance with the supported commander's priorities and plans in OEF.

The sourcing of the OEF equipment requirement was accomplished using a combination of assets available in theater, mainly Iraq, that were mission capable or able to be brought to mission capable status in time to meet the OEF requirement, planned procurements, in stores assets, and through global sourcing from home station units.

21. Senator BAYH. General Chiarelli and General Amos, have any units in Afghanistan reported that they have been unable to conduct their missions due to a lack of supplies and equipment?

General CHIARELLI. A review of readiness reports for units operating in Afghanistan from October 2009 to March 2010 indicates no Army units reported an inability to perform their assigned mission due to a lack of supplies or equipment. Headquarters, Department of the Army and U.S. Army CENTCOM work very hard to ensure that required equipment is on hand upon unit arrival in Afghanistan.

General AMOS. No Marine Corps units have reported that they have been unable to conduct their missions due to a lack of supplies and equipment. This is not to say readiness challenges do not exist for our units in Afghanistan. Although collectively our deployed forces continue to report the highest levels of readiness, it is also true that readiness challenges do exist for some units in Afghanistan and from time to time these units may experience a slight degradation in capability. Battle damage due to enemy action and the harsh operating environment are the prime factors; however, at no time have these factors prevented a unit from accomplishing its mission. A robust forward in stores program and principle end item (PEI) rotation process are designed to mitigate these challenges to our forward deployed units.

22. Senator BAYH. General Chiarelli and General Amos, to what extent will the troop increase in Afghanistan be dependent on equipment retrograded from Iraq, and is there a risk the equipment needed from Iraq will not be available in the planned timeframes to support the Afghanistan troop increase?

General CHIARELLI. The Army has carefully developed a plan to resource equipment needed in Afghanistan from both domestic production and Iraq retrograde. Of the equipment required to resource the Afghanistan surge, 85 percent will come from domestic production and 15 percent from Iraq retrograde. We are confident these resource quantities will be met, given that the Army has thoroughly analyzed the availability and throughput capability for theater refurbishment.

General AMOS. Approximately 40 percent of the equipment in Afghanistan came from within theater, mainly from Iraq. This equipment was mission capable or able to be brought to mission capable status in time to have met the OEF surge requirement.

23. Senator BAYH. General Chiarelli and General Amos, what effect, if any, will use of equipment from Iraq to Afghanistan have on the plans to reset equipment for use in other future contingency operations?

General CHIARELLI. The expansion in Afghanistan will create a decline in national level (depot) reset requirements and production in the short term. Additionally, there will be an increased requirement for theater refurbishment of equipment as specific items are moved from Iraq to Afghanistan. We believe this will cause a delay in the Army achieving balance within 12 to 18 months.

General AMOS. The Marine Corps had initially forecasted to complete OIF ground equipment reset actions in fiscal year 2012; however, due to operational necessity, equipment scheduled for retrograde from OIF in 2009 for reset beginning 2010, was diverted to OEF. As a result there are impacts to the reset plans, timeline, and budget required to execute reset; these impacts are in the process of being identified and analyzed.

Because the Marine Corps held large quantities of equipment retrograded from Iraq to support the increased footprint in Afghanistan, the reset of a significant portion of equipment used in Iraq has been deferred beyond 2011. The majority of equipment that remained in theater consists of armored vehicles, including most of our deployed medium tactical fleet, our entire fleet of MRAP vehicles, light armored reconnaissance vehicles, and some theater-specific items.

While the decision to leave wheeled vehicle fleets and other critical items in theater enabled a quick and seamless transition from Iraq to Afghanistan, those same assets drive a significant portion of the Marine Corps' total reset liability and depot maintenance costs. Foregoing reset actions now (e.g. field or depot-level maintenance) will undoubtedly result in higher than normal equipment wash-out rates and more costly depot repairs once the equipment is eventually able to be reset.

The initial planning has commenced for drawing down forces in Afghanistan, which will follow the same planning process as was used for Iraq's drawdown. Equipment requiring reset actions will be included in the development of an OEF equipment reset plan and be retrograded to the maintenance depots at either Albany, GA or Barstow, CA or sent to other Service depots or commercial sources of repair for depot maintenance, modernization and rebuild, or field level maintenance repair actions. Following appropriate maintenance and repair actions, equipment will be returned to Ready For Issue (RFI) condition and is used to source Marine Corps equipment requirements in accordance with the Commandant of the Marine Corps' equipment priorities.

24. Senator BAYH. General Chiarelli and General Amos, to what extent will the United States provide equipment to coalition forces, and what impact will this have, if any, on the flow of U.S. forces into Afghanistan?

General CHIARELLI. The U.S. Army provides equipment to our coalition partners using congressionally-granted authorities that will have no impact on the flow of U.S. forces into Afghanistan. It is in the best interest of our Nation to support our coalition partners with equipment, when feasible.

In Afghanistan, we are building coalition partner capabilities in two ways. First, we are utilizing the authority granted under section 1202 of the National Defense Authorization Act (NDAA) for Fiscal Year 2007, whereby we can loan certain types of equipment (such as Up-Armored HMMWVs, crew-served weapons, protective masks, and add-on armor kits) for up to 1 year to our coalition partners. Second, for other types of equipment outside the scope of section 1202, we utilize Acquisition and Cross-Servicing Agreements to loan equipment to our coalition partners.

In Afghanistan, we are also enabling the Afghanistan National Security Forces (ANSF) to build their Minimum Essential Capabilities (MEC) through the following three authorities: Excess Defense Articles (EDA) (section 516 of the Foreign Assistance Act of 1961); Non-Excess (section 1234, NDAA for Fiscal Year 2010); and Sale from Stock (section 21 of the Arms Export Control Act).

In Iraq, we are transferring certain equipment to the Government of Iraq (GoI) to ensure they achieve their required MEC. As with the ANSF in Afghanistan, we are executing these equipment transfers through multiple authorities: EDA (section 516), Non-Excess (section 1234), and Sale from Stock (section 21). Additionally, we are also using Foreign Excess Personal Property (Federal Property and Administrative Services Act of 1949, as amended (40 U.S.C. 511–514)) authority to transfer operational bases to the GoI.

General AMOS. The Marine Corps has provided equipment to seven coalition nations contributing forces to Afghanistan and will continue to do so when tasked by the Joint Staff to the greatest extent possible without degrading our own ability to successfully accomplish our assigned mission. This level of commitment will not impact the deployment or employment of Marine Corps forces into Afghanistan.

The Marine Corps has provided a significant quantity of vehicles and garrison equipment from stores within the CENTCOM AOR to the Georgian battalion serving as part of the Marine Expeditionary Force. Types of equipment provided from stores within theater include: MRAP vehicles, night vision devices, MRAP ambulances, force tracking systems, tactical radios, tactical trailers, GPS systems, medical supplies, IED jammer systems, and miscellaneous garrison equipment. The Marine Corps has also provided equipment under the Coalition Operational Needs Statement (CONS) process to the following coalition partner nations: Croatia, Czech Republic, Latvia, Georgia, Portugal, Polish, and Romania. The Marine Corps will maintain its combat readiness notwithstanding transferring equipment to coalition forces.

ADDITIONAL CONTRACTING CONCERNS

25. Senator BAYH. General Chiarelli and General Amos, further complicating DOD's redeployment from Iraq is the fact that DOD will be simultaneously transitioning several major support contracts in Iraq, including the Logistics Civil Augmentation Program (LOGCAP) contract, during the height of the redeployment, which may lead to interruption of services. What actions are the Services taking to mitigate the potential adverse impact of these contract transitions during the drawdown?

General CHIARELLI. The Army strategy to transition from LOGCAP III to IV in Southwest Asia was built on two fundamental principles: to minimize the effect on the operational commander in the field, and to make sound business decisions in order to be good stewards of resources. We built our transition plan to start in the most benign environment (Kuwait) and progressively move to the most challenging theaters (Afghanistan and Iraq). Our plan allowed us to build upon lessons learned as we progressively increased contract task order scale, scope, and complexity.

In February 2010, the Rock Island Contracting Center, a subordinate command of the Army Contracting Command, awarded a LOGCAP IV task order to Kellogg Brown and Root Services (KBR) for the provision of Corps Logistic Support Services, Postal Services, and the Theater Transportation Mission in Iraq. KBR conducts a phased transition to the new task order beginning 15 May 2010; the projected completion date is 1 September 2010. This will complete transition of one of the two remaining LOGCAP III task orders in Iraq.

ARCENT conducted the Business Case Analysis (BCA) on whether to transition the remaining LOGCAP III task order (for Base Life Support) in Iraq LOGCAP IV, and the Office of the Deputy Assistant Secretary of the Army for Cost and Economics validated the methodology and results. The Army used that BCA to determine the best course of action for BLS in Iraq. At this time, the final decision on whether to transition the BLS task order from LOGCAP III to IV is still pending.

General AMOS. The drawdown of the Marine Corps component from Iraq and subsequent transition to operations in Afghanistan was conducted seamlessly and did not result in a curtailment of support contracts such as the LOGCAP. Marines operating in Afghanistan continue to benefit by LOGCAP support services; the LOGCAP is currently managed by the U.S. Army.

26. Senator BAYH. General Chiarelli and General Amos, what specific factors are the Services considering as it weighs whether to proceed with the transition to the new LOGCAP contract for base and life support in Iraq?

General CHIARELLI. While examining whether to proceed from LOGCAP III to LOGCAP IV, the Army considered the following factors: the operational impact of any transition, the BCA of alternative courses of action, and the ability of the LOGCAP III contractor to perform the mission.

Headquarters, U.S. Forces-Iraq assessed the operational impact of a possible transition. Headquarters, ARCENT conducted a BCA, and the Office of the Deputy Assistant Secretary of the Army for Cost and Economics validated the BCA. The BCA assessed four courses of action using a list of operational and financial criteria. The criteria included: timing—executable within existing security agreement timeline; sufficiency—provides the required level of base life support services in Iraq; legality—meets the Federal Acquisition Regulation requirements; and funding—sufficient funding available. The BCA analysts weighed the criteria based on their relative importance to each other. The Defense Contract Audit Agency provided advisory services to the ARCENT Comptroller in support of the analysis. DOD Inspector General and the Defense Contract Management Agency (DCMA) also reviewed the BCA and endorsed its conclusions.

DCMA continues to assess the ability of the current LOGCAP III contractor to perform the mission. In March 2010, the Administrative Contracting Officer advised the Procuring Contracting Officer that KBR's accounting, estimating, and purchasing systems, as well as its cost accounting standards disclosure statements, were adequate and in accordance with applicable regulations.

General AMOS. The Marine Corps continually seeks ways to increase its combat potential within programmed resource allocations. The use of contractors in combat theaters of operations such as Iraq and Afghanistan has allowed the Marine Corps to effectively release military units for other missions or to fill support shortfalls. The Department of the Army-managed LOGCAP includes all pre-planned logistics and engineering/construction-oriented contingency contracts actually awarded, and peacetime contracts which include contingency clauses. LOGCAP is primarily designed for use in areas where no bilateral or multilateral agreements exist. LOGCAP support services are also used effectively during CONUS mobilizations to assist support bases in preparing forces for mobilization.

SUPPORT FOR URGENT NEED AND NONSTANDARD EQUIPMENT

27. Senator BAYH. General Chiarelli and General Amos, approximately $11.7 billion of equipment in Iraq currently belongs to military units and will be returning with those units when they redeploy to the United States. The remainder includes theater provided equipment comprised of $10.2 billion in standard military gear and about $2.9 billion in nonstandard gear. As we increase troop levels in Afghanistan, the Army and Marine Corps have been adjusting their plans to redeploy equipment from Iraq. Some of this redeploying equipment, which was scheduled to return to the United States, is now being redirected to units headed to Afghanistan. In addition, some forces will move directly from Iraq to Afghanistan. Can you tell me to what extent the theater-provided equipment in Iraq will be returned to the United States for reset versus being repaired or reset in theater before being shipped to Afghanistan to support the surge there?

General CHIARELLI. Every piece of equipment being redirected from Iraq to Afghanistan will be inspected and refurbished as necessary to ensure its serviceability before arrival in Afghanistan. We are not planning to ship any equipment currently in Iraq to the United States for reset and then transport the same equipment to Afghanistan. Shipping to, and reset in, the United States would consume too much time for this to be a viable option. Some equipment that is currently inducted in national-level depot reset, however, may be available in time for shipment to Afghanistan to meet requirements.

General AMOS. All theater provided equipment (TPE) carried by Marine Corps forces in Iraq was turned over to the Army prior to redeployment. The Marine

Corps' Marine Expeditionary Force (Forward) (MEF (Fwd)) in Afghanistan carries limited amounts of TPE as part of its deployed equipment density list (EDL). As was the case in Iraq, all TPE in Afghanistan is provided to the Marine Corps by the Army. Upon redeployment, or as TPE is no longer required for deployed operations, it will be returned to the Army. All other equipment on the MEF (Fwd) EDL—whether it is standard or "non-standard" equipment—is currently planned for redeployment to CONUS and reset.

28. Senator BAYH. General Chiarelli and General Amos, to what extent are we pulling from our prepositioned equipment to support the surge in Afghanistan?

General CHIARELLI. Over the past 2 years, more than 2,600 pieces of APS equipment have been issued in support of operations in Iraq and Afghanistan. The use of this APS equipment resulted in delaying the completion of rebuilding the APS–5 Heavy Brigade Combat Team (HBCT) by 1 year, from March 2010 to March 2011. Examples of equipment drawn are tactical wheeled vehicles (TWV), trailers, engineer equipment, material handling equipment, communication equipment, and generators. We are planning to address these shortages through repaired and reset equipment retrograded from Iraq, as well as equipment coming from depots and new production.

General AMOS. For Afghanistan, MCPP–N provided 41 principal end items to support the establishment of MEB–A in January 2010. Meanwhile, there were 298 principal end items downloaded at Blount Island Command that were shipped to Afghanistan to also support MEB–A.

Equipment from MPSRON–1 was required to outfit new units standing up fiscal year 2007 and fiscal year 2008 as part of our end strength increase to 202,000 marines. Equipment from MPSRON–2 was offloaded to support OIF II.

29. Senator BAYH. General Chiarelli and General Amos, will the TPE returning from Iraq be repaired or reset in theater to replace prepositioned equipment drawn to support the Afghanistan surge?

General CHIARELLI. Yes, prior to TPE being completely retrograded out of theater, CENTCOM will make determine if the equipment can be repaired in theater to be sourced against a theater requirement, to include specific APS needs. We have already begun using repaired TPE (i.e., vehicles, radios, generators, and other support equipment) to fill some of our APS shortages. We will continue to use a combination of repaired and reset equipment retrograded from Iraq, as well as equipment coming from depots and new production to replace our prepositioned equipment.

General AMOS. All TPE carried by Marine Corps forces in Iraq was turned over to the Army prior to redeployment. The Marine Corps' MEF (Fwd) in Afghanistan carries limited amounts of TPE as part of its deployed EDL. As was the case in Iraq, all TPE in Afghanistan is provided to the Marine Corps by the Army. Upon redeployment, or as TPE is no longer required for deployed operations, it will be returned to the Army. All other equipment on the MEF (Fwd) EDL—whether it is standard or "non-standard" equipment—is currently planned for redeployment to CONUS and reset.

30. Senator BAYH. General Chiarelli and General Amos, what are the plans for the reset and sustainment of the almost $3 billion in nonstandard gear that we have rapidly acquired to support urgent warfighter needs?

General CHIARELLI. We fully recognize that Non-Standard Equipment (NS–E) has played a significant role in enhancing the Army's capabilities. The Army has established a process called "Capabilities Development for Rapid Transition (CDRT)," to determine the long-term plan for NS–E, which classifies NS–E into three categories:

(1) Acquisition Program Candidates (APC): This is equipment which has been determined to have long-term applicability to Army equipping requirements, and so will be assigned to a program manager for movement through the formal Joint Capabilities Integration and Development System (JCIDS). All APC equipment will be reset upon its return and will eventually be issued to units in accordance with an approved Basis of Issue Plan (BOIP). The Army will manage these capabilities like any other acquisition program, with sustainment planned as part of the systems lifecycle.

(2) Sustain: This is equipment found to be useful for current operations in Afghanistan and Iraq, and so will be reset and continue to be used in OEF and Operation New Dawn (OND). When no longer required in OEF and OND, it may be placed in War Reserve or Operational Project Stocks, or may be disposed of, depending upon how current the technology remains.

(3) Terminate: This is equipment that the Army has determined is no longer militarily useful, and will therefore be disposed of. If feasible, disposal might be through Foreign Military Sales (FMS).

General AMOS. The Marine Corps principally uses the Expeditionary Force Development System (EFDS) to determine requirements for warfighting capabilities, to include equipment fielded by nonstandard methods. That equipment is typically fielded via either the Service's Urgent Needs Process (UNP) or the Joint Urgent Operational Needs (JUON) process. EFDS, conducted throughout each POM cycle, includes a bottom-up component that reviews each item of NS–E, first with respect to the capability gaps those items are intended to resolve. If validated, they are approved as entries to the MAGTF Gap List (MGL) by the Marine Requirements Oversight Council (MROC) led by the Assistant Commandant of the Marine Corps. Solution strategies are then developed to address each gap, which might include new technologies. If the particular item of NS–E is judged the best plan to provide a solution, it is included on the MROC-approved MAGTF Requirements List (MRL). Finally, the MRL is used to identify and prioritize initiatives for inclusion in the upcoming POM. In every case, investment in NS–E depends upon the establishment of that particular item as an enduring Marine Corps requirement. The Marine Corps will address the reset of NS–E once CD&I has determined what equipment will remain a part of the Marine Corps inventory.

31. Senator BAYH. General Chiarelli and General Amos, have you determined how much of this NS–E has proven useful and therefore should be reset and sustained? If not, what are your plans for this equipment and where are you in executing that plan?

General CHIARELLI. The Army has established the CDRT to determine the long-term plan for NS–E. Through this program, NS–E will be classified into three categories:

(1) APC: This is equipment which has been determined to have long-term applicability to Army equipping requirements, and so will be assigned to a program manager for movement through the formal JCIDS. All APC equipment will be reset upon its return and will eventually be issued to units in accordance with an approved Basis of Issue Plan (BOIP). The Army will manage these capabilities like any other acquisition program, with sustainment planned as part of the systems lifecycle.

(2) Sustain: This is equipment found to be useful for current operations in Afghanistan and Iraq, and so will be reset and continue to be used in OEF and OND. When no longer required in OEF and OND, it may be placed in War Reserve or Operational Project Stocks, or may be disposed of, depending upon how current the technology remains.

(3) Terminate: This is equipment that the Army has determined is no longer militarily useful, and will therefore be disposed of. If feasible, disposal might be through FMS.

The Army has coordinated and synchronized processes at every level to properly account for and dispose of equipment. We have established metrics for monitoring our progress and are currently on track in capturing accountability and disposition of our equipment.

General AMOS. A large percentage of NS–E has proven very useful to our Marine Corps forces operating in theater. And, the investment of those nonstandard items for future use depends upon the establishment of the particular item as an enduring Marine Corps requirement.

The Marine Corps uses the EFDS to determine requirements for warfighting capabilities, to include equipment fielded by nonstandard methods. That equipment is typically fielded through what is known as the UNP or the JUON process, which includes a bottom-up review of each item of NS–E. If validated, the equipment is approved as entries to the Marine Air-Ground Task Force (MAGTF) Gap List by the MROC. If the NS–E is determined to be an enduring requirement, it is included on the MROC-approved MAGTF Requirements List. The MAGTF Requirements List is then used to identify and prioritize initiatives for inclusion in the upcoming POM.

The Marine Corps is continuing to determine plans for the use of nonstandard items. However, current estimates project that approximately 47 percent of all equipment repaired in 2010 will be repaired either at a depot or field level maintenance facility, and 36 percent of the returning equipment will be replaced. The remaining percentage includes items for which no reset action will be taken. This includes theater-specific items which have no intended usage beyond OIF, or items that can be placed directly back into the Marine Corps inventory with no further maintenance action required.

67

32. Senator BAYH. General Amos, the Marine Corps seems to be facing a lot of unanswered questions that will affect its total requirement for equipment reset. The Marine Corps is requesting billions of dollars to repair its battle-worn equipment, but at the same time there are questions regarding whether the Marine Corps should be procuring new lighter equipment to support it expeditionary roots. To what extent does the Marine Corps know what equipment it will reset through new procurement, rather than through repair and recapitalization?

General AMOS. The reset cost model shows what equipment is in the MARCENT AOR and how the Marine Corps projects how they will reset that equipment. Reset includes the projection of field level maintenance, depot level maintenance, or new procurement to replace items based upon the developed reset cost model. The reset of ground equipment returning from the MARCENT AOR will be challenging as we rebalance resources to support ongoing combat operations, rearm, and reposition forces around the world.

As we retrograde and redeploy, a significant number of principal end items (PEI) must be reset in a timely manner to sustain continued operations, reset home station units and strategic programs such as our MPF. The reset of ground equipment returning from combat generally falls into four categories. They are: (1) procurement/replacement; (2) depot maintenance; (3) field maintenance; and (4) no maintenance required. Each category has a separate logistics action. The initial assessment of equipment being redeployed takes place in theater by forward deployed elements of Marine Corps Logistic Command (MCLC). Using a triage methodology, we determine the type of reset action required and take appropriate measures based on that assessment. Some equipment that is determined to be beyond repair will be disposed of in theater. Equipment that is economical to repair will be directed to an appropriate level maintenance facility, typically here in CONUS. Where necessary, the Marine Corps Systems Command (MCSC) will procure replacements for equipment which is beyond economic repair or obsolete. New procurement will play a major part in force modernization.

Equipment retrograded or redeployed from theater is inspected to determine if depot level repairs are required. The use of DOD core depot maintenance capabilities play a critical role in the reset of ground equipment. The goal of depot operations is to restore equipment to full capability as quickly as possible. Ground equipment repaired at designated depot-level repair activities will normally undergo 100 percent overhaul/rebuild. However, Inspect and Repair Only as Necessary (IROAN) and Selective Overhaul and Repair (SOAR) programs are viable options when determined to be a more effective and efficient means to return equipment to full mission capability and back into the hands of marines.

33. Senator BAYH. General Amos, how much of the Marine Corps equipment returned from Iraq was actually in good enough condition that it could be repaired and sent to Afghanistan?

General AMOS. Approximately 40 percent of the equipment in Afghanistan came from within theater, mainly from Iraq. Maintenance was conducted in Kuwait and then the required equipment was sent from Kuwait to Afghanistan. Because so much of the OIF equipment was sent to OEF, total reset actions have been deferred until we begin to drawdown our presence in Afghanistan. Equipment from OIF which was not redirected, returned to CONUS to be inducted into the reset process. As the reset process continues, that equipment will continue to be fielded across the enterprise to fill equipment requirements in accordance with the CMC Priority List.

34. Senator BAYH. General Amos, how did the Marine Corps make up the difference, and what is the status and plans for the Marine Corps equipment that was not diverted to Afghanistan?

General AMOS. Marine Corps forward deployed forces have the resources and equipment needed to conduct operations in support of OEF, but this has come at the expense of our home station, nondeployed units. For example, equipment used to support OIF that was scheduled to go through a depot overhaul has now been redirected to support OEF. As a result, we expect much higher than normal washout rates and more costly depot repairs when the equipment is eventually reset. This increased cost will be significant considering that over 40 percent of the equipment in Afghanistan was sourced from the CENTCOM theater (most of that coming from Iraq). Of the equipment that was retrograded to CONUS a significant portion was deemed obsolete or unsuitable for future use by the Marine Corps. In addition to shifting equipment from Iraq to Afghanistan, we drew heavily from the home station, nondeployed units. This resulted in an additional 5 to 10 percent decrease in equipment supply readiness for home station units, which directly impacts our preparedness for contingencies beyond Afghanistan. In short, we have assumed considerable risk within our nondeployed operational units where EOH currently averages 60 percent of the requirement.

Prior to the decision to deploy additional forces to OEF, the Marine Corps planned on performing depot maintenance on over 12,000 retrograded items, and field maintenance on over 24,000 items in fiscal year 2010. Due to the diversion of equipment to support our increased footprint in Afghanistan, we now expect that depot maintenance will be performed on approximately 6,100 retrograded items, and field maintenance on approximately 10,000 items in fiscal year 2010.

The process of reset execution is further integrated via the Marine Corps Logistics Command-led Enterprise Level Maintenance Program (ELMP). This is a comprehensive program that plans, programs, budgets for, and executes requirements for depot level maintenance. Once retrograded equipment is repaired through depots or via field maintenance, the process of filling equipment requirements is guided by the Commandant of the Marine Corps Equipment Priority List.

NAVY CHANGES IN CREW SIZE

35. Senator BAYH. Admiral Greenert, in the interest of increasing efficiencies and saving costs, the Navy has implemented several initiatives over the past several years, including reducing the size of crews assigned to surface combatants, shifting from hands-on to more computer-based training for basic engineering and other courses. At the same time, ships are facing increased mission requirements, such as for force protection and ballistic missile defense (BMD). To what extent has the Navy evaluated the impact of these changes in crew size and training on the ability of ships to maintain readiness, perform all required missions, and pass all required inspections?

Admiral GREENERT. Navy has incorporated the manpower requirements associated with force protection and BMD within our ship manpower documents across the surface force where applicable. Additionally, Navy has addressed the impacts of reduced crew manning. Within Program Review 2011, we have added 16 Engineman billets in LSD 41 class ships and 35 Machinist Mate billets in LHD 1 class ships to mitigate some impacts of optimal manning crew reductions. We are also evaluating the feasibility of restoring manpower within other surface ships.

Navy has focused efforts to deliver additional training to the waterfront and leveraged lessons learned to establish a blended training solution, which combines computer based training with traditional instructor-led training that, includes seminars and practical application in laboratories featuring hands-on training using both equipment and high fidelity simulators. This method utilizes the cost benefits of computer-based training to produce a more competent sailor. Billets for afloat-training have been increased to provide the warfighter increased access to subject matter experts while in port or during local operations. New programs, such as Advanced Warfare Training, taught by the Center for Surface Combat Systems, deliver waterfront training to the sailor to build confidence in maintaining the combat systems suite, operator proficiency, and the ability to work in a team environment.

AIR FORCE KEY ENABLERS

36. Senator BAYH. General Chandler, given the growing reliance on the Air Force to provide key enabling support capabilities to ongoing operations, such as military police and engineers, what impact has this had on force readiness?

General CHANDLER. The reliance on the Air Force to provide key enabling support capabilities through Joint Expeditionary Taskings (JET) degrades overall Air Force unit readiness by diminishing from organized, trained, and equipped unit numbers. For each augmentee that is tasked, an Air Force capability is degraded by not having its full complement of deployment ready personnel. For example, over the last year, the Air Force provided on average 1,025 personnel to fill military police (MP)-like capabilities. This amounted to roughly 25 percent of the total deployment requirements for Air Force Security Forces. These missions have included Police Transition Teams, Detainee Operations, Law and Order Detachments, and the like. In addition, augmentee sourcing is generally supported by Field Grade Officers and Senior Noncommissioned Officers (NCO), which adversely affects unit leadership, training, and capability. As an example, Civil Engineering officers are 1 of 11 stressed officer career fields and 8 of 17 stressed enlisted career fields are within Civil Engineering. Air Force end strength does not account for augmentee tasks which are over and above postured capability. In addition to MP and engineers, augmentees tend to be tasked from high-tempo capability areas such as Intelligence, Communications, Logistics Readiness, et cetera, further exacerbating sustainment of rotational sourcing.

37. Senator BAYH. General Chandler, given that these requirements are expected to continue, does the Air Force have plans to adjust its force structure to increase the inventory of these capabilities?

General CHANDLER. The Air Force is "all in." We size our human capital inventory based on long-term stability needs, therefore the Air Force does not plan to increase the inventories in these capabilities. We are taking steps to mitigate the high tempo on individual airmen. We continue to execute enlisted retraining programs both for first-term airmen and NCOs and are implementing a formal officer crossflow program to do the same for our officer force. We have protected high OPTEMPO career fields where possible from force management actions as we strive to meet overall end strength. These efforts will help maintain the proper inventory in enabling support capabilities and shape the force to meet current and emergent Air Force missions.

38. Senator BAYH. General Chandler, on April 2, at an Air Force Association-sponsored breakfast, Air Force Chief of Staff General Schwartz told reporters, "a service life extension program (SLEP) for aging F–15 and F–16 fighters would cost about 10 to 15 percent of what it would costs to buy new aircraft." Yet my staff has been told that to execute SLEP and increase from 8,600 flying hours to 10,000 flying hours will cost approximately $25 million per aircraft, while the cost of a new aircraft is approximately $42 million. This doesn't make fiscal sense. What is the engineering data and explanation behind the comments made by General Schwartz?

General CHANDLER. SLEP of current fighters provides essentially the same capability as new fourth generation fighters. The Air Force determined that SLEP costs about 10 to 15 percent of new aircraft based upon a comparison of current estimates for procurement of new fourth generation fighters (F–15E+, F–16 B50+, F/A–18 E/F) and a POM quality estimate for F–16 B40/50 SLEP (structure and avionics). The estimate of 10 to 15 percent is considered to be in the heart of the envelope of procuring new aircraft after considering many variables including quantity, multi-year versus single year procurement, and structural upgrade only versus modernization. New aircraft such as the F–16 B50+ range in price from $54.3 million to $59.8 million and new F–15+ from $76.4 million to $87.3 million; the cost to SLEP an F–16 B40/50 is $8.69 million per aircraft, all in base year 2010 dollars. SLEP cost estimates were provided by F–16 System Program Office, and included structural upgrade (SLEP), Active Electronically Scanned Array (AESA) radar, Center Display Unit (CDU), ALQ–213 EW Management System (EWMS), and Integrated Broadcast Service (IBS). Costs were validated by the Air Force costing agency and the Government Accountability Office (GAO) has reviewed them. The quoted figure of $25 million per aircraft SLEP is a Navy estimate for the F–18.

Bottom line, the cost of a SLEP depends on the modernization options selected but 10 to 15 percent of the cost of new procurement bounds most options.

39. Senator BAYH. General Chandler, have these figures of 10 to 15 percent been validated by DOD and by the Capability Assessment and Program Evaluation (CAPE) office or anyone else?

General CHANDLER. The CAPE office has not validated these numbers, but the Air Force costing agency and the GAO have reviewed them. Results of these reviews are pending.

40. Senator BAYH. General Chandler, currently, the Air Force may deploy individuals or parts of units to meet the requirements of combatant commanders. However, I'm concerned it does not reflect the impact of these deployments in reporting the readiness of nondeployed units. Specifically, for readiness reporting purposes, a nondeployed unit reports as if it has all its personnel and capabilities even though some may be deployed. Doesn't this mask the true readiness of Air Force units?

General CHANDLER. Joint Staff Status of Resources and Training System (SORTS) guidance (CJCSM 3150.02) allows the counting of personnel as 'available' if they are available within the forecasted mission or alert response time. For those units that have a mission response time that would permit its deployed personnel to be ready to redeploy to another contingency within the unit's mission response time, it is appropriate for them to count those personnel as available. For those personnel that would not be available within mission response time, units count them as unavailable and this is reflected in their overall SORTS rating. In addition, the Joint Staff guidance assumes that appropriate deployment orders have been received. By adhering to the Joint Staff guidance, the true readiness of Air Force units is presented to senior leadership for contingency sourcing, and the readiness of Air Force units is not masked. While we currently adhere to CJCSM 3150.02, the Air Force believes it can improve its readiness reporting and is undertaking an effort to develop an improved reporting process.

REDUCTION IN ARMY READINESS

41. Senator BAYH. General Chiarelli, while we work to support the surge of forces in Afghanistan and the drawdown in Iraq, we are reliant upon sufficient ground transportation capabilities for the movement of soldiers, equipment, and supplies. The fiscal year 2011 budget indicates that there will be a 2-year gap in the procurement of 34-ton flatbed semitrailers as well as similar pauses in other classes of heavy ground transportation assets for the Army. How does the Army plan cover this procurement shortfall?

General CHIARELLI. The Army has met its fiscal year 2011 requirement for the 34-ton flatbed trailer and is not projected to procure more trailers at this time. We currently are authorized 8,001 trailers and have 8,632 on-hand.

The Army plans to procure new Palletized Load System trucks through fiscal year 2011, Heavy Equipment Tractors through fiscal year 2012, Heavy Expanded Mobility Tactical Trucks Light Equipment Tractor and Load Handling System Trucks through fiscal year 2016, and the 40-ton trailers through fiscal year 2016. This will continue until the Army meets its acquisition objective for each of these systems. Additionally, the Army will focus on Heavy Tactical Vehicles and Trailers through fiscal year 2025 to extend the service life of its vehicles through recapitalization and modernization of older truck variants to the current armor-capable configurations. The Army will reduce sustainment costs by divesting the oldest vehicle and trailer variants that are excess or are being replaced by new production.

42. Senator BAYH. General Chiarelli, what is the projected rate of loss for these types of trailers both to obsolescence and hostile action?

General CHIARELLI. Since 2007, the washout rate for 34-ton flatbed semitrailers at our depots is 1.5 percent. We do not have a reported combat loss of these trailers since 2007. In 2007, three 34-ton flatbed semitrailers were lost to combat operations, and in 2006, four were lost to combat operations.

43. Senator BAYH. General Chiarelli, how many 34-ton flatbed semitrailers, if any, will be left in Iraq and therefore unavailable for use in Afghanistan?

General CHIARELLI. Afghanistan is our first priority for the redistribution of equipment coming out of Iraq. Any 34-ton flatbed semitrailers that are not mission essential in Iraq will be sent to support operations in Afghanistan as required. We do not plan to leave any 34-ton flatbed semitrailers in Iraq.

44. Senator BAYH. General Chiarelli, why is the Army opening competition for one type of trailer (M872A5, 34-ton) but procuring another (M871A3, 22-ton) via the General Services Administration (GSA) schedule?

General CHIARELLI. The M871A3 is a commercial 22½ ton trailer that has been altered and modified to include military specific requirements such as a blackout lighting system trailer, lifting and tie down provisions, stream/river fording capability, prime mover compatibility, and can transport up to one 20-foot International Organization for Standardization (ISO) container or cargo. 10 U.S.C. 2304 and 41 U.S.C. 253, requires, with certain limited exceptions, that contracting officers shall promote and provide for full and open competition in soliciting offers and awarding government contracts. In the case of the M871A3, the Army is procuring the trailer via the GSA Schedule because it is readily available and GSA is listed as an acceptable competitive procedure in accordance with Federal Acquisition Regulation (FAR) 6.102(d)(3). The configuration of the M871A3 available on the GSA Schedule has been tested to verify conformance to the Army's required performance capabilities and Type Classified.

The Army requirement for the 34-ton M872 trailer is to transport a single 40-foot or two 20-foot ISO containers, palletized cargo, or light combat or tactical vehicles. Unlike the M871A3, the M872A4 does not have a GSA option that meets the Army's requirement to transport a single 40-foot or two 20-foot ISO containers. Therefore, the Army must compete its future procurements of M872 Series 34-ton semitrailers as prescribed by law and in the FAR.

45. Senator BAYH. General Chiarelli, do the flatbed semitrailers procured off the GSA Schedule need to meet the same testing and performance requirements as those which are procured on a competitive basis? If not, why not?

General CHIARELLI. Yes, the flatbed semitrailers procured off the GSA Schedule need to meet the same testing and performance requirements. The M871A3s that the Army is procuring off the GSA Schedule were extensively tested by the Army at the Aberdeen Test Center from May 1999 through January 2002. The performance requirements to which the M871A3s have been procured were addressed within a GSA commercially-available performance specification. This trailer specification was modified to address military-specific performance requirements such as a blackout lighting system, trailer-lifting and tie-down provisions, ammunition transport capability, an upgraded suspension system to handle the rigors of off-road tactical mobility, and painting with Chemical Agent Resistant Coating (CARC).

———

QUESTIONS SUBMITTED BY SENATORS EVAN BAYH AND ROLAND W. BURRIS

MARINE CORPS RESET

46. Senator BAYH AND SENATOR BURRIS. General Amos, the Marine Corps seems to be facing a lot of unanswered questions that will affect its total requirement for equipment reset. The Marine Corps is requesting billions of dollars to repair its battle-worn equipment, but at the same time there are questions regarding whether the Marines should be procuring new lighter equipment to support it expeditionary roots. To what extent does the Marine Corps know what equipment it will reset through new procurement, rather than through repair and recapitalization?

General AMOS. The Reset Cost Model shows what equipment is in the MARCENT AOR and how the Marine Corps projects will reset that equipment. Reset includes the projection of field level maintenance, depot level maintenance, or new procurement to replace items based upon the developed Reset Cost Model. The reset of ground equipment returning from the MARCENT AOR will be challenging as we rebalance resources to support ongoing combat operations, rearm, and reposition forces around the world.

As we retrograde and redeploy, a significant number of principal end items (PEI) must be reset in a timely manner to sustain continued operations, reset home station units and strategic programs such as our MPF. The reset of ground equipment returning from combat generally falls into four categories. They are: (1) procurement/replacement; (2) depot maintenance; (3) field maintenance; and (4) no maintenance required. Each category has a separate logistics action. The initial assessment of equipment being redeployed takes place in theater by forward deployed elements of MCLC. Using a triage methodology, we determine the type of reset action required and take appropriate measures based on that assessment. Some equipment that is determined to be beyond repair will be disposed of in theater. Equipment that is economical to repair will be directed to an appropriate level maintenance facility, typically here in CONUS. Where necessary, the MCSC will procure replacements for equipment which is beyond economic repair or obsolete. New procurement will play a major part in force modernization.

Equipment retrograded or redeployed from theater is inspected to determine if depot level repairs are required. The use of DOD core depot maintenance capabilities play a critical role in the reset of ground equipment. The goal of depot operations is to restore equipment to full capability as quickly as possible. Ground equipment repaired at designated depot-level repair activities will normally undergo 100 percent overhaul/rebuild. However, IROAN and SOAR programs are viable options when determined to be a more effective and efficient means to return equipment to full mission capability and back into the hands of marines.

47. Senator BAYH AND SENATOR BURRIS. General Amos, how much of the Marine Corps equipment returned from Iraq was actually in good enough condition that it could be repaired and sent to Afghanistan?

General AMOS. Approximately 40 percent of the equipment in Afghanistan came from within theater, mainly from Iraq. Maintenance was conducted in Kuwait and then the required equipment was sent from Kuwait to Afghanistan. Because so much of the OIF equipment was sent to OEF, total reset actions have been deferred until we begin to drawdown our presence in Afghanistan. Equipment from OIF which was not redirected, returned to CONUS to be inducted into the reset process. As the reset process continues, that equipment will continue to be fielded across the enterprise to fill equipment requirements in accordance with the CMC Priority List.

48. Senator BAYH AND SENATOR BURRIS. General Amos, how did the Marine Corps make up the difference, and what is the status and plans for the Marine Corps equipment that was not diverted to Afghanistan?

General AMOS. Marine Corps forward deployed forces have the resources and equipment needed to conduct operations in support of OEF, but this has come at the expense of our home station, nondeployed units. For example, equipment used to support OIF that was scheduled to go through a depot overhaul has now been redirected to support OEF. As a result, we expect much higher than normal washout rates and more costly depot repairs when the equipment is eventually reset. This increased cost will be significant considering that over 40 percent of the equipment in Afghanistan was sourced from the CENTCOM theater (most of that coming from Iraq). Of the equipment that was retrograded to CONUS a significant portion was deemed obsolete or unsuitable for future use by the Marine Corps. In addition to shifting equipment from Iraq to Afghanistan, we drew heavily from the home station, nondeployed units. This resulted in an additional 5 to 10 percent decrease in equipment supply readiness for home station units, which directly impacts our preparedness for contingencies beyond Afghanistan. In short, we have assumed considerable risk within our nondeployed operational units where EOH currently averages 60 percent of the requirement.

Prior to the decision to deploy additional forces to OEF, the Marine Corps planned on performing depot maintenance on over 12,000 retrograded items, and field maintenance on over 24,000 items in fiscal year 2010. Due to the diversion of equipment to support our increased footprint in Afghanistan, we now expect that depot maintenance will be performed on approximately 6,100 retrograded items, and field maintenance on approximately 10,000 items in fiscal year 2010.

The process of reset execution is further integrated via the Marine Corps Logistics Command-led ELMP. This is a comprehensive program that plans, programs, budgets for, and executes requirements for depot level maintenance. Once retrograded equipment is repaired through depots or via field maintenance, the process of filling equipment requirements is guided by the Commandant of the Marine Corps Equipment Priority List.

ISSUES WITH READINESS REPORTING

49. Senator BAYH AND SENATOR BURRIS. General Chiarelli, General Amos, Admiral Greenert, and General Chandler, I can understand how a unit commander knows his or her unit the best. And in reporting their unit readiness through the Defense Readiness Reporting System (DRRS) we capture not only whether they are ready, but ready for what. My concern is that should they be allowed to subjectively upgrade if the statistics and data do not support a higher unit readiness rating?

General CHIARELLI. The unit status report is intended to reflect the unit commander's personal assessments and individual judgments. Clearly there are circumstances where a unit commander subjectively upgrades even when the currently measured statistics and data do not support a higher unit readiness rating. For example, a unit may be short some of its Modified Table of Organization and Equipment (MTOE) required items; however, the commander, based on his or her knowledge of the unit's current training proficiency and the availability of other equipment items, assesses that the missing equipment items do not significantly degrade the ability of the unit to accomplish its core functions or increase its vulnerability, and upgrades the overall C-level assessment accordingly. Similarly, the unit commander may subjectively change the "Assigned Mission Level (A-level) to reflect unit training proficiency that is not measured otherwise. Reports are processed through command channels so that commanders at higher levels can review the report for accuracy and provide additional comments, if necessary. Currently, Army Regulation 220–1 allows any unit commander to subjectively upgrade or downgrade the overall readiness assessment (C-level and A-level) by one level unilaterally. In general, two level changes require the approval of the commander at the next higher level. Three level changes require Headquarters, Department of the Army (HQDA) approval. This policy is intended to balance the desire to support commander prerogatives with the need to provide the timely, accurate, and objective reports prescribed by Congress in the 1999 NDAA.

General AMOS. While we believe we have a very good readiness reporting system, we also believe that no one knows and understands the readiness and capabilities of his or her unit better than that unit's commander. If a commander has a strong and compelling reason to override the readiness rating of his or her unit based on objective inputs, the commander should be able to do so.

73

Our readiness reporting policy provides specific guidelines for when and why commanders can use the override function. Reports are reviewed for accuracy throughout the chain of command all the way up to the Headquarters Marine Corps level. In their commander's comments, commanders must clearly articulate the reasons for their subjective upgrade (or downgrade) to provide balance to their report. This human dimension in our readiness reporting is important; ultimately the commander is entrusted and responsible for the readiness of his or her unit and we believe the commander should have the final say on how ready his or her unit is.

Admiral GREENERT. The commander's assessment represents their first-hand knowledge of the unit's readiness, which is primarily based on information about the resources available to support and accomplish the mission. DRRS-Navy (DRRS–N) makes available to the commander information from authoritative data sources that reflect the status of those resources (Personnel, Equipment, Supply, Training, Ordnance, and Facilities) that help assess Mission Essential Tasks (MET) that each ship, unit, or squadron is required to perform to support their core mission areas. The commander must balance his/her overall knowledge of the full spectrum of resources that support the required capabilities, with the experience factor relative to the reliability of equipment/systems when making the assessment. These experienced commanders have received many years of training, and their judgment is an exceptional resource and an important factor in the most effective evaluation of readiness. This judgment can either lead them to assess a readiness level higher or lower than the data may otherwise support. In addition, senior commanders have access to the readiness information from their subordinate units in DRRS–N. This promotes open dialogue about any questionable assessments, and it also serves as means for monitoring the quality of readiness.

General CHANDLER. There is no subjective upgrade of the unit readiness in the DRRS; the commander's assessment is subjective by the very design of the system. Each unit has a core METL which contains several METs. Each MET is assessed against a variety of measures, usually objective, but some of them may be subjective as well. These objective and subjective measures are used by the commander to inform his overall assessment; there is no published DOD or Air Force guidance equating individual MET assessments to a commander's overall assessment. Because of the complexity of unit readiness, commanders are permitted to use their experience and judgment, in addition to the factors that make up the SORTS subarea assessments, when making their overall unit readiness assessment.

50. Senator BAYH AND SENATOR BURRIS. General Chiarelli, General Amos, Admiral Greenert, and General Chandler, my concern is that we may be masking true readiness at the unit level and as that information is passed up the chain of command to the Joint Staff, combatant commanders, and JFCOM, that those assessments and abilities to respond to mission requirements may not possess absolute clarity. I'll give you an example: SOCOM does not allow commanders to subjectively upgrade their unit readiness reporting status. Why do conventional forces allow subjective upgrades and as a result of that are we not masking true readiness reporting?

General CHIARELLI. The responsibilities and authorities for implementing and enforcing various readiness reporting requirements are shared among the Chairman, the Secretary of Defense, the combatant commanders and the Service Secretaries in accordance with existing law and policy. Title 10 U.S.C. establishes that the SOCOM Commander is responsible to ensure the combat readiness of assigned forces and for monitoring the mission readiness of all special operations forces, restrictions on subjective changes for Army Special Operations Forces are within his authority. Current Army policy restricts, but does not prohibit, subjective changes to the overall readiness assessments contained in unit status reports. While the commander of a conventional Army unit may subjectively change his overall assessment, he is required to clearly explain and justify the subjective change in mandatory comments, and he cannot change the objective resource measurements that reflect the current status of personnel and equipment. Unit status reports are processed through command channels, and all subjective changes to overall readiness assessments are clearly identifiable to commanders at higher levels with those management oversight responsibilities.

General AMOS. The Marine Corps believes that no one knows and understands the readiness and capabilities of his or her unit better than the unit commander. If a commander has a strong and compelling reason to override the readiness rating of his or her unit based on objective inputs, the commander should be able to do so. There are sometimes other factors to consider other than objective inputs exclusively, such as unit morale or a commander's training and judgment applied to a specific situation.

Our readiness reporting policy provides specific guidelines for when and why commanders can use the override function. In their commander's comments, commanders must clearly articulate the reasons for their subjective upgrade (or downgrade) to provide balance to their report. Reports are reviewed for accuracy throughout the chain of command all the way up to the Headquarters Marine Corps level.

This human dimension in our readiness reporting is important; ultimately the commander is entrusted and responsible for the readiness of his or her unit and we believe the commander should have the final say on how ready his or her unit is.

Admiral GREENERT. The commander's assessment represents their first-hand knowledge of the unit's readiness, which is primarily based on information about the resources available to support and accomplish the mission. DRRS–N makes available to the commander information from authoritative data sources that reflect the status of those resources (Personnel, Equipment, Supply, Training, Ordnance, and Facilities) that help assess METs that each ship, unit, or squadron is required to perform to support their core mission areas. The commander must balance his/her overall knowledge of the full spectrum of resources that support the required capabilities, with the experience factor relative to the reliability of equipment/systems when making the assessment. These experienced commanders have received many years of training, and their judgment is an exceptional resource and an important factor in the most effective evaluation of readiness. This judgment can either lead them to assess a readiness level higher or lower than the data may otherwise support. In addition, senior commanders have access to the readiness information from their subordinate units in DRRS–N. This promotes open dialogue about any questionable assessments, and it also serves as means for monitoring the quality of readiness assessments overall.

General CHANDLER. Joint Staff SORTS guidance (CJCSM 3150.02) allows commanders to subjectively assess their unit's readiness up or down to permit commanders to use their judgment and consider factors outside of the strict factors that make up the personnel, equipment, and training ratings. The Air Force has three major commands who have supplemented SORTS reporting guidance and do not allow their commanders to subjectively assess up. However, the Air Force is going to address this policy with the major commands to ensure standardization across the Air Force.

The following are a few of the reasons provided in Air Force SORTS guidance (AFI 10–201), that are not accounted for elsewhere, for why a commander may assess up or down: inspection results, personnel turnover rates, unusually high/low morale, demonstrated maintenance surge capabilities, modification programs, and the ability of contractors or foreign nationals to provide services.

This is not a masking of true readiness. Readiness, by its nature, is subjective. Objective measures are used to inform the commander's subjective assessment.

51. Senator BAYH AND SENATOR BURRIS. General Chiarelli, General Amos, Admiral Greenert, and General Chandler, how does our current readiness reporting system account for new and urgent operational need items such as the MRAP and M–ATV, and how are they being tracked and implemented into your MTOE?

General CHIARELLI. AR 220–1 establishes requirements for units to report an "Assigned Mission Level" (A-level) following the formal assignment of a mission for planning or execution. The A-level is supported by an Assigned Mission Equipment Level" (AME level) that is intended to reflect the current availability to the unit of the specific equipment items required for the assigned mission. While many of these mission-required equipment items will reside on the unit's MTOE, several equipment items may not, especially if they are "theater-unique" and/or if the unit has been assigned to accomplish a nontraditional mission (for example, a field artillery unit assigned a security force mission). The Army Tasking Authority—the command or force provider that formally assigned the mission to the unit—is responsible to establish or convey the specific resource requirements for the mission to the unit. Resource requirements that exceed or differ from those documented on the unit's MTOE or that will require an urgent operational need statement (ONS) require Headquarters, Department of the Army (HQDA) approval. Frequently, HQDA preapproves MRAPs and M–ATVs for missions via Mission Essential Equipment Lists (MEEL). Subsequently, these MEELs and ONS are considered during the force development process to determine whether any future MTOE adjustments are necessary.

General AMOS. Marine Corps policy ensures each UNS item is appropriately categorized in our supply and maintenance systems of record. The readiness of these items is tracked closely through these systems by both forward deployed commanders and the Service Headquarters. Although UNS items are not identified as mission essential equipment (MEE) or PEIs per Marine Corps policy, those UNS items which are deemed key readiness drivers, as in the case of MRAPs and M–ATVs (as of February 2010), are treated as significant military equipment and tracked in our current readiness reporting system as PEIs.

Admiral GREENERT. DRRS–N documents readiness across all resource pillars (Personnel, Equipment, Supply, Training, Ordnance, and Facilities) for each specific platform. This is accomplished after the Navy METs (NMET) have been loaded for the specific unit identification code (UIC) employing the equipment. Although DRRS–N is not designed to track equipment below the UIC-level, Navy is developing a Global Force Management (GFM) Organization Server that will track force structure below the UIC-level. The GFM Org server will be fully operational in March 2011.

General CHANDLER. Our current readiness reporting system does not treat new and urgent operational need items differently than other items. All new equipment is added to equipment lists and tracked in the same manner. Our SORTS reporting system accounts for new items once they have been included on the Design Operational Capability (DOC) statements. Units would then report the equipment condition ('R' rating) or the supplies on hand ('S' rating) of that equipment. The DRRS would account for new items after they have been included as part of a MET. Units would then report against specific measures that would quantify a standard for that equipment.

QUESTIONS SUBMITTED BY SENATOR RICHARD BURR

DWELL TIME FOR MAJOR COMBAT UNITS

52. Senator BURR. General Chiarelli, the 2009 Quadrennial Defense Review (QDR) assumed that the Armed Forces must be prepared to respond to a range of contingencies similar to what we have faced over the past 8 years. In contrast, we've heard testimony over the past 2 years from the Chief of Staff of the Army that: "The Army is out of balance. ... Overall, we are consuming readiness as fast as we can build it. These conditions must change. Institutional and operational risks are accumulating over time and must be reduced in the coming years." In your opinion, does the QDR adequately address the issue of restoring the current unit combat readiness in the Army?

General CHIARELLI. Yes, it does adequately address the issue of restoring current unit combat readiness in the Army. A priority objective of the defense strategy articulated during the QDR is to prevail in today's wars. The 2010 QDR recognizes that years of war have significantly stressed our military personnel and their families, especially our ground forces. The 2010 QDR notes that, "As we finish well in Iraq and shift the main effort to Afghanistan, we have the opportunity to begin resetting and reconstituting our units and, as dwell time increases, reduce stress on our servicemembers and their families." The Chairman of the Joint Chiefs of Staff, in his assessment of the 2010 QDR, notes that, "Now and for several years upon completion of operations we must reset equipment lost through combat and the strain of today's wars. Our success in these and other missions depends upon obtaining sufficient, timely funding to reset the force and restore readiness and a responsible withdrawal from Iraq." We concur with the assessments of the Secretary of Defense and the Chairman. Within the Army, as time between deployments increases, soldiers and units will begin to restore their readiness and capability for the full-spectrum of challenges envisioned by the defense strategy. For the past several years, the demand for Army forces has exceeded the sustainable supply of those forces, limiting soldiers and units to prepare only for their next assigned mission in Afghanistan or Iraq, at the expense of the broader range of capabilities for which their specific unit was designed. As we reestablish balance between operational demands and our sustainable supply of trained and ready soldiers and units, we also intend to limit deployment duration to not more than 9 months and increase time between deployments to at least 27 months to permit soldiers, units, and families adequate time to recover and reset from challenging deployments, and more fully prepare for an uncertain and dynamic future.

53. Senator BURR. General Chiarelli, can the Army achieve its dwell times goals with the current force structure assuming similar demands on the force?

General CHIARELLI. The global demand for Army forces exceeds available resources. The Army is out of balance and is consuming readiness as fast as it can be built. This imbalance is driven by the need to respond to current demands at the expense of preparing for future conflicts. This limits the Army's strategic depth in terms of capabilities and in the quantity of forces available to respond to unexpected contingencies. The Army's plan to reduce risk to the force and achieve its dwell time goal assumes a reduction in demand for Army forces.

EQUIPMENT IN THEATER

54. Senator BURR. General Amos, MV–22 mission capable rates in Afghanistan have been about 70 percent despite extraordinary efforts to provide parts and maintenance capability in excess of the requirements for routine deployment of the aircraft. Despite the hostile environment of Afghanistan that contributes to lower mission capable rates, such a relatively low mission capable rate for a new platform raises questions about the sustainability of the MV–22 over its life cycle. What are the Marine Corps and the contractors involved doing to improve the mission capable rate of the MV–22?

General AMOS. The V–22 readiness challenges are being met by addressing the three readiness elements: reliability, maintainability, and supply support.

The core reliability of some components has already been fixed and programmed or implemented on the production line. The Marine Corps, AFSOC, and NAVAIR have reprioritized existing funding to retrofit those changes that affect the highest degraders. NAVICP is funding redesign of several other degraders. Future funding through HQMC Aviation is planned to bring these and other redesigns to the fleet.

Significant improvement to maintenance procedures, troubleshooting tools, and organic repair capabilities are keeping components on the aircraft longer or closer to the flightline for repair.

Some of these improvements have a direct impact on supply support and operating costs. In addition, NAVICP and DLA continue to work closely with industry to shift high-cost consumable parts to low-cost repairs (over 400 items to date). Refinement of contracting vehicles by NAVICP, investment in parts procurement, and closer management by the prime contractors of their suppliers are expected to have a telling impact in the near future.

Most of these adjustments and direct improvements have been implemented recently, and are just beginning to yield. As the more prevalent supply support improvements take hold, we expect to see a wider and more dramatic impact.

In summary, the aircraft continues to prove itself exceptionally effective and survivable. The Marine Corps, AFSOC, the naval supporting commands, and industry are committed to bringing the readiness and operating cost in line.

ACCESS TO HEALTH AND MENTAL HEALTH CARE

55. Senator BURR. General Chiarelli, I am very concerned about the adequacy of TRICARE networks to meet the health and mental health needs of our servicemembers and their families, especially in light of the stress of deployments and exposure to combat. In January this year the New England Journal of Medicine reported that "prolonged deployment was associated with more mental health diagnoses among U.S. Army wives."

A new GAO report describes several factors of continuing concern regarding access to care: instances of lack of willingness by providers to accept new TRICARE patients; a lack of awareness and acceptance by providers of the TRICARE program; and low reimbursement rates. How confident are you that the TRICARE networks are attracting sufficient numbers of health and mental health care providers to provide the services that soldiers and their families need?

General CHIARELLI. The Army is confident that TRICARE Management Activity (TMA) will continue traditional and creative efforts to attract network health and mental health providers. The Army works closely with TMA in their efforts to provide the services necessary to meet the needs of soldiers and their families. As required by law, TMA regularly monitors both network provider acceptance of TRICARE and beneficiaries' access to care.

TMA has developed and expanded behavioral health (BH) services that include two new online video behavioral health programs to help eliminate obstacles to seeking BH treatment. The two programs, TRICARE Assistance Program (TRIAP) and Tele-behavioral Health, are available to Active Duty servicemembers and their families. Through these programs soldiers and families can access licensed BH counselors for short-term, real-time, face-to-face confidential counseling utilizing video technology, and software such as Skype or iChat.

TRIAP expands access to existing BH services by using audiovisual telecommunications systems such as video chat and instant messaging to access existing BH centers within the TRICARE region. It also expands access to the BH call centers and counseling services. It is available 24 hours a day, 7 days a week, with no limits to usage. No notification about those seeking counseling will be made to their primary care managers or others, unless required by the counselor's licensure (spouse abuse, et cetera). Beneficiaries may access TRIAP from any location provided they have the necessary hardware and software. Telebehavioral health is also available throughout the United States. This program involves medically supervised, secure audio-visual conferencing between beneficiaries and an offsite licensed BH provider.

Additional opportunities to expand TRICARE BH exist with the use of virtual technologies, but require legislative relief to State licensure restrictions on TRICARE certified providers. Under current statutory restrictions, TRICARE network providers cannot conduct virtual BH interviews and counseling across State borders unless they are located at a Federal installation (DOD, VA, et cetera). This severely limits our ability to fully utilize these BH professionals. Legislative relief authorizing TRICARE certified providers to connect with our beneficiaries/patients from their private practice offices will increase assets available to meet the BH needs of soldiers and their families.

OPERATIONAL IMPACT OF TRAUMATIC BRAIN INJURY

56. Senator BURR. General Chiarelli, according to a recent study by the Institute of Medicine, an estimated 10 to 20 percent of OEF and OIF Army and Marine Corps servicemembers have sustained mild traumatic brain injury (TBI) that has been associated with various long-term health outcomes. What are the operational and readiness impacts of mild TBI and concussion among deploying forces?

General CHIARELLI. Many of the recommendations made in the 2008 report by the Institute of Medicine, Gulf War and Health: Volume 7, Long-term Consequences of Traumatic Brain Injury, have already been adopted by DOD. The Institute of Medicine's (IOM) recommendations are consistent with reports by the Defense Health Board and the Army TBI Task Force. Currently, approximately 87 to 90 percent of TBI cases in the Armed Forces involve mild TBI, also known as a concussion. The majority of these servicemembers return to full duty when their symptoms resolve with minimal operational impact. Some of the health outcomes mentioned in the IOM study such as depression and memory problems could impact operational readiness either within the few months following the injury or in some cases a few years later while the servicemember is still on Active Duty. Studies are underway. However, we currently do not have sufficient scientific information to quantify the full impact of this issue. To address more immediate concerns of our soldiers, the Army has taken action to protect the force. In late 2009, we implemented our "Educate, Train, Treat & Track" TBI management strategy to improve early recognition of signs and symptoms for these injuries. Efforts are underway to adopt this strategy across DOD for all deployed forces.

Many of the long-term health outcomes cited in the IOM report such as dementia, Parkinson's, and Alzheimer's disease may not manifest until possibly decades after the injury. Understanding the long-term impact requires longitudinal studies including the one currently underway that will evaluate 1,600 servicemembers with TBI over the next 15 years. We are taking steps to ensure that soldiers involved in events that may cause mild TBI are well-documented, even if they are not experiencing any immediate symptoms. Emerging knowledge regarding the long-term health outcomes associated with mild TBI will continue to be reported as scientific literature advances in this area.

57. Senator BURR. General Chiarelli, how effectively have the resources provided by Congress been used to mitigate the effects of mild TBI?

General CHIARELLI. The funds provided by Congress have been highly effective in mitigating the effects of mild TBI both through equipment and material solutions designed to prevent injury and through medical advances to improve our diagnostic and treatment capabilities. Since September 2007, these resources have funded more than 350 staff members dispersed among 52 programs across the U.S. Army Medical Command to address the effects of TBI. This funding has ensured the development and fielding of the latest protective equipment to mitigate the effects of blasts and other injuries that may result in a mild TBI. Quality of care has been improved by developing clinical practice guidelines, obtaining state-of-the-art equipment for TBI care, funding basic and applied research to advance medical practices, and improving education and training for providers treating mild TBI. Additionally, these resources have enabled the Army to lead the way in developing TBI management protocols for our deploying soldiers. Efforts are underway to codify these protocols into a DOD Directive Type Memorandum for all deployed forces.

58. Senator BURR. General Chiarelli, what is the way forward to ensure that soldiers in the field are adequately screened and, if necessary, removed from combat roles in order to recover from mild TBI or concussion?

General CHIARELLI. The new DOD policy being worked will mandate that all servicemembers who are exposed to concussive events be removed from combat roles for a minimum of 24 hours and undergo immediate medical screening. This will improve clinical management of concussed patients through detailed care algorithms which will assist healthcare providers by guiding medical evaluations and referrals to the next echelon of care. This pending policy will mandate rest periods, prohibit all sports and activities with risk of concussion until medically cleared, direct the use of standardized educational sheets, and implement a protocol to manage recurrent concussion.

Deployed medical providers are using new screening resources while researchers are developing more promising neurocognitive assessment tools. One of the most commonly-used screening tools, the Military Acute Concussion Evaluation (MACE) has recently been improved. In addition, 43 Automated Neuropsychological Assessment Metrics (ANAM) computer systems have been deployed to Iraq and Afghanistan, outfitted with additional commercial assessment software to extend their capability. Test administration has been improved, with training products that focus on accuracy and effectiveness of both the MACE and the ANAM. Emerging technologies such as teleneurology, teleneuropsychology, brain imaging, biomarker detection, and automated quantitative electroencephalography promise to dramatically improve future mild TBI screening, detection, and treatment capabilities.

59. Senator BURR. General Amos, how will the Marine Corps be able to meet these extensive and costly war-related funding needs within the normal DOD budget which is only projected to grow about 4 percent in fiscal year 2010?

General AMOS. TBI is a defense-wide funded program and the Office of the Secretary of Defense (OSD) has the lead for all war-related funding requirements and research as it pertains to TBI. The Marine Corps funding for any medical treatment is through Navy medicine and is not part of the Marine Corps budget.

INCREASE IN SUICIDES

60. Senator BURR. General Chiarelli, another tragic consequence of the OIF and OEF deployments is an increase in suicide. Yesterday, the Army released suicide figures for the month of March: 13 potential suicides among Active Duty soldiers, and 8 potential suicides among Reserve component soldiers not on Active Duty. How do these numbers compare with previous years?

General CHIARELLI. From calendar year 2005 through calendar year 2010, Active Duty soldiers averaged 10 suicides in the month of March; 7 soldiers died by suicide in March 2005; followed by a slight decrease in March 2006 to 5 suicides. For March 2007, the number nearly doubled to 9 suicides, followed by an incremental increase to 11 suicides in March 2008. There were 13 suicides in both March 2009 and March 2010.

For Reserve component soldiers not on Active Duty, there was an average of 5 suicides in the month of March during the period calendar year 2005 through calendar year 2010. Only 1 Reserve component soldier not on Active Duty died by suicide in March 2005. Incremental increases occurred in March 2006, with 3 suicides and March 2007, with 5 suicides. March 2008 experienced a decline to 3 suicides. For March 2009 and March 2010, 7 and 8 soldiers died by suicide, respectively.

RESET COSTS AND THE SHIFT OF WAR FUNDING TO THE BASE BUDGET

61. Senator BURR. General Amos, I have a question about estimated costs to reset combat units in the Marine Corps. In your written testimony, you state: "we estimate the cost of reset for the Marine Corps to be $8 billion, of which $3 billion is requested in the fiscal year 2011 OCOs and an additional $5 billion reset liability will be addressed upon termination of the conflict." In last year's hearing, you estimated approximately $20 billion for replacing, repairing, or rebuilding equipment to reset the Marine Corps equipment stocks to acceptable readiness levels. Please give an update on the dramatic decrease in the estimate.

General AMOS. The Marine Corps' reset estimate did not decrease. The $20 billion mentioned in last year's testimony was an overall snapshot of the total reset requirement, to include what has been appropriated from fiscal year 2006 to fiscal year 2009 and what was required in fiscal year 2010 and beyond. Since testifying last year, combat operations have continued and our overall reset estimate has grown to $24 billion. This number includes $16 billion received through fiscal year 2010, a $3 billion fiscal year 2011 request, and a $5 billion future years reset liability.

62. Senator BURR. General Amos, is the Marine Corps being asked to scale back its requirements for reset based on budget realities, or is there another explanation?
General AMOS. No, the Marine Corps is not being asked to scale back its requirements for reset based on budget realities.

63. Senator BURR. General Amos, in your opinion, will the Marine Corps be able to continue funding reset from the OCO account?
General AMOS. Yes, as long as the Marine Corps is engaged in combat operations, and under the current rule set, there will be a requirement to fund the repair and replace of equipment directly used in combat through the OCO account.

64. Senator BURR. General Amos, you also mention in your testimony that the Marine Corps has revised its unit tables of equipment (T/Es) to accurately reflect the challenges and realities of the 21st century dispersed battlefield and estimated the cost associated with the revised T/Es to be $5 billion. Is this amount in addition to the reset costs?
General AMOS. Yes, this estimate is in addition to reset costs. The Marine Corps' equipment sets have been modified based on the lessons we learned in OIF and OEF about what we need to be ready for future operations. The cost to make these necessary changes to our equipment sets is currently estimated to be $5 billion.

65. Senator BURR. General Amos, will the Marine Corps fund this from base budgets or the OCO account?
General AMOS. The Marine Corps will have to fund the shortfalls for operational units in dwell through the base budget as this requirement does not meet the criteria to be included in the OCO budget.

66. Senator BURR. General Amos, how quickly do you need to have this funding in place to ensure marines have the updated list of equipment to be able to use in Afghanistan?
General AMOS. Marines next to deploy and those already in Afghanistan have the equipment they need to be successful. However, operational units in dwell have suffered because their equipment sets and training gear has been pushed to Afghanistan. These units in dwell currently have limited training capabilities until they are back in the predeployment training cycle.

RESET FOR THE RESERVE COMPONENT

67. Senator BURR. General Chiarelli, in your written testimony, you state that in order to restore the Army's full operational depth by fiscal year 2012, the Reserve component, that is our National Guard and Reserve Forces, must continue a transition from a Strategic Reserve to an Operational Force, thus allowing the Army "recurrent, assured, and predictable" access to the Reserve component to meet operational requirements. Since the Army expects the National Guard to be a full partner in the ARFORGEN model, do Guard and Reserve units get the same priority for equipment reset and resourcing?
General CHIARELLI. Yes, the Reserve component units redeploying from contingency operations are given the same priority as they move through the ARFORGEN Model as Active component formations. The process for reset is the same except that the timeline for Reserve component units to complete reset operations is 365 days as opposed to 180 days for an Active component organization. The difference in reset timelines is based on Reserve component organizations having a longer programmed dwell time between deployments (4 years) versus only 2 years between deployments of Active component formations.

68. Senator BURR. General Chiarelli, given the dedicated call to duty of National Guard units across the country for service in Iraq and Afghanistan, are the historic complaints of the National Guard getting the hand-me-down or older equipment from the Active Army a vestige of the past?
General CHIARELLI. Yes. Modernizing the Army National Guard (ARNG) is critical for transformation to an Operational Reserve. The ARNG equipment funding averaged $5.7 billion per year for fiscal years 2006 to 2010, a 256 percent increase over the $1.6 billion the ARNG received in fiscal year 2005. In fiscal years 2011 to 2015,

the Army programmed an additional $12.4 billion for the ARNG, which will significantly increase its capabilities. At the end of March 2009, the ARNG EOH was 77 percent, with a projected growth based on current procurement plans to 83 percent by the end of 2017. The EOH rate for Critical Dual Use equipment will increase from 83 percent in 2009 to 87 percent by March 2011.

69. Senator BURR. General Chiarelli, in your constant review of readiness rates, do you see any glaring discrepancies in the relative readiness of Active units versus Guard and Reserve units? If so, what are they and how can they be mitigated?

General CHIARELLI. There are differences between the primary readiness drivers for Active and Reserve components. Active units report equipment availability as their primary readiness driver, followed by soldier availability. Conversely, Reserve component units cite soldier availability (availability of qualified and trained soldiers) as the primary driver, while equipment availability is cited infrequently. Over time, the trends for these drivers have remained essentially stable.

The ARFORGEN process is how the Army mitigates these issues. Active component units essentially migrate equipment from units in the reset phase to support immediate warfighting requirements. Meanwhile the Reserve components cross-level personnel from nondeployed or reset units to support immediate operational requirements. Additionally, implementation of the 180-day TRICARE Early Eligibility program and modifications to the Reserve Health Readiness Program have improved Reserve component personnel readiness.

70. Senator BURR. General Chiarelli, of the $13 to $14 billion per year you have suggested for additional funding provided for reset, how will that amount be equitably distributed among the Active and Reserve components?

General CHIARELLI. OCOs funding for equipment reset is determined by the number and types of units scheduled to redeploy each year. The Army National Guard receives direct distribution of funding from the Army Budget Office to complete their reset mission. Army Reserve units complete their reset mission at the appropriate demobilization sites and funded accordingly. Army equipment reset requirements are historically made up of 20 to 25 percent Reserve unit requirements. Based on current ARFORGEN projections, the Army estimates that 20 percent of equipment reset funding will go to Guard and Reserve equipment in fiscal year 2011 and fiscal year 2012. The Army will continue to support all components to ensure equipment readiness is restored and ready for the next contingency.

AIRCRAFT MAINTENANCE CHALLENGES FOR THE AIR FORCE

71. Senator BURR. General Chandler, your written statement identified concerns with the availability rates of certain types of aircraft. Specifically, you stated: "the B-1, B-52, and F-15E did not meet aircraft availability standards due to maintenance and depot-related issues." Please describe what types of maintenance and depot issues are affecting availability rates.

General CHANDLER. The B-1 not mission capable maintenance rate is well above projections due to manpower shortages and inexperienced technicians. A primary driver is preparing and recovering aircraft going to and coming from the area of responsibility. In addition, many mid-level maintenance NCOs have left the B-1 over the past 4 years due to manning cuts and ops tempo challenges and that expertise is not easily replaced. Depot possessed aircraft rates are high because the Air Force opted to give combatant commanders greater capability by modernizing systems like the radar, the engine digital controller, and the inertial navigation system. These modernization efforts sacrifice short-term aircraft availability so the warfighter gains enhanced capability.

The B-52 aircraft availability standards are lower than projections because of the number of aircraft in depot possessed status. The NDAA for Fiscal Year 2008 prohibited reductions in the B-52 fleet. As a result, there was a bow wave of aircraft requiring programmed depot maintenance. Depot rates have been at 20 percent since the first quarter of fiscal year 2009. In addition, future capability modifications and normal weapon system depot overhaul requirements will continue to impact aircraft availability through the Future Years Defense Program (FYDP).

The F-15E aircraft availability standards were affected because of higher depot possessed time due to ongoing major depot-level upgrades to systems like the Satellite Communication Radio, Joint Helmet Mounted Cueing System, and Advanced Display Core Processor. The associated pre- and post-depot maintenance activities supporting these modifications have also contributed to the lower aircraft availability. As with the B–1, the Air Force capability enhancements decision was made to sacrifice short-term availability for increases in capability and lethality.

72. Senator BURR. General Chandler, what are the current mission capable rates for each of those aircraft?

General CHANDLER. The current mission capable rates for the B–1, B–52, and F–15E for fiscal year 2010 (October 2009 through 31 July 2010) are 49.6 percent, 72.75 percent, and 74.44 percent, respectively.

73. Senator BURR. General Chandler, please explain what the Air Force is doing to overcome these challenges.

General CHANDLER. Although the B–1 is currently not meeting the aircraft availability goal, we expect to see modest improvements in aircraft availability across the FYDP. Improvements are anticipated in a number of ways. First, as aircraft return from depot status; second, as high velocity maintenance process improvements are implemented at the bases; and third, as surplus fighter manpower is moved into the bomber career field.

For the B–52, we expect the depot rate to decrease as the program office collaborates schedules and repair requirements with the depot to expedite the burn down of the programmed depot maintenance backlog. We expect the B–52 to meet its availability standard in fiscal year 2011.

For the F–15E, depot rates will improve as modifications are completed. We are aggressively working a mitigation strategy to reduce not mission capable maintenance time in several ways. First, we are taking an enterprise view to implement common F–15E inspections in an effort to relieve maintenance man-hours due to duplicate scheduled inspections. Second, we are leveraging availability improvement initiatives with emphasis on system enhancement, sustaining engineering, reliability centered maintenance, and engine component improvement. Third, we are conducting a quarterly Commodity Supply Supportability Review to address commodities shortfall and long-term system reliability issues impacting mission capability rates.

74. Senator BURR. General Chandler, you also go on to state: "the F–22 fell short of the projected availability due to low observable maintenance requirements. Recent improvements in many F–22 system components and increased durability of low observable materials resulted in a 32 percent reduction in maintenance man-hours per flying hour." Please explain the extent to which the F–22 fell short of the projected availability.

General CHANDLER. F–22 aircraft availability was 53.6 percent for fiscal year 2009, slightly below the program's original projection of 55.7 percent. The fiscal year 2009 shortfall was primarily due to unexpected wet weather-related reliability issues while deployed to Andersen Air Force Base Guam. Several avionics components experienced water intrusion and humidity problems but we've improved water drainage and already fielded some modified, humidity-resistant components. For fiscal year 2010, the fleet's aircraft availability is currently averaging 54.5 percent versus the 57.1 percent projection. The newly identified damage limits for low observable coatings in the engine exhaust cavity have also caused an approximate 3 percent decrease in aircraft availability as suppliers work to meet the new parts demand. However, it should be noted that this issue does not prevent affected aircraft from flying training missions.

75. Senator BURR. General Chandler, please provide an update on the current mission availability rates for the F–22 from the past 2 years to the present.

General CHANDLER. The mission capable rates for the F–22 were 51.05 percent in fiscal year 2008, 53.14 percent in fiscal year 2009, and 53.64 percent in fiscal year 2010 (current as of 31 Jul 2010).

76. Senator BURR. General Chandler, what maintenance challenges other that low observable surfaces is the Air Force facing to maintain the readiness of the F–22 fleet?

General CHANDLER. Our biggest current challenge is water intrusion and humidity-related reliability of the avionics systems. In addition to improving water drainage, we have already fielded some modified, humidity-resistant components. Recent results from our deployment to Andersen Air Force Base Guam indicate that the fixes we incorporated were successful.

Another priority has been to improve sub-system reliability. To gain access to failed parts, maintenance personnel often have to remove low observable panels creating the requirement to repair the low observable coatings after replacement of the failed part. By improving sub-system reliability, we can improve the overall weapon system availability rate. The newest aircraft (lot 8) that include the latest reliability improvements are demonstrating significantly better mean time between maintenance rates. The older aircraft (lot 7 and below) are being retrofitted with the more reliable parts and will also benefit from an increase in reliability.

77. Senator BURR. General Chandler, are maintenance man-hours affected by where the F–22 is stationed? If so, is the Air Force looking at restationing F–22s?

General CHANDLER. There is no apparent correlation between maintenance man-hours and where F–22s are currently stationed. As a result, the Air Force is not looking at restationing F–22s for maintenance reasons.

M–4 CARBINE REPLACEMENT

78. Senator BURR. General Chiarelli, a vital component of maintaining the readiness of our Armed Forces is ensuring our men and women in uniform are provided the best equipment available. Following reports of malfunctions and reliability concerns from the field, the Army has begun a process to determine whether the currently fielded M–4 carbine is the best weapon available to our soldiers, whether it needs modifications, or whether an entirely new carbine is required. Please provide an update as to where this process stands.

General CHIARELLI. The Army has a dual path strategy to improve the carbine for our soldiers. The Army recently approved a new requirement for a carbine that will be the basis for a carbine competition in the near future.

Concurrently, the Army has approved enhancements to the M4 carbines that are currently being produced and we are working towards retrofitting improvements to all M4 carbines that have already been fielded. This is an ongoing process. The Army has continued to test and upgrade the carbine since its adoption. For example, since 1991 more than 8 million rounds have been fired in product improvement testing. As a result of this testing, over 62 performance enhancing improvements have been incorporated into the carbine design to include the trigger assembly, extractor spring, recoil buffer, barrel, chamber, and bolt. These improvements have made a significant increase to the reliability of the weapon. The Army recently approved a heavier barrel, a full auto trigger mechanism, and an ambidextrous fire control selector to incorporate into the current M4 series production.

DEMAND FOR CIVIL AFFAIRS AND PSYCHOLOGICAL OPERATIONS UNITS

79. Senator BURR. General Chiarelli, given the environment in which our forces are operating today, there is increasing demand on the unique capabilities brought to bear by civil affairs (CA) and psychological operations (PSYOP) teams. Originally composed primarily of Reserve component forces, the Army has begun growing the first Active Duty CA brigade to support general purpose forces and plans continued growth in organic CA support to SOCOM. What is your assessment of the progress in the growth in CA?

General CHIARELLI. The Army is on track to meet OSD-directed growth for CA. During its most recent force structure analysis, the Army approved an increase in CA capacity for the general purpose force and Special Operations Force. For the general purpose force, the Army will activate its first Active component brigade headquarters and one Active component CA battalion in fiscal year 2011. By fiscal year 2015, the Army will activate a total of five Active component CA battalions into a fully operational brigade.

The current force structure of Special Operations CA units consists of one brigade headquarters and four battalions comprised of four companies each. The Army plans on adding a fifth battalion in fiscal year 2012, a company to each of the five battalions, and a sixth team to each company. When programmed growth is completed, the brigade will consist of one brigade headquarters and five battalions composed of six companies with six teams each.

Additionally, the Army is adding a ninth CA brigade to the Army Reserve effective fiscal year 2011 which will increase rotational depth to the general purpose force.

To facilitate growth in the total CA force, the Army is addressing CA training capacity as well as the size of the proponent office for CA. These adjustments to the generating force will increase student throughput and provide more robust oversight over Army CA training and education.

80. Senator BURR. General Chiarelli, has the Army encountered any issues in meeting the demand for CA and PSYOP units?

General CHIARELLI. Yes, there have been issues meeting the overseas contingency operations demands for CA and PSYOP units. Currently, 100 percent of the general purpose forces CA and PSYOP assets are in the Army Reserve. The demand for both types of units grew quickly and put major strains upon the U.S. Army CA and PSYOP Command. This command routinely mobilized CA units with less than 36 months dwell, and on occasion with less than 24 months dwell. PSYOP units dwell ratio was even lower, with many being under 24 months. Occasionally the Army used "in lieu of" sourcing solutions to fulfill CA requirements. For example, seven Army Reserve chemical companies were mobilized and deployed in lieu of CA companies to meet CA force requirements.

81. Senator BURR. General Chiarelli, do you foresee a need to grow CA and PSYOP forces beyond currently programmed levels?

General CHIARELLI. There is no anticipated growth for CA or PSYOP forces beyond the current programmed levels, which are scheduled through fiscal year 2015. When programmed growth levels for CA and PSYOP are completed in fiscal year 2015, the requirements to either increase or sustain CA and PSYOP capabilities will be in accordance with the strategic guidance given by the Secretary of Defense to meet operational demands. We will continue to track and assess operational demands ensuring the Army has the right CA and PSYOP mix for the future.

ROTARY LIFT SHORTFALLS

82. Senator BURR. General Chiarelli, the demands of nearly 8 years of sustained combat operations in Iraq and Afghanistan have placed an enormous burden on airlift assets, particularly rotary lift. Given the remote locations in which our forces often operate, the availability of these aircraft is vital to moving personnel, providing logistics, and for the replenishment of supplies. DOD is aware that current demand far exceeds supply. The 2010 QDR calls for a substantial increase in key enabling assets for general purpose forces and special operations forces, including an expansion of Army pilot training, the creation of a 13th Active component combat aviation brigade, as well as growth of the 160th Special Operations Aviation Regiment. While these are welcome steps and will provide long-term relief, what steps, if any, can be taken in the near- to mid-term to mitigate the shortfall of rotary lift assets in Afghanistan?

General CHIARELLI. Currently, the three Combat Aviation Brigades (CAB), additional aviation formations, and a limited number of Operational Readiness Float (ORF) aircraft deployed in Afghanistan are meeting operational demands. We began increasing aviation capability in 2009 with the deployment of a second CAB to Afghanistan. This summer we will deploy a third CAB to Afghanistan, along with additional medical evacuation (MEDEVAC) and CH–47 heavy lift assets.

83. Senator BURR. General Chiarelli, if our withdrawal from Iraq continues as planned, what is the estimated lag time before we see an increase in airlift capacity in Afghanistan?

General CHIARELLI. Currently the Army is not planning on transferring aviation capability from Iraq to Afghanistan. We significantly increased rotary wing capability in Afghanistan over the past 18 months. This summer we will have a total of three CABs plus additional MEDEVAC and CH–47 heavy lift assets in Afghanistan to meet combatant commander requirements.

84. Senator BURR. General Chiarelli, given the enormous demand in theater, are there sufficient aircraft at home station to fulfill the requirements of the nearly 1,400 pilots trained annually by the Army?

General CHIARELLI. Yes. The ARFORGEN process allows the Army to cross level aircraft throughout its institutional training posts/sites and installations to meet requirements. A fine balance has been struck in the distribution of aircraft between the institutional and the operational force. The Army will continue to reset and reposition aircraft as required to meet our training and operational needs.

85. Senator BURR. General Chiarelli, is the Army experiencing any problems recruiting or retaining pilots?

General CHIARELLI. No. The Army continues to have more officer and warrant officer candidates than there are requirements or opportunity for training. Additionally, we have experienced a general increase in aviator retention over the past several years.

NAVY STRIKE FIGHTER GAP

86. Senator BURR. General Amos and Admiral Greenert, the Strike Fighter gap is also a readiness issue. The Navy has testified that the so-called fighter gap or shortfall of Strike Fighter aircraft on aircraft carriers and expeditionary squadrons for the Marine Corps rose from 146 to 177 aircraft—primarily due to the F–35 delivery ramp reduction of 55 aircraft and removing the assumption of aircraft reaching 10,000 flight hours. Is the Navy taking appropriate action to mitigate the gap and the operational implications of that gap?

General AMOS. The Department of the Navy is today projecting a shortfall of about 100 Strike Fighters in the 2018 timeframe which includes some aircraft service life extension (SLEP) to 10,000 flight hours. This projection is based on an excursion from the Inventory Forecasting Tool (IFT) Version 18. Based on the projected shortfall, the Navy continues to identify further opportunities to reduce its impact. It is possible to manage the Strike Fighter shortfall through the application of management levers both in the near- and long-term. Examples of management levers are the Marine Corps modifying it's F–35 transition plan by transitioning some Hornet squadrons earlier and leveraging the service life remaining in the AV–8B fleet, the Navy accelerating the transition of five legacy F/A–18C squadrons to F/A–18 E/F, and transitioning two additional F/A–18C squadrons to F/A–18 E/F using the remaining attrition F/A–18 E/F Reserve aircraft, and reducing the Navy Unit Deployment Program (UDP) and USMC Expeditionary F/A–18 A+/C/D squadrons from 12 to 10 aircraft per squadron. Although global demand may not allow for implementation of some of these levers in the near-term, changes in the operational environment in the future may allow additional flexibility in their implementation. As we go forward, we are considering all options to manage our inventory and balance risk, including SLEP to some number of F/A–18 A–D aircraft to extend their service life to 10,000 flight hours and optimizing depot efficiencies. SLEP analysis continues and will be introduced in the fiscal year 2012 President's budget request.

The Navy continues to rigorously manage the service life and warfighting effectiveness of each of our legacy Hornets, Harriers, and Super Hornets to ensure the maximum contribution to the Nation's security for the taxpayer dollars invested.

Admiral GREENERT. The Navy anticipates a decrease in our Strike Fighter inventory of about 100 aircraft that will peak at the end of this decade. We are addressing this inventory decrease through aggressive and precise management strategies that include service-life extension programs to prolong the use of existing F/A–18 A–D aircraft, reducing the number of aircraft available in our nondeployed squadrons to the minimum required, accelerating the transition of seven legacy squadrons to F/A–18 E/F Super Hornets (using F/A–18 E/F attrition aircraft in two cases), and maximizing depot level throughput to return legacy Strike Fighter aircraft to the fleet more quickly. Collectively, these measures will extend the service life of our legacy aircraft and make the projected inventory decrease manageable.

87. Senator BURR. General Amos and Admiral Greenert, is the Marine Corps taking appropriate action to mitigate the gap and the operational implications of that gap?

General AMOS. The Marine Corps is closely managing the flight hours and fatigue life of our tactical aircraft. Since 2004, we have provided guidance and actions to optimize aircraft utilization rates while maximizing training and operational opportunities. The F/A–18 A–D Inventory Management Forecasting Tool is used to project the combined effects of TACAIR transition plans, retirements, attrition, and pipeline requirements on the total F/A–18 A–D aircraft inventory. The model is updated with the most recent data and forecasts the Strike Fighter inventory compared to the existing requirements. Critical model variables include JSF deliveries, force structure, usage rates, life limits, depot turnaround time, Fatigue Life Expended (FLE), catapult launches and arrested landings, and field landings.

Faced with a forecast based on current assumptions that indicates an increased shortfall, the Navy has continued to identify further opportunities to reduce its impact. The Marine Corps has modified its F–35 transition plan by transitioning some Hornet squadrons earlier and leveraging the service life remaining in the AV–8B fleet. Management levers have been identified: accelerating the transition of five legacy F/A–18C squadrons to F/A–18 E/F; transitioning two additional F/A–18 C squadrons to F/A–18 E/F using the remaining attrition F/A–18 E/F Reserve aircraft; and reducing the Navy UDP and Marine Corps Expeditionary F/A–18 A+/C/D squadrons from 12 to 10 aircraft per squadron. Some of these measures are dependent on reduced demand in Global Force Management (GFM) requirements.

Admiral GREENERT. The Navy and the Marine Corps are working closely together to address the Navy Strike Fighter gap. I believe the Marine Corps is closely managing the flight hours and fatigue life of our tactical aircraft. Since 2004, they have provided guidance and actions to optimize aircraft utilization rates while maximizing training and operational opportunities. The F/A–18 A–D Inventory Management Forecasting Tool is used to project the combined effects of TACAIR transition plans, retirements, attrition, and pipeline requirements on the total F/A–18 A–D aircraft inventory. The model is updated with the most recent data and forecasts the Strike Fighter inventory compared to the existing requirements. Critical model variables include JSF deliveries, force structure, usage rates, life limits, depot turnaround time, FLE, catapult launches and arrested landings, and field landings.

Faced with a forecast based on current assumptions that indicates an increased shortfall, the Navy has continued to identify further opportunities to reduce its impact. The Marine Corps has modified its F–35 transition plan by transitioning some Hornet squadrons earlier and leveraging the service life remaining in the AV–8B fleet. Management levers have been identified: accelerating the transition of 5 legacy F/A–18C squadrons to F/A–18 E/F; transitioning 2 additional F/A–18C squadrons to F/A–18 E/F using the remaining attrition F/A–18E/F Reserve aircraft; and reducing the Navy UDP and Marine Corps Expeditionary F/A–18 A+/C/D squadrons from 12 to 10 aircraft per squadron. Some of these measures are dependent on reduced demand in Global Force Management (GFM) requirements.

88. Senator BURR. General Amos and Admiral Greenert, does the Navy have the adequate carrier air wings to satisfy the needs of 11 aircraft carriers?

General AMOS. The Marine Corps provides Marine Fighter/Attack squadrons in compliance with the Tactical Air Integration MOA, and we defer to the Navy for sufficiency of the number of Carrier Air Wings.

Admiral GREENERT. Yes. Our Carrier Air Wings Fleet Readiness and Training Plan is tailored to complement the training and maintenance requirements for our 11 Carrier Air Wings. We will manage our tactical aviation inventory to ensure we have the number of aircraft required to support our deployable Carrier Air Wings.

IMPACT OF FORCE STRUCTURE CAPS IN AFGHANISTAN

89. Senator BURR. General Chiarelli, I've been told that, as a result of the cap of 30,000 troops placed by the President on General McChrystal's plan for surge operations in Afghanistan, many of the requests for forces currently being received by the Army from field commanders are for individual augmentees versus major units. The ARFORGEN model was not created to manage the dwell time and availability of individual soldiers. What is the long-term impact to Army unit readiness of having to satisfy requests for small units and individual augmentees for deployment to Afghanistan?

General CHIARELLI. Requests for small units and individual augmentees exacerbate manning challenges, forcing the Generating Force and other nondeploying units to be billpayers for deployed manning requirements. The Army continues to focus on force structure, ensuring that units are designed to meet current needs and are manned and equipped to accomplish those missions. Most importantly, the Army is building a supply-based force that provides a constant supply of organizations with organic capabilities to operate in a joint and expeditionary role and meet combatant commander requirements.

90. Senator BURR. General Chiarelli, since the Army has traditionally trained as large units, and a commander assesses the readiness of an unit as a whole, how is the training of individual augmentees accomplished to ensure mission success?

General CHIARELLI. Once selected for either an individual manning requirement on a Joint Manning Document or an ad hoc requirement, an individual soldier is provided the requisite training as specified by either military occupational skill proficiency standards or by requirements specified in the request for forces (ad hoc requirement). In the case of a Joint Manning Document, an individual soldier selected for the requirement is assumed to be competent in his duty position and military occupational skill. The soldier then processes through the Fort Benning Continental United States (CONUS) Replacement Center, which provides a program of instruction based upon theater-specific individual required training requirements. In the case of an ad hoc requirement, an individual soldier may get paired with a team for the full requirement and the training received would be accomplished per the training specified in the corresponding request for forces. For example, training team members (comprised of individual soldiers) which support nearly all of the security force assistance requirements in the CENTCOM area of responsibility would go to an Army-designated training location to receive their theater-specific individual required training and also their request for forces specified training. Once the training is completed at both the replacement center and the specified training location, the Army component that has the designated training and readiness oversight certifies the individual and/or the ad hoc requirement for deployment.

91. Senator BURR. General Chiarelli, how do requests for individual augmentees affect the assessment of Army goals for dwell time?

General CHIARELLI. While the Army has full visibility of individual augmentation requirements as they are processed to fill either a Joint Manning Document or an ad hoc requirement, the assessment of Army goals for dwell time are computed based upon unit, MTOE, structure vice providing a factor which computes a percentage of personnel loss due to these unprogrammed shortfalls. However, current manning guidance ensures soldiers deploying have the appropriate dwell time; exceptions to dwell time requirements must be approved by the first General Officer in the chain of command. The Army system for individual augmentation conducts its analysis for specific requirements across the entire Army Active component structure and selected commands are tasked for individual soldiers based upon a leveling of the requirement to mitigate a significant loss to any one unit. This system, as structured, limits effects which would detract from Army goals for dwell time.

MANNING FOR COMBAT UNITS DEPLOYING TO AFGHANISTAN

92. Senator BURR. General Chiarelli and General Amos, in review of current readiness rates, I note that both the Army and the Marine Corps are committed to deploying units overseas which are 100 percent, or close to 100 percent manned. While I commend this track record, I am concerned about exactly when those new personnel are arriving into the unit. Specifically, if they arrive too late to take part in unit training and mission rehearsal exercises, what is the risk to them and the unit?

General CHIARELLI. Unfortunately this does occur; some personnel turnover after mission rehearsal exercises is unavoidable. However, we make every effort to minimize this and are establishing metrics to ensure we monitor and limit this turbulence on the unit and individuals. As to the risk to them and the unit, I would say it is manageable. For example, our current manning guidance ensures that every Active component BCT and CAB achieves at least 90 percent overall assigned strength and a minimum of an 80 percent fill of Field Grade Officers, Company Grade Officers, and Senior NCOs not later than 45 days prior to their Mission Rehearsal Exercise. So for the most part, the unit is set with sufficient leadership when it conducts this training. Additionally, units and installations conduct pre-deployment training for all late arrivals which covers a variety of required individual tasks, such as weapons training, first aid, combat lifesaver, combat stress courses, and cultural and geographic instruction. This training has become a crucial element to prepare late arriving and replacement soldiers for deployment.

General AMOS. The Marine Corps has developed extensive manpower processes that enable us to focus our resources on deploying units. This process allows us to conserve and staff our units 180 days prior to deployment to support training and mission rehearsals as well as our deployment cycles. All marines receive the required pre-deployment training prior to deploying. We are confident that these efforts will meet long-term operational manpower demands.

93. Senator BURR. General Chiarelli and General Amos, given our surge operations in Afghanistan, is this phenomenon trending negative or holding steady?

General CHIARELLI. This trend is currently holding steady. The Army's supply of forces is fixed, so a reduction in the demand for brigades in one theater has been replaced with increased demand in another—the result is no net change. For fiscal year 2010, we are achieving those manning goals I previously discussed for the majority of our deploying units. However, achieving the fill levels for specific field grade officers and some low density skilled soldiers remains a challenge. Until the global demand for forces reaches a sustainable level, we will continue to be challenged to synchronize all the critical readiness resources early enough to allow the necessary time to collectively train prior to deployment.

General AMOS. Due to our improvements in manpower processes, we have not trended negatively, but have achieved a holding steady status.

94. Senator BURR. General Chiarelli and General Amos, do each of your Services have goals for certain manning levels prior to unit deployment to ensure unit integrity and performance? If so, what are they?

General CHIARELLI. Yes, currently the Army, utilizing the ARFORGEN model, focuses human and material resources on those deployed and/or deploying Army units to resource them to the highest readiness levels before they deploy. This ARFORGEN focused manning is event-driven and applies to all brigade-sized units. Units will be manned and prioritized based on major readiness exercises and deployment latest arrival dates.

The Army goal is for every Active component BCT and CAB to achieve 95 percent deployable strength by the latest arrival date, with a minimum acceptable deployed strength of 90 percent. In order to achieve this goal, the Army must overman BCTs to a minimum of 105 percent and CABs to a minimum of 100 percent assigned strength not later than 90 days prior to their latest arrival date. This overmanning compensates for the increasing nondeployable population and ensures units can meet the deployed strength benchmarks. Additionally, there are also specific goals for the manning levels of Field Grade Officers, Company Grade Officers, and Senior NCOs that vary by unit type. The Army goal is for every Active component BCT and CAB to achieve a minimum of 80 percent fill of field grade officers, company grade officers, and senior NCOs 45 days prior to their Major Readiness Exercise.

General AMOS. The Marine Corps has established staffing levels to support deploying units with a primary focus on unit integrity to positively impact combat performance. We have achieved this by developing a holistic implementation process that assigns not only staffing allocations by unit, but also by grade and primary occupational specialty. Our combat units are staffed to deploy with their manning document combat allocations thereby ensuring appropriate levels of combat power.

95. Senator BURR. General Chiarelli and General Amos, are these goals being met?

General CHIARELLI. During fiscal year 2010 year-to-date, 11 of the 13 BCTs met the minimum 90 percent deployed strength requirement at the latest arrival date. The two that missed that benchmark achieved the minimum 90 percent deployed strength requirement within 30 days after the latest arrival date. Additionally, during this timeframe, all four of the CABs exceeded the minimum 90 percent deployed strength requirement at the latest arrival date.

General AMOS. Yes, the staffing of our combat units is one of our primary concerns. We are committed to meeting our manning and staffing goals to ensure unit combat effectiveness.

MARINE CORPS TRAINING FOR FULL SPECTRUM OPERATIONS

96. Senator BURR. General Amos, during last year's hearing in response to a question on the focus of training on preparing for ongoing operations, specifically, the extent of skill degradation given the shift in focus, you responded that Marine Corps Training and Education Command is sponsoring a Training Reset Study, which would provide a recommended training posture for the future. Is this study completed? If so, please provide a summary of its conclusions and recommendations.

General AMOS. The Training Reset Study provides the Marine Corps survey and interview-based data in determining the appropriate balance between the skills that are being trained in support of OEF and required core competency training. The study identifies this balance through its response to questions contained in the study objective and the development of a draft training reset posture.

From a training perspective, what constitutes resetting the force?

- Broad consensus that resetting the force is a function of standards-based training built around core METLs, Training and Readiness Manuals, and application of the Systems Approach to Training and Unit Training Management.

What do the operating forces think the Marine Corps should focus on?

- Surveys point to a need to refocus on unit and individual skills in combined arms and amphibious operations while continuing to train COIN skills.

What should be done at the Service level to make this happen?

- Rigorous application of the existing Marine Corps training system to refocus on core skills and provide appropriate focus on COIN.
- Continue to conduct Enhanced Mojave Viper or an appropriately modified version of the exercise based on current threats. Enhanced Mojave Viper is described as "striking a good balance between irregular and conventional tactics," and has value beyond current operations.

- The draft Force Generation Order (FGO) provides a structured approach "to improve both the efficiency and the effectiveness by which units are prepared for deployment."
- Limitations to resetting the force are:
  - Time to train (dwell)
  - Requirements to train for current operations
  - Inter-Service coordination to refocus skills in amphibious operations

What should be done at the unit training level?

- Reinforce and expand as required the training systems outlined per existing Marine Corps Orders and the draft FGO.
- Focus on resetting individual skills in unit training management.

The Draft Training Reset Posture Statement captures the key elements for successful training reset:

> The Marine Corps will reset training, consistent with the Commandant's Vision and Strategy 2025, to optimize the MAGTF for operations against hybrid threats in complex environments without sacrificing conventional capabilities. Training reset will be accomplished through the rigorous application of the Marine Corps training system.

REMOTELY PILOTED AIRCRAFT SQUADRON MANNING

97. Senator BURR. General Chandler, regarding remotely piloted aircraft (RPA) operations, I noticed in your written testimony that you state: "Remotely piloted aircraft currently provide 41 continuous combat air patrols to U.S. CENTCOM. This number will grow to 50 by the end of fiscal year 2011, and to 65 by the end of fiscal year 2013." I have heard that these growing requirements are taking its toll on aircrew readiness, data collection, and maintenance personnel that support the CAPs. Is the Air Force in the process of assessing the right size of a RPA squadron to result in an OPTEMPO that is sustained over the long-term?

General CHANDLER. In order to sustain the OPTEMPO over the long-term, the Air Force has assessed the right size of an active duty RPA squadron to be five CAPs worth of personnel, aircraft, and equipment. Additionally, the required crew ratio is 10 pilots and 10 sensor operators for each MQ–1 or MQ–9 combat air patrol.

98. Senator BURR. General Chandler, when will these assessment be completed and subsequently RPA squadron manning adjusted?

General CHANDLER. Since the assessment was completed, the Air Force has been training aircrew at a sustainable rate in order to grow RPA squadrons to the 10:1 crew ratio. The Air Force will steadily improve the crew ratio, while meeting all operational combat air patrol requirements and balancing the need to assign RPA aircrew to various overhead requirements, such as rated staff positions.

99. Senator BURR. General Chandler, will additional RPA squadrons be required?

General CHANDLER. Additional RPA squadrons will be required to meet operational combat air patrol requirements. The Air Force plans to create three new RPA squadrons at bases to be announced. Also, two existing RPA squadrons at Creech AFB will move to other bases in the future. Finally, the Air National Guard plans to stand up RPA squadrons at up to five additional locations.

AMPHIBIOUS FLEET AFFORDABILITY AND READINESS

100. Senator BURR. General Amos and Admiral Greenert, the Navy's plan for a 33-ship amphibious fleet, according to the Navy's budget proposal, represents the limit of acceptable risk in meeting the requirement to deliver two Marine expeditionary brigades in a forcible-entry operation. Is the Marine Corps' desire for 38 ships affordable and are there ways to mitigate that risk when considering the entire shipbuilding plan?

General AMOS. Without a top line increase and/or a reprioritization of missions and capabilities that form the basis of the Navy's shipbuilding plan, the requirement for 38 amphibious assault ships outlined in our February 2010 report to Congress is unaffordable. The Navy and Marine Corps have determined a minimum force of 33 ships represents the limit of acceptable risk in meeting the 38-ship amphibious force requirement for the Assault Echelon in a 2 Marine Expeditionary Brigade forcible entry operation. A 33-ship force comprised of 11 LHA/D amphibious assault ships and a mix of 11 LPD 17 amphibious transport docks and 11 LSD(X) dock landing ships would be sufficient to support forcible entry operations with acceptable risk in the speed of arrival of combat support elements of the MEB. We have examined ways to mitigate risk within the context of the entire shipbuilding plan and determined that sustaining a minimum of 33 amphibious ships is adequate within today's fiscal limitations.

Admiral GREENERT. The 38-ship force identified by the Marine Corps represents the lift capacity necessary to support 2.0 MEB operations including all of their Combat Support and Combat Service Support needs across their full range of expected missions. This risk/force level is inconsistent with the risk levels accepted by the remaining naval forces. Therefore, the Commandant and CNO reached an agreement to benchmark the amphibious force at 33 ships and accept a modicum of risk in the extent of combat support equipment available within the Assault Echelon (AE) forces and to move that equipment in conjunction with follow-on force equipment. Specific decisions made in support of this agreement are:

- The Navy plans to procure an LHA 6 class ship in fiscal year 2011 and its 11th LPD 17 class amphibious transport dock in fiscal year 2012. LSD(X), replacement for the existing LSD 41 class, will begin in fiscal year 2017.

  - The Navy determined the LHA 6 class amphibious assault ships previously designated for the MPF (Future) (MPF(F)) would serve more effectively in the AE force where they could be employed in Marine forcible-entry operations. Within the context of the 30-year Shipbuilding Plan, these AE amphibious ships will be procured in fiscal year 2011, fiscal year 2016, and fiscal year 2021.
  - The Navy begins procurement of LSD 41 class replacement, LSD(X), in fiscal year 2017, on a 2-year build cycle.

- The Amphibious Lift Enhancement Program (ALEP) provides additional lift capacity, but does not factor in meeting the Marine Corps' 2.0 MEB AE requirement.

  - ALEP is designed to fill the gap in vehicle square feet stowage.

- The Navy plans to procure three Mobile Landing Platforms (MLP) as well as the three previously appropriated T–AKEs. These augmented Maritime Prepositioning Squadrons (MPS) enhance the afloat prepositioning capacity and will support the Marine Corps 2.0 MEB lift requirement by enabling a reinforcing MEB to "marry up" ashore with its equipment from one of the three MPS squadrons. The augmented MPS facilitate the routine employment of prepositioned equipment in a variety of activities across the range of military operations (ROMO) and mitigate the risk of lower than desired amphibious ship inventory levels.

101. Senator BURR. General Amos and Admiral Greenert, are the requirements for more amphibious ships greater because at least 15 to 20 percent of the amphibious fleet is not deployable because they are in shipyards undergoing maintenance and repair?

General AMOS. The requirement for amphibious ships outlined in our 7 January 2009 report to Congress assumes that amphibious ships are not operationally available due to maintenance approximately 10 percent of the time. Due to the current maintenance challenges faced by the *San Antonio* class, amphibious shipping is trending near 75 percent availability vice the 90 percent planned. We would work to improve operational availability to close to the 90 percent level instead of increasing our force structure requirement to offset a significantly lower operational availability. This will require increased resources specifically maintenance funding for the upkeep of amphibious ships.

Admiral GREENERT. No. Under normal circumstances, no more than about 10 percent of the amphibious fleet is undergoing significant maintenance and repair that would preclude operational availability in the event of a national crisis. While there may be instances when greater than 10 percent of the force is undergoing maintenance, we are confident this assumption is consistent with the long-term availability of amphibious ships for contingency operations.

The requirement for amphibious ships outlined in the January 7, 2009, Report to Congress on Naval Amphibious Force Structure and the Annual Report to Congress on the Long Range Plan for Construction of Naval Vessels for fiscal year 2011, calls for a force of 33 total ships (11 LHA/LHD, 11 LPD, and 11 LSD). Under normal circumstances, 29 to 30 are available for tasking, enough to support MEBs while accepting risk in the arrival of combat support and combat service support elements of the MEB.

Without accepting this risk, the full requirement would be 38 ships. However SECNAV, CNO, and CMC agree that the 33-ship force equates to an acceptable level of risk, as stated in the January 7, 2009, Report to Congress on Naval Amphibious Force Structure.

102. Senator BURR. General Amos and Admiral Greenert, the serious engineering problems on LPD–17 class ships gives rise for a concern about a broader readiness problem. While the recent commissioning of the USS *New York* in New York City harbor was great for the Navy, the ship cannot get underway because of mechanical failures in the main propulsion engines, generators, and failing piping welds that make the ship unsafe to operate. The LPD–17 amphibious ship program has more challenges than we had hoped. Are we seeing a systemic problem with the readiness of the Navy's amphibious ships?

General AMOS. No deployments have been missed. However, there has been multiple negative impacts due to unscheduled maintenance requirements during work ups and more importantly, during deployments.

26th MEU: (LF5th Flt 2010–01)

- *San Antonio* had to be swapped with *Ponce* due to *San Antonio* non-mission capable and unscheduled maintenance. Loss of C2 and cargo space.

15th MEU (Westpac 2010)

- *Peleliu* main feed pump repair caused a 2-day delay in deployment.
- *Dubuque* had to return to port 2 days early during PTP due to engineering casualty. Potential impact on availability to Certex.

31st MEU (Spring Patrol 2010)

- MEU deployed aboard two-ship ARG (*Essex* and *Tortuga*) due to maintenance availability. MEU CDR reports "the MEU will not be immediately capable of performing all METs and core capabilities due to significant remain behind equipment and personnel." RBE includes: Artillery Battery detachment, al CBRN gear, 21 HMMWVs, 14 MTVRs. Degraded TSC capability and risk to USPACOM contingency response. *Denver* is undergoing scheduled maintenance and *Harpers Ferry* is conducting a PACFLT directed TSC event.

24th MEU (LF5th Flt 2010)

- *Nassau*: Failure to install full GIG–E backbone. Significantly degraded C2 infrastructure: limited bandwidth, outdated switches, minimal VTC capability, and extremely limited VOSIP capability. Intermittent connectivity has significantly impacted and degraded execution of several missions.
- *Wasp*: Degraded combat systems. NASSAU substitution requiring MEU and reduced C2 capability (LHA vs. LHD).
- *Mesa Verde:* Outdated VTC capability. Installed VTC incompatible with current systems. Mission degradation.

11th MEU (WESTPAC 2009–02)

- *Bon Homme Richard*: Mechanical failure that caused a 6-day delay in deployment.

31st MEU (Fall Patrol 2009)

- MEU deployed without *Essex* due to scheduled maintenance. Degraded TSC capability and risk to USPACOM contingency operations.

13th MEU (WESTPAC 2009)

- *Boxer* experienced 40 days of degraded or no fixed wing capability due to flight deck surfacing issues that were deferred due to budget constraints. Flight deck was shut down while in CENTCOM AOR.
- *Comstock* missed 12 days of work up at sea days, unreliable for 50+ days of PACOM transit resulted in 19 day extended in-port maintenance call while in theater, totally of 81 days out of action.

15th MEU (WESTPAC 2009–02)

- *Dubuque* experienced ruptured boiler. Required 3 to 4 weeks of repair in Bahrain. Limited MEU participation in Exercise Infinite Moonlight and impact on capability to back load in case of contingency.

26th MEU (LF5th Flt 2008–01)

- *San Antonio* experience engineering lube oil system failure. *San Antonio* was pier side at Bahrain non-mission capable for 1 month.
- *San Antonio* experienced a stern gate casualty causing a 2- to 3-day delay in deployment.

- *San Antonio* missed a total of 30 days of PTP/operational employment in support of embarked forces.

Admiral GREENERT. No. While we have seen some recurring material issues in LPD 17 class ships, the problems associated with a new construction ship are not indicative of a systemic problem with the amphibious ship readiness of the existing fleet.

MINE RESISTANT AMBUSH PROTECTED VEHICLES

103. Senator BURR. General Chiarelli, in response to the increasing threat posed by improvised explosive devices (IED) in Iraq, DOD initiated a rapid acquisition strategy to field a more survivable, mine resistant ambush protected (MRAP) vehicle. As a result, DOD has purchased approximately 12,000 MRAPs saving countless American lives. Now the question is how the Army plans to integrate a platform designed to meet an urgent wartime requirement into its long-term modernization and sustainment strategy. What is the Army's plan for the integrating MRAP vehicles into its ground vehicle strategy, particularly with regard to the Joint Light Tactical Vehicle (JLTV)?

General CHIARELLI. The Army's 2010 draft TWV Strategy is informing the MRAP Study II, in conjunction with the TWV Study III. MRAP Study II acknowledges changes since the original 2009 MRAP Study I results and DP 147 and will seek to place more MRAPs on Tables of Organization and Equipment, use more MRAPs as substitutes for LTV/JLTV mission roles, and examine the use of MRAP as Data Interchange platforms. Preliminary analysis indicates the likelihood that MRAP reuse goals will be achieved and has also identified the value of implementing certain MRAP upgrades that will result in greater capability. Initial results are expected in October 2010, and final results no later than 31 Dec 2010. We expect to meet the Army's TWV Strategy goals with a mixed fleet of vehicles capable of meeting the spectrum of DOD contingency plans.

104. Senator BURR. General Chiarelli, does the Army plan to integrate all 12,000 vehicles into its long-term inventory? If so, how will this affect inventory issues such as APS and motor pool space constraints?

General CHIARELLI. The Army's 2010 draft TWV Strategy is informing the MRAP Study II, in conjunction with the TWV Study III. MRAP Study II acknowledges changes since the original 2009 MRAP Study I results and DP 147 and will seek to place more MRAPs on Tables of Organization and Equipment and into the APS and have others reserved for sustainment stocks. APS as a program will also receive some additional vehicles which must be reviewed to ensure they are supportable within the current global APS infrastructure, and any improvements required to meet that supportability are identified and resolved. Those platforms that go into units may require a change to current motor pools and some maintenance procedures.

105. Senator BURR. General Chiarelli, the MRAP program was initiated as a joint program but will shift to the individual Services in fiscal year 2012, where the Army will assume budgetary control over its MRAP fleet, including its significant sustainment costs. Do you have any estimates on future costs associated with sustaining the MRAP fleet?

General CHIARELLI. A final decision on when to transfer the MRAP program to individual Service control has not been made. The Under Secretary of Defense (Acquisition, Technology, and Logistics) will select a path forward for transitioning the joint program to another program management construct based on events rather than purely time. Given the rapid acquisition and fielding of MRAP vehicles to meet urgent warfighter requirements, long-term sustainment costs are also unknown at this time. The Army will have more clarity on long-term sustainment costs upon approval of Army Campaign Plan (ACP), which allocates ~15,000 enduring force MRAP vehicles between APS, Army organizations, and training/war reserve stocks. The final allocation will significantly impact future sustainment cost estimates since vehicles stored in APS have a significantly lower operational tempo and sustainment costs compared to vehicles used on a regular basis in units. The Army will also conduct a fiscal year 2011 Sustainment Readiness Review (SRR), which is a post deployment review to assess the performance of the MRAP support system. The SRR will evaluate the actual performance against predicted parameters and thus provide better insight on the path forward for future MRAP sustainment, to include costs.

106. Senator BURR. General Chiarelli, how does the Army plan to absorb these costs, particularly as we transition from OCO dollars to base budget dollars?

General CHIARELLI. Given the rapid acquisition and fielding of MRAP vehicles, long-term sustainment costs are unknown at this time. Until we have clarity on future MRAP sustainment, to include funding requirements, we cannot provide a feasible plan to absorb the costs. We expect to know more after the Under Secretary of Defense for Acquisition, Technology, and Logistics (USD(ATL)) selects a path forward for transitioning the joint program.

107. Senator BURR. General Chiarelli, how will this affect other Army priorities, such as its modernization efforts?

General CHIARELLI. The Army will develop and field an affordable and interoperable mix of the best equipment available to allow soldiers and units to succeed in both today's and tomorrow's full-spectrum military operations. We will continuously modernize a balanced set of equipment—including MRAPs—to meet current and future capability needs through a combination of upgrade, recapitalization, refurbishment, and technology insertion. As 21st century threats emerge and adjust, and force requirements evolve in response to that future operational environment, the Army will fund, field, and distribute capabilities—using the ARFORGEN model—in accordance with the Army Resourcing Priorities List to ensure that deployed soldiers have the best possible equipment.

NONDEPLOYABLE SOLDIERS

108. Senator BURR. General Chiarelli, you mentioned in your statement that the nondeployable rate for our soldiers increased from 9.92 percent in fiscal year 2007 to 12 percent in fiscal year 2009. What is the current level of nondeployable soldiers?

General CHIARELLI. For fiscal year 2010 year-to-date, the current level of nondeployable soldiers is 14.11 percent.

109. Senator BURR. General Chiarelli, do you see this level decreasing?

General CHIARELLI. Based on past and current trends, I do not anticipate nondeployable levels to decrease in the near-term. A key factor in the recent increases in nondeployable rates has been the sustained high levels of demand. Additionally, the reduction of Stop Loss has caused a corresponding increase in nondeployables based on voluntary separations and retirements. As demand decreases, we would expect to see an eventual stabilization and ultimate decrease in nondeployable rates over the long-term.

110. Senator BURR. General Chiarelli, in addition to the temporary increase in end strength of 22,000, what steps are being taken to address the nondeployable levels?

General CHIARELLI. After 9 years of war, the health of our All-Volunteer Force is showing signs of stress. From a tactical perspective, commanders at all levels are actively engaged in identifying nondeployable soldiers and, in the case of temporary nondeployable conditions, linking the soldier with the requisite resources necessary to resolve the nondeployable condition. From a strategic perspective, the Army staff is focused on policy and implementation decisions necessary to dampen the nondeployer rates in our units and to gain better visibility on the health of the force.

Specifically with regard to medical nondeployers, my staff is engaged in numerous efforts to improve medical readiness policies and processes. These efforts are synchronized across four lines of operations (Systems, Training, Policy, and Processes) and focused on our desired end-state to man an expeditionary Army with soldiers who are medically deployable while preserving the All-Volunteer Force. Our actions in this realm are built upon four primary objectives: to develop a medical Common Operating Picture; to train our leaders and medical professionals on medical readiness policies and procedures; to determine what impact worldwide deployability should have on soldier retainability; and to standardize and streamline medical board processes across all components. Over time, increased visibility combined with improved policy and streamlined processes will combine to decrease nondeployer rates.

111. Senator BURR. General Chiarelli, what effect has the temporary increase in end-strength had on ensuring units are capable of deploying?

General CHIARELLI. The Temporary End Strength Increase (TESI) has provided us with the operational flexibility to over-man units and achieve deployed strength benchmarks, compensating for nondeployable soldiers and the reduction of Stop Loss. During fiscal year 2010 year-to-date, 11 of the 13 BCTs and all 4 of the CABs met the minimum 90 percent deployed strength requirement at the latest arrival date. The two BCTs that missed that benchmark achieved the minimum 90 percent deployed strength requirement within 30 days after the latest arrival date.

112. Senator BURR. General Chiarelli, do you see a need to make the temporary increase of end-strength permanent?

General CHIARELLI. No. The TESI is a temporary solution to a temporary problem. TESI was designed to improve the fill of deploying units by mitigating the effects of the increase in nondeployable soldiers, Stop Loss elimination, and wounded warriors, which were a result of the operational demand for forces in support of OIF and OEF. Our vision of the future manning environment is predicated on the projected reduction in demand in fiscal year 2012 and the plan to completely eliminate Stop Loss by March 2011. Any significant changes in demand or other key variables may affect our end-strength requirements.

MARINE CORPS TRAINING ON GUAM

113. Senator BURR. General Amos, the Marine Corps has indentified the ability to train on Guam, or nearby islands, at the unit level as a major requirement to support the relocation of Marine forces to Guam. Will the Marines require small arms training sites on Guam, or can this training be accomplished solely on Tinian?

General AMOS. Yes, the Marines will require small arms training sites on Guam to sustain core competencies in order to meet the operational requirements of the combatant commander. This training cannot be accomplished solely on Tinian as it is the type of training that marines will conduct on a daily/near-continuous basis. The types of ranges being planned for on Guam support basic, individual skills—those essential warfighting skills that make us marines—that all marines are required to use on an annual basis, at a minimum, for readiness sustainment. Additionally, the ranges currently planned on Tinian under the current environmental impact statement (EIS) do not support medium or heavy caliber ammunition as required for the multi-purpose machine gun range. Based on the frequency of range use, the number of Marines relying on these ranges for annual qualifications, and the enduring presence the Marine Corps intends to have on Guam, we have determined that it is critical to build these ranges at the location where marines live and work.

114. Senator BURR. General Amos, what level of training and arms can be used? In other words, will Marines have to travel off Guam to train in order to deploy? If so, where would the Marines have to go to train?

General AMOS. On Guam, the marines will primarily conduct live-fire qualification and sustainment training with individual weapons and crew-served weapons. Those Marine Corps forces relocating from Okinawa to Guam will have to travel off-island to accomplish requisite core competency training. This is because the current EIS does not provide for a high explosive, dud-producing impact area, amphibious landing beach or higher level collective training ranges the Marine Corps forces need to sustain core competencies. The Marine Corps ultimately desires to conduct core competency training in areas that minimize travel time and reduce operational non-availability. Commonwealth of the Northern Marianas Islands (CNMI) provides land space reasonably close enough to ensure Guam-based marines sustain the core competencies that cannot be met on Guam on a regular basis.

115. Senator BURR. General Amos, how is this pre-deployment training requirement met for those marines assigned to Okinawa now?

General AMOS. The Marine Corps' Pre-Deployment Training Program consists of four blocks of training. Blocks I and II are conducted by unit commanders at home station and are designed for individuals and small units. Blocks III and IV are progressive training for entire units culminating in a final exercise testing the unit's capability to function as a cohesive team.

The Marine Corps does deploy complete units from ground, aviation, and logistics combat elements from Okinawa, as well as smaller enabler detachments, to Afghanistan in support of OEF. These units complete pre-deployment training in the same manner as CONUS-based units, including block IV mission rehearsals and assessments at Twentynine Palms, CA, or at approved alternate training venues.

The Marine Corps also deploys marines from Okinawa to serve as Afghanistan and Iraqi training teams who also conduct pre-deployment progressive Block training that finishes with either a home station or CONUS based mission rehearsal and assessment.

Units rotating to Okinawa on the UDP complete Blocks I and II prior to arrival in the same manner as CONUS-based units. Units rotating to Okinawa as part of the 31st MEU also complete individual and small unit training. Additionally, designated units complete specialized training with the first Special Operations Training Group (SOTG), Camp Pendleton, CA, prior to arrival in Okinawa. The Maritime Reaction Force (MRF) platoon training is one example.

116. Senator BURR. General Amos, what steps, including an EIS and military construction (MILCON), would be needed to improve training on and near Guam?

General AMOS. The May 2006 Realignment Roadmap delineates specific Marine Corps units to permanently relocate from Okinawa to Guam. The Guam realignment EIS, conducted by the Joint Guam Program Office, includes analysis of live-fire and non-fire training activities to support limited individual and collective training. The DOD considers Marine Corps training requirements in the Pacific beyond what is being analyzed in the Guam realignment EIS to be part of a much broader picture that must take into account DOD's global posture. The Marine Corps considers training of the MAGTF elements relocating to Guam tied to the movement of those forces: development of training capacity must align with force flow in order to sustain readiness for relocating units. MILCON for ranges will need to be synchronized with force flow such that units arriving on Guam will have ranges available to sustain readiness.

PACOM has determined that there is an ongoing need to reassess current training locations and to develop additional training capacity for higher-level core competency training in the Western Pacific. PACOM will conduct a joint training review to address longstanding training deficiencies in the Pacific. This review will specifically evaluate the needs for additional training facilities in the CNMI and other locations in the Western Pacific to address individual, collective, and MAGTF training requirements for Marine Corps and joint forces in the area. Initial analysis has identified Tinian and Pagan as potentially suitable for training forces aboard Guam for individual, collective, and MAGTF-level training requirements. However, the full environmental impact analysis must be completed in order to accurately determine Tinian and Pagan's suitability to meet these training requirements.

117. Senator BURR. General Amos, what is the timeline for establishing these improved training facilities?

General AMOS. Programming for training ranges and areas under the Guam EIS are budgeted to begin with potential land acquisition in fiscal year 2012 and construction to begin thereafter. PACOM is budgeted to receive $30 million in fiscal year 2011 to conduct the Pacific Training Study that will examine training potentialities in the CNMI.

IMPACT TO READINESS FROM OFF-SHORE DRILLING

118. Senator BURR. General Chandler, the President recently announced his support for new off-shore drilling initiatives. As you may know, the issue of drilling in the Eastern Gulf of Mexico has raised concerned within DOD over potential impacts to the test and training air ranges in that area. Some of this concern has been addressed with recent negotiations with the Department of the Interior (DOI) about acceptable methods of drilling. What is the current position of the Air Force concerning the issuance of additional leases in the Eastern Gulf of Mexico to support off-shore drilling operations?

General CHANDLER. The Air Force has participated in the DOD's efforts to identify compatibility issues with drilling in the Gulf of Mexico. Our most recent initiative assessed the Gulf for potential operational impacts from energy development. The Air Force did not designate any areas as completely incompatible with oil exploration and drilling. However, we noted stipulations that should be included in any DOI lease that would protect the military mission. These stipulations include periodic evacuations and hold-harmless agreements, similar to those employed near space launch ranges.

In our operational impact findings, we noted that while no single area is incompatible with drilling, that could change as development ensues. The nature of current Air Force operations in the Gulf allows for some geographic flexibility in the scheduling of missions. The effect of pinning missions into smaller areas is: (a) more missions in the remaining areas, and (b) potential "incompatible" designations in the remaining areas. The Air Force will remain engaged with DOD and its partners to ensure that current and future operational impacts, both specific and cumulative, are taken into consideration during energy siting decisions.

119. Senator BURR. General Chandler, what are the current concerns about the impact to military readiness?

General CHANDLER. The Air Force has participated in DOD's recent initiatives to identify operational compatibility issues with development on the Outer-Continental Shelf. Our concerns in the Gulf of Mexico are primarily related to the potential restrictions on current and future operations, test, and training resulting from development. The Air Force identified lease stipulations that could overcome these concerns. The stipulations were: (1) some restrictions on permanent above-surface structures; (2) periodic evacuations with proper notification; and (3) hold-harmless agreements for property damage. These stipulations have been used near launch facilities on both coasts. While damage from debris is unlikely, our commitment to safety requires that certain areas remain free of bystanders during certain missions.

In short, the physical presence of a drilling structure in the Gulf of Mexico is unlikely to be incompatible with Air Force operations as long as that structure does not result in new restrictions on our current and future operations.

AV–8B HARRIER AIRCRAFT SUSTAINMENT

120. Senator BURR. General Amos, it is my understanding that the current pace of operations in Iraq and Afghanistan has significantly increased the utilization of the Marine Corps AV–8B aircraft above the planned usage. Because of the need to keep the AV–8B in service until we transition to the F–35 Joint Strike Fighter (JSF), various levels maintenance are needed to keep this aircraft flying. How would you recommend the current AV–6B sustainment strategy be improved in order to reduce maintenance turnaround time and enhance readiness?

General AMOS. In contrast to other legacy platforms, the life limits of AV–8B major airframe components are now being defined by FLE rather than flight hours. This means the Harrier's airframe can be in service significantly beyond the projected out-of-service date of fiscal year 2022. Emergent avionics obsolescence and subsystem issues, engine, and engine accessory supportability, all of which are addressed by the Readiness Management Program and Engine Life Management Program, will have the greatest impact on AV–8B long-term sustainment.

The Harrier Fleet is currently inventory-constrained. Ongoing efforts to streamline the Planned Maintenance Interval (PMI) process are a key element to reducing depot turnaround time, thereby limiting the number of aircraft out of service and mitigating inventory shortfalls. PMA–257 and Fleet Readiness Centers (FRCs) East and Southwest signed a Performance Based Agreement that assigns FRC–E as the PMI–2/3 Single Process Owner starting in fiscal year 2011. Additional efforts to reduce turnaround time involve improving existing processes and awarding a long-term Performance Based Logistics contract through DLA to improve material availability.

READINESS RISK FOR COMBAT AIR FORCES

121. Senator BURR. General Chandler, you state in your written testimony for this hearing the following: "By accelerating the planned retirement of 257 legacy fighter aircraft, we are committed to a smaller, but more capable fifth-generation fighter force. These retirements freed more than 4,000 personnel to operate RPA and to process, exploit, and disseminate intelligence. This shift accepts a moderate amount of warfighting risk due to decreased capacity, but is necessary to move forward to more capable and survivable next generation platforms." Can you explain what you mean by a moderate amount of warfighting risk?

General CHANDLER. Risk definitions are derived from the Chairman of the Joint Chiefs of Staff Risk Assessment process. The broad definition of moderate risk is that forces, capabilities, and effects, required or implied, will likely be provided in an effective and timely manner; but may be delayed, are less than optimally configured, or could entail increased tactical losses than if fully funded. This will not jeopardize operational or strategic success. Aircraft inventories will need to be aggressively managed to maintain primary mission aircraft inventories and timelines may require an extension, but strategic objectives are likely to be met.

122. Senator BURR. General Chandler, is the Air Force working with the Joint Staff and the combatant commanders to mitigate the risk of decreased capacity?

General CHANDLER. When preparing the fiscal year 2010 President's budget, the Secretary of Defense provided guidance to the Services to assess, balance, and adjust manned, short-range fixed-wing capacity. After conducting a thorough examination of the current and future strategic environment, the Air Force determined that a window of opportunity existed in the near-term to accelerate the retirement of approximately 250 of its oldest legacy fighters. The Air Force coordinated this plan across all major commands in the Active Duty as well as the Air National Guard and Air Force Reserve. This plan was briefed to the Joint Staff and the Unified Combatant Commanders or their designated representatives, and their concerns about the plan were either directly addressed with Air Force leadership or with the Secretary of Defense.

123. Senator BURR. General Chandler, how long do you expect the Air Force to assume this risk?

General CHANDLER. As stated in the Combat Air Forces Restructuring Congressional Report submitted in February 2010, the Air Force increased the level of risk to achieve National Defense Strategy (NDS) objectives in the 2010 to 2020 timeframe to build a smaller, but more capable force. This revised force structure along with investments to modifications, preferred munitions, and key enablers will serve as a capabilities-based bridge to an increasingly fifth generation fighter force structure. These actions will posture the Air Force fighter fleet to better enable the joint force in pursuit of NDS objectives in the 2020 to 2030 timeframe and beyond—coincident with an increasingly dangerous MCO environment.

124. Senator BURR. General Chandler, what are Air Force plans in the long term to reduce or eliminate this warfighting risk?

General CHANDLER. The Air Force will aggressively manage its budget to comply with the DOD fiscal year 2011 President's budget guidance to procure F–35 aircraft at a rate of 80 per year starting in fiscal year 2016. The Air Force is also investigating modernization and SLEPs for its legacy fighter fleet to increase capability and maintain capacity. Additionally, the Air Force is reviewing options to field survivable, long-range surveillance and strike aircraft as part of a comprehensive, phased plan to modernize the bomber force. These risk reduction efforts are part of an enterprise-wide Total Force effort to ensure the Air Force meets current and future emerging missions. The Air Force is ready to execute the President's guidance to make the most of our allocated resources and to work as a member of the joint team to accomplish our Nation's military objectives.

ARMY REQUIREMENTS FOR THE CLOSURE OF GUANTANAMO BAY

125. Senator BURR. General Chiarelli, I have a question about pending Army requirements related to Guantanamo Bay (GTMO). As you probably know, I do not support bringing suspected terrorists to the United States, let alone spending this kind of money to attempt to recreate the state-of-the-art detention facility we already have in GTMO. But the OCO portion of the President's budget request for fiscal year 2011 includes $350 million in a transfer fund for the detention facilities at GTMO, provides funding to make improvements at the Illinois State Prison at Thomson, IL, in the amount of $150 million, and includes another $158 million for information technology improvements at the Rock Island Arsenal, IL, to support DOD detainee operations at Thomson. The Army will be the executive agent for this operation. Has the Army determined how many military personnel will be assigned to Thomson and where will they be housed?

General CHIARELLI. The Army participated in several preliminary planning sessions and developed a very tentative plan for manning the Thomson facility should the decision be made to use that facility to house Guantanamo Bay detainees. Our basic planning figures include approximately 1,000 military and civilian personnel at Thomson, and up to 500 military and civilian personnel at Rock Island Arsenal, to support the detainee operations mission.

A plan to house military personnel and their families will be developed based on housing market analyses in the vicinity of Thomson and Rock Island. If military housing is required, it will be constructed at a later date.

126. Senator BURR. General Chiarelli, has the Army planned for the commitment of manpower and resources to support the mission at Thompson?

General CHIARELLI. Yes, the Army conducted planning with OSD, but no commitment for manpower and resources were allocated to support the mission at Thomson.

127. Senator BURR. General Chiarelli, does the request for funding include funding for military housing and other base support facilities at Thomson and Rock Island for the Army personnel that will be stationed to support the new facility?

General CHIARELLI. The funding request associated with the potential relocation of Guantanamo Bay facilities was developed by OSD. I am not able to provide any information with regard to that request.

ARMY GREEN AMMUNITION

128. Senator BURR. General Chiarelli, the Army has been developing a more effective and lead-free bullet to replace the currently fielded M855 5.56mm round for several years, commonly referred to as green ammunition. The initial plan was to field the first installment of 20 million green rounds late last summer but this was delayed as a result of significant testing failures, particularly when the rounds were exposed to high temperatures. Are you confident this ammunition will be ready for combat by June of this year, as earlier stated by the Army?

General CHIARELLI. The temperature issue experienced with the M855A1 Enhanced Performance Round (EPR) has been corrected. The Army has begun to issue the M855A1 to our soldiers in Afghanistan, packaged for use with the M16 rifle and M4 carbine. Early reports we have received about the cartridge's performance have been very favorable. The Army has produced and accepted over 45 million M855A1 EPR cartridges and 1.1 million EPR cartridges have been airlifted through Kuwait and are now in Afghanistan. Additionally, 4.6 million EPR cartridges have arrived via sealift to the CENTCOM area of operations (AO); 14.5 million cartridges are scheduled to arrive in the CENTCOM AO by October 12 and another 7 million are now planned for delivery in late December.

129. Senator BURR. General Chiarelli, are you confident that the green ammo provides a comparable performance to other rounds currently being fielded by other Services, including the SOST round being acquired by the Marine Corps and SOCOM?

General CHIARELLI. The M855A1 EPR cartridge is an improved version of the M855 cartridge that is fired from the M4 carbine and M16 rifle. The M855A1 incorporates a product improved projectile and improved propellant which provides significantly enhanced performance against a wide variety of targets. The M855A1 provides improved hard target capability, more consistent performance against soft targets, improved accuracy, and reduced muzzle flash. These performance improvements were incorporated without an increase to cartridge weight or size. Approval of the M855A1 for fielding for use in the M4 carbine and M16 rifle has been requested. The M855A1 outperforms the Special Operations Science and Technology cartridge (SOST) in accuracy, and terminal consistency against soft targets. The M855A1 meets the Army requirements of perforating 3/8 inch steel and matches the 5.56 mm M856 trace whereas the SOST does not. The M855A1 also has better performance against Kevlar, and against concrete masonry than does the SOST.

QUESTIONS SUBMITTED BY SENATOR JAMES M. INHOFE

PERSONNEL READINESS AND SERVICEMEMBER HEALTH

130. Senator INHOFE. General Chiarelli and General Amos, the military's strength is in its soldiers, the families, and the Army civilians who support them. With over 2 million service men and women having deployed to support the war on terror, indicators of that strain or stress on the force have begun to surface such as increase in suicide rates and divorces, retention, and recruiting challenges. What is your assessment of the health and quality of the Army and Marine Corps?

General CHIARELLI. Our soldiers, families, and civilians are clearly stressed and fatigued by nearly 9 years of combat. The Army is out of balance, and that balance needs to be restored to sustain this All-Volunteer Force for the long haul. Yet, through it all, our Army remains amazingly resilient, determined, and extraordinarily effective. Today, our soldiers have more expertise, education, training, and capabilities than ever before, and in fiscal year 2009, our incoming Active component soldiers had the highest high school diploma rates since fiscal year 2003.

General AMOS. As a Force, our Marines Corps units in the field are performing brilliantly and are consistently proving that they can absorb the stress and accomplish the mission. However, I am concerned about the impact of stress on the individual marine and his/her family. Each month, we monitor behavioral factors, such as divorce and suicide for signs of increased stress on marines and their families, and although there was a slight decrease in the divorce rate—from 3.7 percent in fiscal year 2008 to 3.6 percent in fiscal year 2009—our suicide numbers are up. These stress factors have my attention and that of senior leadership at the highest level as we refocus our efforts to improve the quality of our prevention and lifeskills training to strengthen the resiliency and coping skills of our marines and their families.

131. Senator INHOFE. General Chiarelli and General Amos, what new initiatives are the Army and Marine Corps implementing to address these stress indicators?

General CHIARELLI. The U.S. Army Medical Command developed the Comprehensive Behavioral Health System of Care Campaign Plan to emphasize identifying, preventing, treating, and tracking behavioral health issues affecting soldiers and families. This campaign establishes an integrated, coordinated, and synchronized comprehensive behavioral health system of care supporting the ARFORGEN model in each of its phases in order to reduce the incidence of behavioral health issues and mitigate the impact of the normal stresses of Army life, deployment, and combat.

The Comprehensive Behavioral Health System of Care Campaign Plan focuses on the standardization and implementation of key soldier/family and civilian support models incorporating screening points, assessment, provider education and self care, tele-behavioral health, and a common information technology platform. Specific components of this campaign plan include Child and Family Assistance Centers that execute a comprehensive plan on the installation that provides direct behavioral health support for Army families and their children. This plan integrates all behavioral health resources under a single umbrella organization to facilitate coordination, and increase capacity and flexibility in delivery of these services. Another central support program is School Behavioral Health Programs that will implement a cost-effective comprehensive array of school behavioral health programs and services to support military children, their families, and the Army community in schools and Child Development Centers. Other key components to this overarching campaign plan include the Army Substance Abuse Program and the self-referral pilot Confidential Alcohol Treatment Education Program now underway at multiple locations.

General AMOS. We are committed to developing resiliency and coping skills in individual marines and their families and have taken the following actions:

- Broadened the scope of our Executive Force Preservation Board that I chair to focus on all behavioral health concerns—such as combat and operational stress; suicide; domestic violence; substance abuse; and sexual assault.
- Initiated the development of a systematic standardized family readiness support system, through the Unit, Personal, and Family Readiness Program, which is designed to work across functional lines to build and sustain the capacity of military families to care for themselves and mutually support one another within the Marine Corps Community. As part of this program, we established over 400 full-time, primary-duty civilian Family Readiness Officers (FRO) to support commanders at the unit level.
- Developed an inventory of LifeSkills training courses that specifically address the challenges of military life, as well as personal and family life to initiate and foster a strong foundation of readiness among our marines and their families.
- To address the increased demands and potential impact of multiple, sustained deployments on both our Active and Reserve component marines and their families we have:
    • Expanded and enhanced our pre-, during-, and post-deployment training to focus on the needs of our constituency;
    • Implemented the Yellow Ribbon Reintegration Program to ensure our Reserve Marines are afforded access to comparable deployed support services as their Active Duty counterparts;
    • Broadened the scope of our Lifestyle Insights, Networking, Knowledge, and Skills (L.I.N.K.S.) training to include marines, children, and extended family members;
    • Incorporated Combat and Operational Stress Control (COSC) into our deployment training cycles.
- Established COSC and Operational Stress Control and Readiness (OSCAR) training as a primary prevention tool to help marines identify and mitigate early signs of stress and to encourage them to seek help within the unit setting. In addition, senior and junior marines are trained and function as OSCAR Mentors. They actively engage marines who evidence stress reactions, liaison with OSCAR Extenders (Navy Corpsmen, Chaplains, and Medical Officers) which provide additional services or referral, if necessary, to a mental health team re-

garding stress problems. These personnel watch over the marines in their units, identify and refer them for help with stress problems, when required, and provide the support needed to get them back to full readiness as quickly as possible. OSCAR Mentors greatly decrease the stigma associated with stress reactions, and help marines take care of their own.

\- Engaged on multiple fronts on suicide prevention:

- • Creating new, dynamic training programs that are targeted toward our marines, NCOs, SNCOs, officers, and family members.
- • Working closer than ever before with the other Services, the DOD, and civilian and Federal agencies to build our programs, share our information, and put our best practices forward.
- • Committed to developing resiliency and coping skills in individual marines.
- • With peer and senior leadership, we are sending the message to every marine that getting help for distress is a duty not an option, and it is consistent with our culture and our ethos to do so.

Disseminating lessons learned from all death briefs and building knowledge and awareness of senior leaders at forums and symposiums.

132. Senator INHOFE. General Chiarelli and General Amos, we have significantly improved the care for our wounded warriors yet we still suffer a significant shortfall in mental health care specialists or providers. What is being done to address the mental health care provider issue?

General CHIARELLI. The Army is using numerous mechanisms to recruit and retain both civilian and uniformed behavioral health (BH) providers including bonuses, scholarships, and an expansion in training programs. The Army Medical Department (AMEDD) has increased funding for scholarships and bonuses to support expansion of our provider inventory. The Secretary of the Army is conducting a comprehensive review of recruiting and retention efforts for mental health providers. This review is nearly complete and will offer additional insights and recommendations to enhance our abilities to attract and keep these professionals within the Military Health System.

Efforts to improve recruitment and retention of military behavioral health providers include the expanded use of the Active Duty Health Professions Loan Repayment Program and a $20,000 accessions bonus for Medical and Dental Corps health professions scholarship applicants. Additionally, the Army implemented an officer accessions pilot program that allows older healthcare providers to enter the Army, serve 2 years, and return to their communities. To improve retention, the Army used a onetime Critical Skills Retention Bonus (CSRB) for social workers and BH nurses and the AMEDD CSRB for clinical psychologists. For our critical civilian workforce, the Army provides centrally funded reimbursement of recruiting, relocation, and retention bonuses for civilian behavioral health providers to enhance recruitment of potential candidates and retention of staff.

Expanding training opportunities has been a significant part of the Army's strategy as well. In partnership with Fayetteville State University, the U.S. Army Medical Command (MEDCOM) developed a Masters of Social Work program which graduated 19 in the first class in 2009. The program has a current capacity of 30 candidates. Additionally, MEDCOM increased the number of Health Professions Scholarship Allocations dedicated to Clinical Psychology and the number of seats available in the Clinical Psychology Internship Program. Prior to 2004 the Army historically trained 12 interns per year and has progressively increased that number, admitting 33 interns in 2009.

General AMOS. To further assist leaders with prevention, rapid identification, and early treatment of combat operational stress, we are expanding our program of embedding mental health professionals in operational units—the OSCAR program—to directly support all Active and Reserve ground combat elements. This is being achieved through realignment of existing Navy structure supporting the operating forces, and increases in the Navy mental health provider inventory. Currently there are six authorized permanent billets, two at each active division. In fiscal year 2011, 23 additional permanent billets will be authorized in the Active and Reserve divisions. Ultimately, each active division will have three mental health providers, and each regiment will have two. In the Reserves, the division will have four providers. OSCAR capability is also being extended to all deploying units by providing additional training to existing medical providers, corpsmen, chaplains, and religious program specialists where available (OSCAR Extenders) as well as to marines and leaders (OSCAR Mentors). These personnel watch over the marines in their units, identify and refer them for help with stress problems, when required, and provide the support needed to get them back to full readiness as quickly as possible. OSCAR Mentors, who have the lead in this process, greatly decrease the stigma associated with stress reacgreeions, and help marines take care of their own. As of 10 Sep, over 400 marines have received training as OSCAR mentors. Training has already been conducted at I Marine Expeditionary Force (MEF), Camp Pendleton and The Basic School, Quantico, VA. In September, II MEF and III MEF will receive OSCAR training. MARFORRES is scheduled to receive training in November.

133. Senator INHOFE. General Amos, both the Army and the Marine Corps are suffering significant OPTEMPOs, though the Army is by far suffering more with 12-month deployments followed by 12- to 15-month dwell times. I have been told that even with the marines on a 7-month deployed, 12-month dwell cycle, that units are still suffering a compressed timeline. What are the issues associated with the 12-month dwell cycle for your marines?

General AMOS. Regarding current deployments, our goal is to achieve a 1:2 deployment to dwell ration for Active-Duty Forces and 1:4 for Reserve Forces. In peace, our goals are 1:3 and 1:5 respectively. The drawdown in Iraq and our current end strength of 202,000 personnel is allowing us to get close to our goal with the current level of marines in Afghanistan. Dwell time is one of the key factors to ensure that unit readiness, recruiting, retention, morale, and family readiness are not adversely affected. Our heavy training focus on counterinsurgency, coupled with short dwell time, limited the ability of the Marine Corps to develop and maintain proficiency in core competencies such as combined arms and amphibious operations. This training deficiency presents significant risk in our ability to support other OPLANs and contingencies, where full spectrum capabilities would be required.

134. Senator INHOFE. General Chiarelli, is the Army Forces Regeneration model working to get us greater dwell times?

General CHIARELLI. ARFORGEN provides an enterprise framework to provide predictable periods of unit availability to manage equipment, and most importantly to manage our soldiers to ensure each unit is manned, equipped, and trained for its assigned mission. Dwell time is primarily a function of supply and demand for forces. As long as demand exceeds sustainable supply, we will experience issues with dwell time. The reduction of the global demand for forces as we move from a surge condition to a steady state condition in this era of persistent conflict will create greater time between deployments. This results in more opportunities for Professional Military Education (PME) and training, maintenance, and to enhance the quality of life for soldiers and their families.

The overarching purpose of ARFORGEN is to provide combatant commanders and civil authorities with a steady supply of trained and ready units to meet operational requirements. These operational requirements focus the prioritization and synchronization of institutional functions to recruit, organize, man, equip, train, sustain, mobilize, and deploy units on a cyclic basis. ARFORGEN's adaptability addresses both emerging and enduring requirements. Simultaneously, Army institutional adaptations to ARFORGEN maximize potential efficiencies while ensuring effective capabilities are built to support operational requirements.

135. Senator INHOFE. General Chiarelli, where do we stand with getting all BCTs to a greater than 12-month dwell time?

General CHIARELLI. As of April 2010, Active component BCTs are operating on a BOG:dwell ratio of approximately 1:1.43 (12 months BOG: 17 months dwell). In fiscal year 2012, the Army anticipates beginning a 1:2 Active component/1:4 Reserve component BOG:dwell and by fiscal year 2014, a soldier will spend 2 years at homestation prior to a deployment. Dwell time for BCTs will improve because of the moderated demand for BCTs.

END STRENGTH

136. Senator INHOFE. General Chiarelli and General Amos, I was pleased to see that both the Army and the Marine Corps have reached their permanent end strength goals, 547,000 and 202,000 respectively. I see the positive effects the temporary increase up to 22,000 is having on the Army but I am concerned that this temporary increase may not be enough. I am concerned because we don't have enough BCTs and Reserve combat teams to meet the demands of Iraq, Afghanistan, and other unforeseen requirements for our military forces. Our forces are stretched thin, yet when disaster occurs, they get the job done as they did in Haiti despite the toll the additional deployments took on our servicemembers and their families.

Are your Services' current end strength goals adequate to meet the current and fore-casted operational needs?

General CHIARELLI. Army end strength goals are adequate to meet current and forecasted operational needs. The TESI authority provided by Congress has enabled the Army to deploy units at acceptable manning strength levels. TESI provides the Army increased operational flexibility, reduction in personnel and unit turbulence, and the predictability for soldiers and their families required to maintain the All-Volunteer Force.

General AMOS. Yes, we believe 202,000 Active-Duty personnel are sufficient to meet our current and forecasted operational needs. Such a force level (i.e., three balanced MEFs) enables the Corps to meet current and future challenges in an increasingly demanding operational environment. It also gives the Marine Corps the capacity to deploy forces in response to contingencies and to support security cooperation efforts with our partners across all theaters.

We believe that 202,000 is the right sized force to achieve our goal of a 1:2 dwell given our current level of commitment to Afghanistan.

- Prior to 202,000, Marine Corps infantry battalions were at a 1:1.1 dwell time. Currently, we are at 1:1.8 dwell for infantry battalions. Factoring in a current steady state commitment of 9 infantry battalions (6 x OEF and 3 x MEU) we expect to achieve a 1:1.9 steady state (RIP TOA period, when battalions overlap, prevents us from getting to 1:2).

Marine Corps forces are multi-capable, transitioning seamlessly from fighting conventional and hybrid threats to promoting stability and mitigating conditions that lead to conflict. By maintaining a 202,000 force, we will continue to improve training, upgrade readiness, and enhance the quality of life for all our marines and their families by allowing them more recovery time between deployments.

This fall, the Marine Corps will be conducting a thorough force structure review to inform decisions about what the Marine Corps will look like in the future. Any recommended adjustments to the force will undergo a thorough vetting and analysis to ensure the Nation's Marine Corps remain ready. Such adjustments will be brought to your attention through Defense Department leadership as situations and events dictate.

137. Senator INHOFE. General Chiarelli and General Amos, despite experiencing exceptional recruiting and retention results, our soldiers and marines continue to show signs of stress due to the tremendous amount of time and sacrifice that has been asked of them. How have we managed to meet or exceed our recruiting and retention goals despite the tremendous stress and burdens shouldered by our troops?

General CHIARELLI. Despite the rigors of serving as soldiers, our Nation's young men and women step forward repeatedly and pledge to serve. They recognize the challenges facing our Nation, answer the call, and continue to become part of something larger than themselves. In addition, the Army has met or exceeded its recruiting and retention goals for several years. This reflects historical trends that show rising unemployment and unfavorable economic conditions lead to improved enlistments and retention. The shift in the economy has also allowed us to raise quality metrics and begin to address other important goals. For example, we were able to decrease and eliminate some key waivers for enlistment and officer program entry. As economic conditions improve, we will monitor trends and make adjustments as required to continue to recruit and retain America's best.

General AMOS. The key to the Marine Corps' recruiting success is its continued focus on finding highly-qualified young men and women who are seeking the challenge of serving their Nation. Continued access to high schools and colleges not only assures that we have access to a quality market that reflects the face of the Nation, but also a market that has the mental abilities to serve in our technically challenging fields such as linguistics, aircraft and electronic maintenance, and intelligence. The catalyst to our recruiting success is a commitment to maintaining a sufficient number of recruiting personnel and adequate advertising funding.

Quality metrics and standards are continuously assessed to ensure that we are meeting our manpower skill level needs. We know through studies that a high school graduate is more likely to complete recruit training. The DOD education tier divisions are appropriately grouped and adequately serve as attrition predictors. Applicants who score in the upper mental categories on the Armed Services Vocational Aptitude Battery have the intellect and mental agility needed to work with today's technology. So far this year, 99.7 percent of our enlisted accessions have been high school graduates and 72 percent have scored in the I-IIIA range, both far exceeding

DOD standards of 90 percent Tier I (high school graduates) and 60 percent Mental Group I–IIIA (upper mental categories) respectively.

The Marine Corps achieved unprecedented levels of enlisted and officer retention during fiscal year 2009 and continues to do so in fiscal year 2010. This effort is critical to the proper grade shaping of the Marine Corps. Enlisted retention provides the Marine Corps essential NCO and staff noncommissioned officer (SNCO) experience and leadership. Increased end strength requirements, properly shaped at the NCO and SNCO ranks, will continue to place significant demands on our retention efforts and will require sustained congressional funding to retain quality marines. Robust Selective Reenlistment Bonuses (SRB) will continue to be critical to sustaining the Marine Corps' success in retaining the leadership and experience needed in a 202,000 Marine Corps.

138. Senator INHOFE. General Chiarelli and General Amos, given that fact that this global war on terror will continue and we will be in Afghanistan for at least the near term, what is the outlook on Marine Corps and Army recruiting and retention?

General CHIARELLI. Since the economic downturn began in December 2007, the Army has met or exceeded its recruiting and retention goals and this trend appears to continue for the near term, reflecting historical trends. The economic environment allows us to reduce incentive amounts and the number of occupation offered bonuses or education incentives. However, we must retain the flexibility to apply incentives as necessary to retain soldiers with critical or specialized skills. The continued authorities and funding of these programs by Congress remain critical to the sustainment of the Army.

General AMOS. A key component of our recruiting success is the Marine Corps' image of smart, tough, elite warriors. The time-proven intangible benefits of service, pride of belonging, leadership, challenge, and discipline are what we offer. The Nation's young people continue to answer the call of duty, responding to these intangibles, even during this time of war. Ample funding to sufficiently engage in targeted recruiting advertising efforts is essential to portraying this image and conveying this message.

As it relates to operational requirements and tempo, one of the key factors to ensure that readiness, recruiting, retention, and morale are not affected is to maintain our goal of a 1:2 or better dwell time throughout the force. We also need to weigh competing operational demands and requirements (e.g. exercise support, expeditionary missions, theater security cooperation, combat operations, et cetera) throughout the total Marine Corps force to ensure there is proper balance.

We continue to experience keen competition from the civilian employment sector. Our enlisted marines develop valuable leadership and technical skills that are highly sought by the private sector. Retaining the proper skills and high quality in our ranks requires a robust SRB program and is essential to our mission accomplishment.

Although overall officer retention is excellent, shortages do exist in certain grades and skills, requiring careful management and innovative solutions. To this end, the Marine Corps has active programs in place, both monetary and non-monetary, to ensure officer retention remains high, e.g. Aviation Continuation Pay and Law School Education Debt Subsidy. Non-monetary programs include voluntary lateral moves, inter-service transfers to the Marine Corps, and the Return to Active Duty program. All of these programs provide incentives to officers for continued service, even in the face of significant operational tempo while giving flexibility to manpower planners to meet requirements across the Marine Corps Total Force.

139. Senator INHOFE. General Chiarelli and General Amos, what is the breakout of the nondeployables and what is the plan to reduce the current rates, specifically in the Army and the Marine Corps?

General CHIARELLI. For fiscal year 2010 year-to-date, the average percentage of a unit's assigned population not deploying at latest arrival date is 14.11 percent. This includes late deployers and soldiers who will not deploy. Medical nondeployers account for one-third of the total nondeployer population—by far the largest single category of nondeployers. For fiscal year 2010 year-to-date, the average nondeployer population includes: 35.2 percent medical; 12.7 percent administrative separations (e.g. unsatisfactory performance, misconduct, hardship); 11.2 percent training; 9.4 percent rear detachment cadre; 5.1 percent dwell time; 2.8 percent parenthood; and 23.6 percent other. Other categories include legal processing, retirement, enlisted expiration term of service (ETS), officer release from Active Duty or unqualified resignation, temporary duty, emergency leave, sole survivor, conscientious objector, and reassignments. The training category applies to soldiers who have not completed required predeployment training. Approximately one-fourth to one-third of the nondeployers at latest arrival date will eventually deploy and join the unit in theater; this includes all of the training category and the dwell time category, as well as a portion of the temporary medical and other categories.

From a tactical perspective, commanders at all levels are actively engaged in identifying nondeployable soldiers and, in the case of temporary nondeployable conditions, linking the soldier with the requisite resources necessary to resolve the nondeployable condition. From a strategic perspective, the Army staff is focused on policy and implementation decisions necessary to dampen the nondeployer rates in our units and to gain better visibility on the health of the force. Specifically with regard to medical nondeployers, my staff is engaged in numerous efforts to improve medical readiness policies and processes. These efforts are synchronized across four lines of operations (Systems, Training, Policy, and Processes) and focused on our desired end-state to man an expeditionary Army with soldiers who are medically deployable while preserving the All-Volunteer Force. Our actions in this realm are built upon four primary objectives: to develop a medical common operating picture; to train our leaders and medical professionals on medical readiness policies and procedures; to determine what impact worldwide deployability should have on soldier retainability; and to standardize and streamline medical board processes across all components. Over time, increased visibility combined with improved policy and streamlined processes will combine to decrease nondeployer rates.

General AMOS. From the Marine Corps' perspective, nondeployables are marines that are captured as fleet patients, prisoners, and trainees (schools 20 weeks or longer). As of 29 August 2010, the above categories comprised 874 marines. The assignable enlisted population on the above date was 160,593 which reflect a 0.05 percent nondeployable population. This headquarters has established manpower procedures that effectively reduce the amount of nondeployable marines to current minimum levels.

EQUIPMENT READINESS

140. Senator INHOFE. General Chiarelli, General Amos, Admiral Greenert, and General Chandler, equipment readiness is becoming more and more of a significant issue across all of the Services. The number one comment that resonates with me is that we are flying, driving, and sailing our equipment well beyond what was originally planned. Our fleets are significantly older, based on when they were first designed and fielded with some dating back to the 1950s. The Marines now have a unique situation where they have to deploy home station equipment to Afghanistan and leave it there for replacing units. The inventory of Abrams, Paladins, and Bradleys, designed some 30 years ago, are on their fourth and fifth modernization program. Marine Corps aviation average an age of 22 years old, bombers 34 years old, Air Force fighters 27 years old, tankers 46 years old, et cetera. While equipment readiness is significantly impacting our operations down range, it will have a larger impact in the out-years, once Iraq and Afghanistan go away. I am convinced that we are going to have a capabilities gap due to our inability to repair and modernize current fleets while simultaneously working on future development and our inability to fund all of this. We are headed down the same road we travel down after every other period of conflict where political focus shifts away from the military and national security, leaving a severely depleted force. What are we doing now to hedge the cost of refitting the force in the next several years?

General CHIARELLI. Congress and OSD have been very supportive of Army reset requirements. The Army is executing deliberate reset plans and is including Lean Six Sigma improvements in its national level reset processes to ensure efficiency and a greater return on investment. Reset is a series of maintenance actions taken to restore equipment to a desired level of combat capability commensurate with a unit's future mission. The Army utilizes reset activities to mitigate the long-term impacts of combat operations to equipment in our inventory. Our national and installation maintenance activities reset approximately 100,000 pieces of equipment and 25 brigades annually.

Also, as part of reset, selected systems returning from combat have been recapitalized. Recapitalization is the rebuild or upgrade of currently fielded systems to ensure operational readiness and a near zero-time and zero-mile system. The Army has taken the opportunity to recapitalize selected systems while the system is undergoing reset. Specifically, in fiscal year 2009, returning Apache helicopters, Abrams tanks, and Bradley fighting vehicles were recapitalized.

Nevertheless, the Army will require reset funding for 2 to 3 years after the completion of OCOs.

General AMOS. The timeline for getting the Marine Corps on track with needed equipment is dependent on the length of time the Marine Corps will be engaged in combat, as well as the amount of procurement funds available through both reset and baseline funding sources. Resetting the Marine Corps under current OCO guidelines is challenging since much of the equipment in the retrograde pipeline is legacy equipment that no longer meets operational requirements. Additionally, we have been unable to procure sufficient equipment to meet table of equipment shortfalls and this negatively impacts readiness. The fiscally constrained baseline budget limits the Marine Corps ability to modernize.

Baseline funding levels and procurement timelines have not kept pace with our increased requirements for additional and updated equipment. Our current equipment posture is particularly vulnerable due to the convergence of our equipment modernization due to changing battlefield requirements, along with the need to rapidly buildup forces in Afghanistan as we simultaneously executed a retrograde from Iraq. Accelerating equipment procurement where feasible and directing OCO funding to a broader enterprise approach gives the Marine Corps greater latitude to realign resources to meet equipment requirements.

It is difficult to predict what the exact Marine Corps reset costs will be since it is unknown how long the Marine Corps will be engaged in combat. The most important thing is that our marines are equipped with the best gear. To do this, additional funding will be required as new threats arise on the battlefield. We know in the near term that we need funding in order to continue to reset equipment that is currently deployed. However, as long as the war continues, our costs will continue to grow.

For Marine tactical aviation assets, the O&S costs on our legacy aircraft across DOD have been increasing an average of 7.8 percent per year since 2000. The operational lifetimes of legacy aircraft are being extended well beyond their original design limits. As a result, we face a daily challenge to maintain operational readiness of our legacy aircraft due largely to the increasing age of the aircraft fleet. Early on it was primarily attributed to the aging avionics systems; lately it is maintenance of the airframe and hardware components that are becoming the O&S cost drivers. Extending the life of an airframe has proven challenging and costly.

The Marine Corps strategy for the last 11 years has been to forgo the continuation of procuring new variants of legacy aircraft and continuing a process of trying to sustain old designs that inherit the obsolescence and fatigue life issues of their predecessors. Instead we opted to transition to a new fifth generation aircraft that takes advantage of technology improvements which generates substantial savings in ownership cost. The capabilities of the F–35B enable the Marine Corps to replace three legacy aircraft types and retain the capability of executing all our missions. This results optimizing and avoiding unnecessary retrofit and reap tangible O&S cost savings.

The Marine Corps will preserve our legacy fleets of Harriers and Hornets with sufficient funding while transitioning to the fifth generation STOVL F–35B. This is the best option to balance the requirement to fulfill operational commitments with legacy aircraft, while funding the development and procurement of new production JSF. We are taking proactive steps today to preserve the legacy fleets, maintain their operational relevance, and continue these efforts until the production of the F–35B is sufficient to fully transition our Harriers and Hornets.

Admiral GREENERT. Reset in stride is how our Navy prepares the fleet to deploy again. Lifecycle maintenance and training between deployments is essential for reset and the ability of our ships, aircraft, and submarines to reach their expected service lives. Although we are on pace to grow our fleet for the next 10 years, the past decade has seen a reduction in our overall fleet size. At the same time, we continue to maintain similar numbers of ships at sea assigned to combatant commanders, which we are servicing with historically low numbers of ships available for at-sea training, exercises, and surge operations. Our fiscal year 2011 budget request balances the need to meet increasing operational requirements, sustain our sailors' proficiency, and conduct the maintenance required to ensure our ships, aircraft, and submarines reach their full service lives.

There are several programs in place to ensure the Navy remains combat effective through the foreseeable future. For instance, the Department continues to rigorously manage the service life and warfighting effectiveness of our legacy Hornets, Harriers, Super Hornets, and Prowlers to ensure maximum contribution to the Nation's security. We are actively pursuing all options to manage our inventory and balance risk, including a SLEP for a number of F/A–18 A–D aircraft to extend their service life to 10,000 flight hours and optimizing depot efficiencies. Additionally, the Navy is redesigning obsolete components to provide for future combat capability growth for all strike aircraft and weapons programs.

Maritime Patrol Reconnaissance Aviation (MPRA) has taken a two-pronged approach to refitting the force while we transition from the P–3C to P–8A. The first is sustaining modernization of the legacy P–3 forces to ensure aircrew safety. In addition, the P–3 is managed through the Global Force Management process to meter remaining fatigue life. The second effort is the prioritization of the P–8A program to bring its significant warfighting capability to the fleet as early as possible. P–8A plans include capability improvements that deliver additional and critical ASW, ASUW and intelligence, surveillance, and reconnaissance (ISR) to forward bases over the next 10 years.

In our shipbuilding programs, we plan to conduct Destroyer modernization in two 6-month availabilities. The first availability is focused on hull, mechanical, and electrical (HM&E) modifications, while the second availability, conducted 2 years later, is focused on combat systems modernization. The program commenced this year and focuses on the Flight I and II DDG 51 ships (hulls 51–78). All ships of the class will be modernized at midlife. Key components of the DDG modernization program include: an upgrade of the Aegis Weapons System to include an Open Architecture (OA) computing environment, an upgrade of the SPY radar signal processor, the addition of BMD capability, installation of the Evolved Sea Sparrow Missile (ESSM), an upgraded SQQ–89A(V)15 antisubmarine warfare system, integration with the SM–6 Missile, and improved air dominance with processing upgrades and Naval Integrated Fire Control-Counter Air (NIFC–CA) capability.

There are similar efforts underway in every facet of our programs. The investments we make today, the recapitalization efforts of tomorrow, and the maintenance of our existing fleet will ensure the Navy has no peer as we move through the future.

General CHANDLER. The Air Force portion of the fiscal year 2011 President's budget reflects tough and thoughtful decisions to carry out the Air Force's mission to fly, fight, and win in air, space, and cyberspace. The proposal reflects our continued commitment to fully fund and support today's global operations while ensuring we are prepared to face the likely challenges and opportunities of the future. This budget continues efforts begun last year to rebalance the force and reform how and what we buy.

The KC–135 comprises almost 90 percent of the tanker fleet and their replacement remains the Air Force's number one acquisition priority. The Air Force released the Request for Proposal for the KC–X in February 2010 and is aggressively working toward awarding a contract later this year.

The Air Force also remains committed to the Joint Strike Fighter program, an essential element of our national security strategy, and a capability needed to defeat 21st century threats. In fiscal year 2011, the Air Force will procure 22 F–35 airframes and is on track to achieve F–35 Initial Operational Capability (IOC) in 2016.

Building upon insights developed during the QDR, the Air Force is reviewing options for fielding survivable, long-range surveillance and strike platform as part of a comprehensive, phased plan to modernize the bomber force. Additionally, funding is provided for the B–1, B–2, and B–52 fleets to sustain and modernize the capabilities of these aircraft while maintaining the viability of long-range strike capabilities.

The budget request includes procurement for 36 MQ–9 Reaper aircraft in the baseline budget and requests 12 additional MQ–9 aircraft in OCO funding. This will increase our ISR Combat Air Patrols (CAP) to 50 surge CAPs by the end of fiscal year 2011 and by the end of fiscal year 2013 we'll be at 65 surge CAPs. The budget also requests four additional RQ–4 Global Hawks and seeks to normalize training and basing posture for the MC–12 Project Liberty.

The Air Force is continuing the development and institutionalization of building partnerships and cyberspace capabilities and integration into the joint structure. The fiscal year 2011 budget request reflects a commitment to cyberspace superiority by expanding rapid cyber acquisition capabilities to keep pace with dynamic adversaries and fast-paced advances in technology. It also reflects our effort to field light mobility and light attack aircraft to increase our ability to work effectively with a wider range of partner air forces.

Finally, the budget proposal also includes enhancements to legacy weapons systems to ensure today's capability will continue to be viable and also compatible with future fifth-generation fighters and developing weapon systems. These enhancements include F–15 fleet modernization and radar upgrades, F–22 common configuration upgrades, and the conversion of one WC–130 to an EC–130 Compass Call. The A–10 Wing Replacement Program (WRP) procures 40 new thick-skin wings as part of a program to modify 233 A–10 aircraft with older thin-skin wings. F–16 aircraft have multiple initiatives to mitigate the cost of retrofitting and ensure viability. The first initiative is the repair/replacement of lower wing skins on Block 30 aircraft, as required. The second F 16 initiative is Full-Scale Fatigue Testing which tests the durability of Block 40/50 airframes to extend the airworthiness certification beyond the 8,000 equivalent flight hour design. The Air Force will also continue to modernize the C–5 Galaxy, C–130 Hercules, and C–17 Globemaster III fleet through programs such as avionics modernization; reliability, enhancement, and reengining; and large aircraft infrared countermeasures. Upgrades to Air Force Command and Control platforms such as the E–3 AWACS will modernize a 1970s-era computer network, eliminate discontinued and obsolete components, and add avionics to comply with Global Air Traffic Management standards.

The last two decades of sustained operations have strained our weapons systems. The Air Force will continue to determine which aircraft it will modernize and sustain and which weapon systems must be retired and recapitalized. These decisions require tough choices, as well as the ability to quickly field systems to meet warfighter needs at an affordable price. The fiscal year 2011 budget helps us achieve the right balance to meet today's commitments while shaping the Air Force for future challenges.

141. Senator INHOFE. General Chiarelli, General Amos, Admiral Greenert, and General Chandler, what is needed from Congress to prevent our rapidly aging planes, helicopters, vehicles, and ships from becoming obsolete?

General CHIARELLI. Army aircraft and vehicles of all types have benefitted from strong support and stable funding from Congress. This strong funding support has allowed the Army to invest in the modernization of our fleets via new production, recapitalization, and program upgrades while keeping an eye on the future by funding research and development efforts.

Examples of incremental modernization of core Army programs include the Stryker combat vehicle, Apache Block III helicopter, and TWV programs. The Stryker was fielded with limited blast and underbelly protection. The Army followed with an appliquè solution (i.e., bolt-on plates) against blast threats, and is currently pursuing an integrated survivability solution effort, including an improved lower hull, crumple zones, welded supports, and energy attenuated seats. To this end, the Army is developing and testing the Stryker Double V Hull survivability initiative which, if proven, will provide improved soldier protection against underbelly IED threats.

Another incremental modernization initiative includes the Apache Block III program. The Longbow Block III will begin inductions in 2010 and field the first unit in 2013, providing significant increases in performance and capability at higher altitudes and temperatures with a full combat load. Advances in technology will provide the Block III with improved manned-unmanned interoperability, weight reduction initiatives, open system architecture, and reduced pilot workload via cognitive decision aiding technologies. It will also provide a net-ready capability that maintains Army interoperability for joint operations and future requirements.

Additionally, the Army will shape its TWV fleet size and mix to ensure long-term affordability through new procurement, recapitalization, divestment, and will leverage existing assets to the greatest extent possible to improve overall fleet capability, while reducing fleet age and operating costs. The JLTV program is an excellent example of such an initiative as it promises game-changing technology for our light TWV fleet and is a critical enabler for the Army to replace a substantive quantity of the High Mobility Multipurpose Wheeled Vehicle fleet starting in fiscal year 2014.

Continued timely funding and support from Congress will ensure our equipment is ready for future missions.

General AMOS. In particular to Marine Corps aviation: We are at a crucial point in Marine Corps aviation as we have embarked on the most aggressive modernization and transition plan in our history. By the mid-2020s, every single aircraft in the Marine Corps will have been replaced with a new model or a new airframe. Everything we are bringing online will fly higher, faster, farther, and longer; carry more than the aircraft it replaces; and operate as a node within a network of fused data which will make us all better warfighters. It is the Marine Corps' desire is to acquire these newer aircraft in accordance with the program of record at the programmed ramp to stand up squadrons in the most efficient manner possible

In particular to Marine Corps ground equipment: Congress has generously supported the Marine Corps' reset efforts in the past to ensure marines have equipment resources necessary to succeed. We are committed to managing these resources wisely as we reset and modernize for the future. As a result of shifting forces to the harsher operating environment of Afghanistan, costs are expected to rise, and continued congressional support of future funding requests will be necessary to improve readiness levels across the Corps. Maintaining our vehicle fleet, in particular, will be challenging as we rebalance resources to support ongoing operations, re-arm, and reposition forces around the world. While it is difficult to predict precisely what future costs will be since it is unknown how long the Corps will be engaged in combat, costs will rise the longer we are at war. We are mindful that the Marine Corps cannot rely on supplemental appropriations for baseline operations. Sufficient funding for the Marine Corps' vehicle fleet is critically important in order to restore our operating forces to a level of combat capability commensurate with future missions.

Admiral GREENERT. Our fiscal year 2011 budget request identifies the resources required to increase fleet capacity, maintain our warfighting readiness, and develop and enhance the Navy Total Force. To appropriately provide a deployed naval force, continued congressional support is required to maintain the current fleet and to ensure existing ships/aircraft reach their expected service lives. Further, we must ensure our recapitalization plans are robust and effective in replacing aging ships and aircraft with more efficient, modernized equipment.

Adequate, sustained funding of the Navy's Maintenance and Modernization Program is necessary to provide for the safe and reliable operation while also ensuring we achieve the expected service life of our aircraft, ships, and submarines, and to efficiently deliver combat ready forces to meet current and future operational requirements.

The Navy remains committed to building a 313-ship fleet by 2020, as detailed in our Long-Range Plan for Construction of Naval Vessels for fiscal year 2011. Our current and future fleet enables us to respond rapidly, decisively, and globally to project power, as we have done in Iraq and Afghanistan, and to deliver humanitarian assistance, as we have done in Haiti, while operating from a small, yet persistent, footprint that does not impose unnecessary political or logistic burdens on other nations. To ensure continued execution of the Maritime Strategy, annual support of the President's budget is paramount.

General CHANDLER. The Air Force's budget proposal reflects a continued commitment to fully fund and support today's global operations while ensuring we are prepared to face the likely challenges and opportunities of the future. Balancing requirements for today and tomorrow determined our recapitalization strategy. The Air Force chose to improve existing capabilities whenever possible and to pursue new systems when required. This recapitalization approach attempts to keep pace with threat developments and required capabilities, while ensuring stewardship of national resources. To ensure our ability to prevent our rapidly aging aircraft from becoming obsolete, we ask that you support the fiscal year 2011 President's budget that requests the resources to accomplish this goal. To point out just a few of these critical programs:

The budget includes enhancements for F–15 fleet modernization and radar upgrades, and F–22 common configuration upgrades to enhance their interoperability and long-term viability. The conversion of one WC–130 to an EC–130 Compass Call helps meet current demand for the Compass Call mission; their utilization rates are currently 2.3 times higher than the C–130 fleet average. The A–10 WRP procures 40 new thick-skin wings as part of a program to modify 233 A–10 aircraft with older thin-skin wings. F–16 Block 40/50 aircraft will undergo Full-Scale Fatigue Testing and F–16 Block 30 lower wing-skin repair will be managed under Consolidated Aircraft Management. Our goal is to extend our fourth generation fighter aircraft service life and capability many years beyond the original service life of the aircraft; this is projected to be at a cost of 10 to 15 percent of a new aircraft. The Air Force will also continue to modernize the C–5 Galaxy, C–130 Hercules, and C–17 Globemaster III fleet through programs such as avionics modernization; reliability, enhancement, and reengining; and large aircraft infrared countermeasures. The Air Force solicits the continued support of Congress as we continue with the C–130 Avionics Modernization Program (AMP). This effort increases reliability, maintainability, and sustainability for the Air Force's 222 C–130H2, H2.5, and H3 Combat Delivery aircraft by installing a common avionics suite and standardized cockpit configuration. Additionally, funding is provided for the B–1, B–2, and B–52 fleets that will sustain and modernize the capabilities of these aircraft maintaining the viability of legacy long-range strike capabilities over the short- to mid-term. Programs include modernizing the B–2 Defensive Management System, a new radar and data link system for the B–52, and an Advanced Extremely High Frequency satellite communications system for the B–2 and B–52. Upgrades to Air Force command and control platforms such as the E–3 AWACS will modernize a 1970s-era computer network, eliminate discontinued and obsolete components, and add avionics to comply with Global Air Traffic Management standards.

The Air Force's proposed fiscal year 2011 budget achieves the right balance between providing capabilities for today's commitments and posturing for future challenges. We respectfully ask that Congress support this budget request to help the Air Force make the most of our allocated resources and to work as a member of the joint team to accomplish our Nation's military objectives.

142. Senator INHOFE. General Chiarelli, General Amos, Admiral Greenert, and General Chandler, the QDR presented the historical standard requirement to be able to contend with two major theaters of war simultaneously. I have heard all of you state that the near-term fight and requirements are impacting our ability to maintain a strategic focus. We no longer maintain a readiness force in the same standard that we did prior to September 11. We are taking equipment from non-deployed units to ensure deployed units are fully equipped, leaving training shortages back home and raising concerns that, once in the area of responsibility, equipment promised will be available and mission ready. In some instances, we have depleted our preposition stockpiles. What is the status for both Army and Marine Corps preposition stocks?

General CHIARELLI. The Army is restoring its prepositioned stock capabilities in accordance with the approved APS 2015 Strategy. Detailed readiness status reports are classified but projected status of fill for APS–3, APS–4, and APS–5 unit equipment sets are as follows:

(1) APS–3 Afloat Theater Opening/Port Opening Package: uploaded on the USNS *Watson* and is currently in the Pacific area of operations after completing a cargo maintenance cycle at Charleston, SC. The TO/PO Package has 97 percent EOH level of fill.

(2) APS–3 Afloat Infantry Brigade Combat Team (IBCT) with motorized augmentation set: projected to upload on two Large Medium Speed Roll-on Roll-off ships in September and November 2010 with a projected >90 percent EOH level of fill. The Army will continue to increase the level of fill prior to upload through available equipment from reset and new production.

(3) APS–3 IBCT with motorized augmentation set: currently located in Kuwait with a 94 percent EOH level of fill; the motorized augmentation set has 99 percent EOH fill. The Army issued medium and heavy TWVs and container handlers in support of the force plus-up in Afghanistan, and will backfill those vehicles with retrograde from the drawdown in Iraq, as well as new production. This IBCT will eventually be uploaded on ships and become the Army's second IBCT afloat, when CENTCOM no longer requires it in Southwest Asia.

(4) APS–4 Korea/Japan HBCT and Sustainment Brigade: this set is fully operational with the HBCT at 98 percent EOH and the Sustainment Brigade at 93 percent EOH.

(5) APS–5 Southwest Asia HBCT with motorized augmentation set currently located in Kuwait: The Army delayed the original fully operational date for 31 March 2010 to March 2011 because of a need to issue medium and heavy TWVs, material handling equipment, and SINCGARS radios in support of the plus-up in Afghanistan. This HBCT currently has an 87 percent EOH level of fill, which includes the Army's most modern tanks and Bradley Fighting Vehicles. The motorized augmentation set has 83 percent EOH fill. The Army plans to fill equipment shortages over the next year from repaired and reset OIF retrograded equipment, depot production, and new procurement.

(6) The APS–5 Infantry Battalion with Forward Support Company and motorized augmentation set: currently located in Afghanistan with 74 percent EOH fill and is planned to be fully mission capable by September 2011, in accordance with the approved APS 2015 Strategy.

General AMOS. The MPF and MCPP–N are currently in a high state of readiness. As of 31 August 2010, MPSRON–1 is currently at 88 percent of its full significant military equipment set; MPSRON–2 is at 77 percent and MPSRON–3 is at 88 percent. MCPP–N is at 60 percent of its equipment set. The MPSRONs are at 100 percent for tanks, assault amphibian vehicles, light armored reconnaissance vehicles and ammunition.

Admiral GREENERT. I defer to the Army and Marine Corps with regard to the status of their preposition stocks.

General CHANDLER. [Deleted.]

143. Senator INHOFE. General Chiarelli, General Amos, Admiral Greenert, and General Chandler, what is the plan to get preposition stockages back to the proper levels?

General CHIARELLI. With full support of our fiscal year 2011 to 2015 Base and OCOs funding requests (~$2.7 billion Other Procurement, Army and ~$4.9 billion Operations and Maintenance, Army), Army Prepositioned Stocks can be restored to full levels by 2015. This assessment includes the future integration of MRAP vehicles and the MRAP-all terrain vehicles into our prepositioned stocks.

General AMOS. Our MPSRONs will be reset with the most capable equipment possible.

The MPSRONs are currently rotating through Maritime Prepositioning Force Maintenance Cycle-10 (MMC–10), with the offload of MPSRON–1 beginning in March 2010. Equipment from MPSRON–1 had been used to support new units being established in fiscal year 2007 and fiscal year 2008 as part of our end strength increase to 202,000. MPSRON–1 has 88 percent of its full significant military equipment set and has one ship of equipment downloaded at Blount Island Command.

MPSRON–2 is expected to be fully reset upon completion of its MMC–10 rotation in fiscal year 2012. Its readiness spiked dramatically—from 49 percent to its current 77 percent—during its rotation through MMC–9.

Admiral GREENERT. I defer to the Army and Marine Corps with regard to the status of their preposition stock levels.

General CHANDLER. [Deleted.]

144. Senator INHOFE. General Chiarelli, General Amos, Admiral Greenert, and General Chandler, after the Vietnam war, we had a hollow force—a force that was not resourced to ensure our military was trained and ready ... it had equipment but the force itself was not prepared for combat. Today we are beginning to see opposite—we have the best trained force in the world, the best warfighters in the world, but we are fracturing that force by not providing them with the equipment to sustain that capability in the short- and long-term. I have started to key in on the words you have used like 'mitigate', 'workarounds', 'risk management', 'well above programmed rates', and 'productive ration'. We have not had significant discussion on the operational risk as it relates to meeting combatant commander warfighting requirements and the NDS. All the Services are wrestling with significant budget affordability issues, equipment, personnel, operations, and maintenance. In terms of overall risk, from each of your perspectives, how are we going to be able to meet the near-term readiness demands associated with the global war on terrorism while still mitigating the risk associated with threats in the future?

General CHIARELLI. The Army has outlined two major priorities: Restoring Balance and Setting Conditions for the Future. To restore balance, we are targeting the four imperatives of Sustain, Prepare, Reset, and Transform. To prepare for the future, the Army is building a versatile force with a balanced mix of multipurpose capabilities and sufficient capacity to execute our doctrine of Full Spectrum Operations, from peacetime engagement to major combat.

At the unit level, our ARFORGEN model progresses units through Reset and Train/Ready phases prior to entering an available (for deployment) phase. This provides the time to recover from the previous deployment and to prepare for the upcoming deployment. As we continue to align our institutional processes and modernization strategy to ARFORGEN, we are enhancing our ability to field the latest equipment, maximize training time, and man units in a timely manner. This model also allows the Army to tailor capabilities and structure of the deploying force to best meet the needs of expected scenarios.

However, the high deployment-to-dwell ratios reduce the available training time for units to train for Full Spectrum Operations, forcing a focus on the needs of the current fight. In order to best prepare for future contingencies, we must increase our dwell time which will enhance our ability to train for a wider range of operations in future deployments. This requires us to fully implement our ARFORGEN model and retain assured access to the Reserve component, which has proven invaluable this past decade.

Continued implementation of our Army Modernization Strategy (AMS) will ensure our force is provided with the best capabilities for meeting the variety of future challenges. The AMS articulates three lines of effort to develop and field a versatile and affordable mix of the best equipment available. First, we will develop and field new capabilities to maintain our advantage over current, emerging, and future threats. Second, we will continuously modernize equipment to meet current and future capability needs through procurement of upgraded capabilities, recapitalization, and divestment of obsolete items. Third, we will align our modernization effort with ARFORGEN to prioritize support to the units in preparation to deploy. This strategy will best prepare us for future threats.

General AMOS. The Marine Corps is able to meet the near-term readiness demands associated with the current conflict and is sourcing its best-trained, most ready forces to meet combatant commander requirements around the globe. The Marine Corps is also posturing itself for the future security environment through a number of important initiatives contained in the Marine Corps Service Campaign Plan. First drafted in 2009 to specifically mitigate future operational risk, the Marine Corps Service Campaign Plan directs commanders to regain/maintain core competency in high-end combat operations, given the current focus on Afghanistan. It also directs reset and modernization efforts as well as closer coordination with the Navy through the establishment of the Naval Engagement Board.

The Marine Corps is also currently engaged in a comprehensive post-OEF posture operational planning effort to define risk to the Service and associated decision points to ultimately allow the Marine Corps to optimally posture itself for the future security environment with adaptive forces that can operate across the range of military operations, given a fiscally-constrained environment.

Admiral GREENERT. Despite the existing fiscally constrained environment, the Navy strives to achieve balance in meeting near-term demands for ensuring the readiness of today's force structure, while concurrently fielding capabilities needed to counter future threats. This balance is achieved by prioritizing Service objectives that are aligned to those directed by the Secretary of Defense. Specifically, the Navy's top priority is to ensure that deployed forces are fully trained, ready to deploy, and supported while on deployment in addressing today's contingencies. This is accomplished by the meticulous management of readiness accounts, resulting in the sufficiency of steaming days, flying hours, and depot level repairs necessary to provide combat-capable units that meet combatant commanders' demands. Additionally, investments for future modernization and procurement are rescoped to field only those capabilities which are associated with the most likely threat scenarios. All of this is enabled by the implementation of improved business practices which result in more effective operation at reduced cost. For example, the Navy Enterprise Resource Planning program will standardize key business practices and achieve cost savings by retiring redundant IT systems; reducing supply inventories; and streamlining business processes. Ultimately, the Navy will meet demands for current readiness and counter future threats by focusing on current operations; addressing the most likely future threats; and obtaining savings from process improvements.

General CHANDLER. Your Air Force is dedicated to maintaining its position as the premier global air power. Over 7 years ago, the Air Force began to take a capabilities-based approach to our force structure. Focused on managing risk and capabilities across the range of military operations, our primary vehicle for assessing capabilities and risk is the Capabilities Review and Risk Assessment. It analyzes our force structure capabilities against the OSD-approved scenarios and cases to identify gaps and shortfalls. We use advanced modeling tools to address sufficiency questions and develop consequence metrics in consultation with the combatant commanders. With this information, we are able to measure operational risk and address investment and force structure decisions. This will ensure our force structure is balanced and effective in all our Nation's potential conflicts in the near- and far-term. However, no amount of cultivation of our forces and capabilities can offset a lack of capital investment. Capital investment will be the primary driver as to how well future risk is mitigated. Specific investment is needed in fifth generation fighters, long-range precision strike systems, and preferred munitions. We also need outlays in ISR and electronic combat capabilities in hostile environments. Finally, investment in bases and hardening and building partnerships with our global friends will help ensure operational risk is mitigated. The challenge will be to accomplish all of this while recapitalizing our aging fleet despite constrained resources. The Air Force's aircraft recapitalization plan is contained in the February 2010 "DOD Aircraft Investment Plan."

145. Senator INHOFE. General Chiarelli, General Amos, Admiral Greenert, and General Chandler, what factor or factors are driving these gaps in our force structure and capabilities?

General CHIARELLI. Today, the Nation faces a wider variety of threats in the contemporary security environment. These threats include not only traditional nation-states, but also transnational violent extremists and terrorists, cyber-threats, WMD proliferation, and hybrid threats. This environment is complicated by our ongoing operations in several theaters which require full-time attention. The nature of conflict today requires a flexible approach to meet these diverse threats and anticipate force requirements. Therefore, the Army's greatest emphasis in preparation for the future is to create a versatile force.

Prevailing in the current fight remains our first priority. Our force generation model, along with modular forces, allows us to tailor our force to the needs of the current fight as units prepare for deployment in the near-term with the resources available. During the training phase, units prepare for full spectrum operations as time allows, building depth for the ability to respond to contingencies. The current methods of assessment, such as the QDR, provide the ability to evaluate our force structure and capabilities as the environment and threat evolve.

General AMOS. From a capabilities development perspective, factors such as lack of adequate funding for sustainment and modernization on aging equipment have created unacceptable risk in operational readiness. This lack of adequate funding has caused a ripple effect in our ability to pursue new initiatives to modernize the force to ensure future required capabilities are in place when needed.

Admiral GREENERT. Gaps in force structure and capabilities are caused by the Nation's need to prioritize winning the current fight, and the need to prepare for current and future challenges within fiscal realities. The fiscal year 2011 President's budget request addresses these gaps, ensuring our ability to remain the most ready, dominant, and influential naval force globally, providing a fiscally sustainable force that balances the level of risk across the fleet. The Navy is focusing investment in multi-mission platforms and technologies that perform vital missions, such as cruise and BMD, undersea warfare, and intelligence collection, and has positioned our Navy to counter both current and future naval threats.

General CHANDLER. The two primary factors are insufficient recapitalization of our force structure over the last two decades and the continued rapid improvements by our potential adversaries. Our fighter and bomber forces (with the exception of the F–22 and B–2) are all fourth generation capabilities aligned against increasingly lethal anti-access environments. Our potential adversaries have learned valuable lessons from Operation Desert Storm, Operation Allied Force, OIF, and OEF about how our forces operate and developed impressive asymmetric capabilities in response. Specifically, they have developed and, in some cases, fielded: mobile, long-range, integrated and highly capable Surface-to-Air Missile systems; mobile, precise short-, medium-, and long-range ballistic missiles; Digital Radio Frequency Memory jammer-equipped aircraft; extensive GPS and communications jamming capabilities; and recently demonstrated anti-satellite capabilities, all designed with our force structure in mind. Our fifth generation capabilities and our current and planned capacity, while highly capable, are steadily losing their asymmetric advantage to our potential adversaries' military advances. We are highly dependent on the F–35 being produced as scheduled. We need to develop a long-range precision strike system as soon as possible. We need to analyze how we base and deploy our strike and bomber assets. Networking and communications threats to the cyber domain have a definite impact on our ability to command and control the battlespace, a capability once nearly uncontested.

Our limitations in the electronic warfare environment are directly tied to responsible retirement of Air Force and joint legacy systems, technology propagation and distribution across international boundaries, and an acquisition system in which timeline and cost are often outpaced by an adversary that rapidly acquires inexpensive commercial off-the-shelf technology. Robust electronic warfare capabilities are critical to maintaining our air superiority asymmetric advantage over any potential adversary. The Air Force has made critical investments to support our motivated contingent of airmen dedicated to winning the current fight as part of the joint team. While important to the wars in Iraq and Afghanistan, some of these capabilities will have less utility against a near-peer adversary's employment of airpower.

146. Senator INHOFE. General Chiarelli, General Amos, Admiral Greenert, and General Chandler, what is your risk assessment (near-, mid-, and long-term) associated with these reduced force structures?

General CHIARELLI. The Army continues to be exposed to risk in the near-term as the demand for forces exceeds sustainable supply. The need to respond to the current conflict has degraded our ability to prepare for future or unforeseen conflicts. This limits the Nation's strategic depth in terms of capabilities and in the quantity of forces available to respond to unexpected contingencies.

The Army's ability to restore balance in the short-term is contingent upon achieving sustainable BOG:dwell ratios of 1:2 for the Active component and 1:4 for the Reserve component. Essential to achieving this are: first, maintaining the TESI implemented this year, which increases the forces available to fully man deploying units, and second, maintaining operational access to the Reserve component. Continued high demand prevents units from receiving all required personnel and equipment early enough in their training cycle to meet readiness gates.

In the mid-term, the Army will need to implement a more sustainable BOG:dwell ratio of 1:3 for the Active component and 1:5 for the Reserve component. This ratio is optimal to balance the demand for forces with the need to reset, retrain, and recover. Additionally, the Army will require reset for a minimum of 2 years after completion of combat operations. Finally, we will need to ensure continued programs that support a quality of life for soldiers and families that is commensurate with their quality of service. These programs are essential to honor the commitments we have to our wounded warriors and families of deployed soldiers, and also to ensure we retain the high quality people we now have in our ranks.

In the long-term, we require continued support for our modernization strategy, to ensure we are prepared to meet the wide variety of challenges we will face.

The Army's plan to reduce risk to the force is contingent upon achieving sustainable deploy-to-dwell ratios, adequately providing for soldiers, civilians, and families, and securing reliable, timely, and consistent funding. In the absence of these needs, risk to the force will remain unacceptably high and compromise our ability to support the joint force.

General AMOS. The Marine Corps will be conducting a force structure review from 14 September to 17 December that will assess the risk and capabilities associated with operating under reduced force structure.

Admiral GREENERT. The Navy has balanced the anticipated risk in the period with the uncertainties of the future to achieve the best balance of missions, resources, and requirements possible. The Navy maintains its ability to win in any conventional campaign in any future scenario. In the near- and mid-term, the Navy is able to meet priority presence requirements and fulfill missions such as BMD, as well. In the long-term, the increased risk brought about from the reduced force structure is acceptable for the force and does not unnecessarily place sailors, marines, or airmen in jeopardy.

The Navy's force structure sustains a day-to-day forward presence in each theater and ensures a credible capability to support related theater campaign plans and to deter or respond to MCOs, consistent with force-sizing guidance in the QDR. It reflects the naval capabilities needed to meet the challenges the Nation faces over the next three decades. The Navy will continue to revisit its force structure, and adjust as necessary, to ensure we are prepared to address current and future threats.

General CHANDLER. In the near-term, the readiness of our Combat Air Forces aircraft is adequate despite challenges from accumulating hours on our fleet faster than envisioned when these aircraft were fielded. The readiness of our Mobility Air Forces remains high while meeting robust and dynamic operational requirements. We continue to strengthen our nuclear enterprise, which remains the number one priority of our Service. Despite 20+ years of sustained Air Force deployments, the personnel and aircraft of the U.S. Air Force are ready to face any challenge with precision and reliability.

In the mid- and long-term we are facing very serious challenges in the Combat Air Forces at the high end of the range of military operations. That is why we chose to accelerate the retirement of approximately 250 legacy fighter aircraft in order to allow us to upgrade remaining legacy aircraft, free manpower to support our growing ISR capabilities, and to bridge to the fifth generation fighter force. This shift accepts a moderate amount of operational risk due to decreased capacity, but is necessary to move forward to more capable and survivable next generation platforms. We also need investment in a long-range precision strike system, preferred munitions, ISR, and electronic combat capabilities that are survivable in a hostile environment. We need investment in forward basing options to help counter growing anti-access threats and we need to build partnerships with our allies to mitigate the vulnerabilities associated with a smaller, but more capable force structure.

[Whereupon, at 4:07 p.m., the subcommittee adjourned.]

○